"Pastors to diverse church com[munities ...] congregants' varied backgrounds, experiences, perspectives, [...] when our people start welcoming, loving, and serving one another across the lines of difference because of Christ, it makes living in the tension not only worthwhile but sacred. To help preachers in our role as facilitators of such communities, Kim and Hoffman have provided a wonderful field guide. I can't recommend *Preaching to a Divided Nation* highly enough."

—**Scott Sauls**, senior pastor, Christ Presbyterian Church; author of *A Gentle Answer* and *Beautiful People Don't Just Happen*

"An issue that matters today is our divided nation, filled with too many divided churches and divided Christians. That is clear to all. For those of us who call Jesus Christ our Lord, we also know the prayer of Jesus 'that they may be one' (John 17:22). But how do we do this? We start with the single most influential time in the church each week: the sermon. But how do we do that practically? In *Preaching to a Divided Nation*, Kim and Hoffman give a useful framework to confront the division in our time with preaching grounded in the Bible's story line and founded on the redemptive work of Christ."

—**Ed Stetzer**, Wheaton College

"*Preaching to a Divided Nation* is a must-read for twenty-first-century Christian leaders. Kim and Hoffman offer an excellent road map for preachers, teachers, and leaders on how to use their voice, pulpit, and platform to heal our country's divides. Get this book and read it with your church staff today!"

—**Michelle Ami Reyes**, vice president, Asian American Christian Collaborative; author of *Becoming All Things*

"Kim and Hoffman know well the challenges facing pulpits in fostering true unity among believers. Rightly, they exhort faithful homileticians to listen to various social perspectives as a means of informing authentic Christian preaching. More now than ever, the preacher's personal development as an emotionally, culturally, and historically intelligent shepherd contributes to the ability to proclaim the Scriptures in a way that makes the church a greater agent of righteousness and love in society. For the sake of the healing of divided nations everywhere, may all preachers eagerly hear this exhortation with ears of grace."

—**Eric C. Redmond**, Moody Bible Institute

"In such a polarizing and fractious time, Christian preachers need resources that bridge divides and remind us that God makes a way out of no way.

Thankfully, Kim and Hoffman's timely new book gives us both. *Preaching to a Divided Nation* is grounded in theory, saturated with Scripture, centered on the gospel, informed by practice, and infused with hope. Job well done!"

—**Jared E. Alcántara**, Truett Theological Seminary, Baylor University

"In a polarized and hostile political, racial, and economic context, preaching has become a challenging and delicate pastoral art. With one simple sentence or sound bite, pastors risk unintentionally dividing their flock in a way that harms not only the local church but also the soul of the pastor. Division hurts all of us. Kim and Hoffman provide a theological framework for preaching while also guiding the pastor to remember that we are but heralds, not heart changers. We've needed a book like this for a long time now, and it comes just in time. If you want a framework for preaching that leads to reconciliation instead of division, this one's for you!"

—**Tara Beth Leach**, author of *Emboldened* and *Radiant Church*

"Preaching has become something of a dreaded task. With self-appointed authorities declaring on social media what pastors should and should not address—and telling people to leave their churches if pastors don't say the supposed right thing—the pastor bears the impossible task of speaking God's Word to a disinterested and divided world. In a day where cultural land mines abound, the preacher can either dismiss the concerns of her congregation as invalid or irrelevant or become a prisoner to the narratives and perspectives of the moment. Kim and Hoffman give us a better way. They excavate a treasury of theological resources to address the chief causes of division and map the terrain of our cultural dynamics and historical context. They teach us to become aware of our own lens as preachers and to rely on the Spirit to breathe the Word of God to the people of God. The result is a stunning, scholarly, current, and critical guide for preachers to take seriously the complexity of preaching in a rapidly changing world."

—**Glenn Packiam**, lead pastor, New Life Downtown;
author of *The Resilient Pastor*

"Our world is divided, our rhythms are disrupted, and the church is distracted. Nothing has more potential to unify us than the life-changing message of the gospel. Kim and Hoffman's approach to preaching is practical and attainable. I'm grateful for their effort in training pastors to bring the redemptive power of the gospel in relevant ways to their communities."

—**Scott Ridout**, president, Converge

Preaching
to a
DIVIDED
NATION

Preaching to a DIVIDED NATION

A Seven-Step Model *for* Promoting **Reconciliation** and **Unity**

Matthew D. Kim *and* Paul A. Hoffman

B
Baker Academic
a division of Baker Publishing Group
Grand Rapids, Michigan

Published by Baker Academic
a division of Baker Publishing Group
PO Box 6287, Grand Rapids, MI 49516-6287
www.bakeracademic.com

Printed in the United States of America

Library of Congress Cataloging-in-Publication Data
Names: Kim, Matthew D., 1977– author. | Hoffman, Paul A., 1977– author.
Title: Preaching to a divided nation : a seven-step model for promoting reconciliation and unity / Matthew D. Kim and Paul A. Hoffman.
Description: Grand Rapids, Michigan : Baker Academic, a division of Baker Publishing Group, [2022] | Includes bibliographical references and index.
Identifiers: LCCN 2021055546 | ISBN 9781540964748 (paperback) | ISBN 9781540965622 (casebound) | ISBN 9781493436705 (ebook) | ISBN 9781493436712 (pdf)
Subjects: LCSH: Preaching—United States. | Reconciliation—Religious aspects—Christianity. | Reconciliation—United States. | United States—Social conditions—21st century.
Classification: LCC BV4211.3 .K552945 2022 | DDC 251—dc23/eng/20220114
LC record available at https://lccn.loc.gov/2021055546

Baker Publishing Group publications use paper produced from sustainable forestry practices and post-consumer waste whenever possible.

22   23   24   25   26   27   28   7   6   5   4   3   2   1

To the remarkable women who have contributed much to our ministry and scholarship:

Aída Besançon Spencer, Senior Professor of New Testament at Gordon-Conwell Theological Seminary
—Matthew D. Kim

Elaine Phillips, Distinguished Professor Emeritus of Biblical Studies at Gordon College
and
Deirdre Brower Latz, Principal of Nazarene Theological College, Manchester, UK
—Paul A. Hoffman

CONTENTS

ACKNOWLEDGMENTS

We would like to thank several individuals who helped us with this project.

Scott M. Gibson, our mentor and friend, brought us together in friendship over twenty years ago by mentoring us at Gordon-Conwell Theological Seminary. He has modeled for us the importance of discipleship, reconciliation, and unity.

Manny Cumplido and Heather Joy Zimmerman carefully read the manuscript and offered numerous helpful suggestions for improving it.

Thomas and Amy Cogdell and Christ the Reconciler Community's prayers and encouragement helped sustain this project.

Trip Wolfskehl used his talents to create the diagrams in this book, for which we are so grateful.

Jared Evan Larson, Matt's research assistant, identified several resources to include in this book.

We give thanks to the tremendous team at Baker Academic, especially Robert Hosack, Eric Salo, Jeremy Wells, Paula Gibson, and Shelly MacNaughton, for shepherding this project with their time, resources, and expertise.

We cannot thank enough Sandra María Van Opstal, Rich Villodas, and Ralph Douglas West, whose sermons showcase their prophetic voices and solidify the need for Christian reconciliation and unity in our world.

This project could not have been completed without the support of our amazing wives, Sarah Kim and Autumn Hoffman. Thank you so much. We love you and are grateful to God for you.

To our sons, Ryan, Evan, and Aidan Kim and Landon and Kelan Hoffman, we love you and are so proud of you. We pray that you'll be agents of reconciliation and unity in your generation.

Finally, we give praise and glory to our triune God—Father, Son, and Holy Spirit—who alone enables the church to be reconciled and unified.

INTRODUCTION

Countless pastors, preachers, teachers, and ministry leaders are dismayed at the dysfunction engulfing the church and the wider culture. Every day, headlines reveal a world divided across ethnic, class, sex, and political lines. We are simultaneously a nation and a church with comparable cavernous disagreements. Make no mistake: these chasms are expanding and feel increasingly insurmountable.

For instance, consider the metastasizing tumor of ethnocentrism. In April 2020, Christopher Wray, the director of the FBI, issued a warning regarding "a potential . . . spike in hate crimes" against Asian Americans due to the COVID-19 pandemic.[1] A short while later, the Anti-Defamation League announced "Antisemitic Incidents Hit All-Time High in 2019."[2] Then, on May 25, 2020, came the horrific video of the murder of George Floyd while in police custody, which catalyzed protests and demonstrations in cities across the globe. Despite the presence of a deadly viral pandemic, thousands marched in the streets chanting, "No Justice, No Peace!" and "Defund the police!" and "Breonna Taylor, say her name!"[3]

1. Griffin Connolly, "Coronavirus: FBI Director Warns of Potential for Spike in Hate Crimes as Anti-Asian Incidents Surge," *Independent*, April 22, 2020, https://www.independent.co .uk/news/world/americas/us-politics/coronavirus-hate-crimes-anti-asian-attacks-fbi-us-cases -a9479191.html. As of May 2021, this dire situation appears to be escalating. See Sam Cabral, "Covid 'Hate Crimes' against Asian Americans on Rise," *BBC*, May 21, 2021, https://www.bbc .com/news/world-us-canada-56218684.

2. "Antisemitic Incidents Hit All-Time High in 2019," Anti-Defamation League, May 12, 2020, https://www.adl.org/news/press-releases/antisemitic-incidents-hit-all-time-high-in-2019.

3. Richard A. Oppel Jr., Derrick Bryson Taylor, and Nicholas Bogel-Burroughs, "What to Know about Breonna Taylor's Death," *New York Times*, April 26, 2021, https://www.nytimes .com/article/breonna-taylor-police.html.

We observe a similar pattern in the widening gap between the upper, middle, and lower economic classes in the most prosperous nation in world history. The numbers don't lie: the stark expanse separating the rich from the poor—known as income inequality—is growing. Oxfam International recently released a report contending that "the world's 2,153 billionaires have more wealth than the 4.6 billion people who make up 60 percent of the planet's population."[4] And the painful truth is that ethnicity and economics remain intertwined. Economist Joseph Stiglitz, a Nobel laureate, states, "There has been no significant closing of the gap between the income of African-Americans (or Hispanics) and white Americans the last 30 years."[5]

Moreover, we cannot ignore the plethora of ways in which the battle of the sexes and gender issues continue to cause rifts in the wider culture, in the church, and in households. Aimee Byrd's recent exposure of evangelical Christians' locker room conversations, which dehumanize and delegitimize the *imago Dei* in females, highlights the hidden myopia of church leaders who fail to see and confess their own harmful, misogynistic, and sexist patterns of thinking.[6] Social ruptures preachers may want to acknowledge and speak to include the Billy Graham Rule; #MeToo and #ChurchToo movements; the #TimesUp movement; LGBTQ+ movements; inequities in position, salary, and promotion; women's roles in ministry; complementarian versus egalitarian debates; and domestic violence. They all have shed light on some disturbing and undeniable abuses of power.

Last, but not least, we must address our toxic political environment. Partisan polarization is the foremost "snowball effect" issue of our time, dominating and devouring every person, policy, and topic in its path. Scholar Lilliana Mason labels partisanship "a mega-identity, with all the psychological and behavioral magnifications that implies."[7] It has given rise to a phenomenon political scientists call "partisan sorting" whereby our political system is fueled by "prejudice and emotional volatility," leading Democrats and Republicans to "loathe" each other.[8] All this friction has exacerbated the racial divides in the

4. "World's Billionaires Have More Wealth Than 4.6 Billion People," Oxfam International, January 19, 2020, https://www.oxfamamerica.org/press/worlds-billionaires-have-more-wealth -than-46-billion-people.

5. Joseph E. Stiglitz, *The Great Divide: Unequal Societies and What We Can Do about Them* (New York: Norton, 2016), 140–41.

6. See Megan Fowler, "How a Reformed Facebook Group's Private Comments Turned into a Public Dispute," *Christianity Today*, July 1, 2020, https://www.christianitytoday.com/news /2020/july/aimee-byrd-genevan-commons-reformed-opc-facebook-comments.html.

7. Lilliana Mason, *Uncivil Agreement: How Politics Became Our Identity* (Chicago: University of Chicago Press, 2018), 14.

8. Mason, *Uncivil Agreement*, 122.

church. In the 2016 presidential election, 81 percent of white evangelicals voted for Republican candidate Donald Trump, whereas 96 percent of Black Protestants voted for Democratic candidate Hillary Clinton.[9] Lord, have mercy.

The bottom line: the church's divisions are real and destructive. They break God's heart, undermine our gospel witness, and contradict the reality of heaven. It appears the bride of Christ is struggling to overcome the diseases of prejudice and polarization. Many Christians are behaving boorishly, failing to exhibit a trace of patience, understanding, compassion, or empathy. Sadly, all too often the nonreligious seem more gracious than those who claim to know Christ.

However, despite the gravity of our current situation, we remain hopeful homileticians—dedicated practitioners who love God and his church. We have not lost our faith, one that is rooted in the cross, the resurrection of Jesus Christ, and God's mission to restore all things. Crucially, we maintain that one upshot of our chaotic and fractious era is that the pulpit, always paramount, has become even more so. That is, pastors, preachers, teachers, and leaders can either inflame our tensions or proclaim the peace and healing Jesus offers. We are convinced that all gospel heralds now have a greater opportunity to intentionally and winsomely use their platforms to proclaim the Holy Scriptures in a way that promotes reconciliation and unity.

The question, of course, is "How?"

While we have no illusions that we can solve every problem, we believe we have some fresh insights to offer the church and the academy. Since we developed our strong, interethnic friendship starting twenty years ago while in seminary, we've spent time navigating the "-ism" rapids—the dangerous currents of ethnocentrism, classism, sexism, and political partisanship, to name a few. This book emerges from our convictions, personal practices, pastoral experience in shepherding and preaching ministries, and academic training and scholarship.

Our goal is to provide some guidance, skills, and tools for those bumping along with us. We anticipate that this book's seven-part framework (see fig. 1) will equip communicators with the necessary resources to succeed. Let's take a moment to briefly chart that course.

Chapter 1 explains the *theological step* of our homiletical model. To preach effectively, the pastor, teacher, or leader must comprehend the narrative arc of Scripture, the relationality of the triune Godhead, how sin fuels alienation

---

9. "An Examination of the 2016 Electorate, Based on Validated Voters," Pew Research Center, August 9, 2018, https://www.pewresearch.org/politics/2018/08/09/an-examination-of-the-2016-electorate-based-on-validated-voters.

Seven Steps to Preaching to a Divided Nation

Figure 1

and division, the reconciling mission of God, and the renewal of all things. The role of the preacher is to identify the prejudicial fruit of sin and magnify the healing power of our holy Redeemer.

Chapter 2 focuses on the *contextual aspect* of our paradigm. A good homiletician cultivates not only a strong cultural intelligence but also historical intelligence on a national and local scale. Unfortunately, the *-isms* that bedevil us at present are not new. When a preacher enters the pulpit, she will be wise to grasp the context and social location of her listeners. A community's memory and current reality are an integral part of the homiletical moment.

Chapter 3 zeroes in on the *personal section* of the model. Mature teachers develop attitudes of self-reflection and repentance. To preach with humility, holiness, and vulnerability, we must be willing to examine our hearts, face our prejudices, and confess our sin to God and to safe friends or accountability partners. Otherwise, our blinders will make our preaching more hypocritical than healing and more condescending than authentic and transformational.

Chapter 4 outlines the *positional step*. Preachers cannot hit the target unless they fully embrace their role as God's human heralds. While preachers must earnestly pray for the unction of God's Spirit to accompany their sermons, it remains the job of the Holy Spirit to bring deep conviction and change. Furthermore, we must recognize that many Christian traditions and denominations believe in the importance of social and political action in the pursuit of justice and reconciliation. In each milieu, pastors and churches must discern the will of God for how they are to declare and enact reconciliation.

Chapter 5 defines the *methodological aspect* of our framework and presents homiletical elements that foster reconciliation and unity in churches and communities. The focus of this chapter will be negotiating centered sets and bounded sets for our congregations as well as preaching on virtue formation.

Chapter 6 offers several *best practices for communicating on divisive topics.* These concrete suggestions for pre-sermon, mid-sermon, and post-sermon practices seek to facilitate this arduous journey and preserve congregational unity amid a diversity of beliefs and opinions.

Chapter 7 presents the *categorical step*, sharing common themes and texts that may prove helpful for preaching on the varied *-isms* of our day. This section is a treasure trove of salient preaching themes and texts. Appendix G contains six sample sermons that illustrate how to effectively communicate on reconciliation and unity, including sermons from the authors as well as from Sandra María Van Opstal, Rich Villodas, and Ralph Douglas West.

The conclusion offers a call to action and an inspiring story of hope. Because our present divides need urgent attention and mending, it's time for a gut check: Who will answer the call to live and proclaim the message, ministry, and identity of reconciliation in a violent and tribal world? The credibility of our witness is at stake. Will we uphold the heart of God and his kingdom priorities from our pulpits?

Finally, we invite you to contemplate the implications of failing to preach reconciliation and unity to a disintegrating culture and church. What compels us to write this book is generational impact. We cannot bear the thought of our children coming of age and assuming leadership roles within a diminished church and divided nation. We refuse to lie down and accept this anathema. A godly legacy and gospel heritage are worth contending for and passing on. So, as you read, you might find it beneficial to make this personal and tangible: visualize a young person you care about deeply—your son or daughter or perhaps a neighbor. You preach for him; you proclaim for her. In the final analysis, it's not about us. We sow and plant, we toil, risk, and invest, for the destiny of those who come after us.

Before you plunge ahead, a word of caution is required. Some facts and concepts in this book might make you feel uncomfortable because they challenge your current base of knowledge or some assumptions you hold regarding life and ministry. This stimulates two responses: a reminder and a suggestion. First, as N. T. Wright observes in his commentary on 2 Corinthians 5:16–6:2, "The world has never before seen a ministry of reconciliation; it has never before heard a message of reconciliation. No wonder the Corinthians found Paul's work hard to fathom. . . . He was behaving like someone . . . who lived in a whole new world."[10] What was true then remains true now: reconciliation and unity are radical, even otherworldly.

Second, for our part, we embrace the exciting possibility that this book may reach a diverse crowd. Kevin DeYoung has proposed a helpful "schema" that outlines four "teams" or "approaches" describing how evangelicals are interpreting and responding to the contentious issues of race, politics, and gender: the "Contrite, Compassionate, Careful, and Courageous."[11] To summarize these four camps, the contrite focus on repentance and restorative justice, the compassionate stress empathy and lament, the careful highlight the need for selective engagement (with primary attention given to theological reflection), and the courageous display a *stand your ground and preach the gospel* posture. Wherever you fall on that spectrum, we suggest that if something we write provokes disagreement in your mind or frustration in your heart, you put the book down and ask yourself, "*What* am I feeling, and *why*?" We urge you to take the requisite time to process your thoughts—both prayerfully and scripturally. It is the better part of wisdom and worth the effort. At least the triune God thinks so: he "bestows his blessing" over the pursuit of reconciliation and unity (Ps. 133:3). Is that not motivation enough?

Now, on to step one.

10. N. T. Wright, *Paul for Everyone: 2 Corinthians*, New Testament for Everyone (London: SPCK, 2004), 65.
11. Kevin DeYoung, "Why Reformed Evangelicalism Has Splintered: Four Approaches to Race, Politics, and Gender," *DeYoung, Restless, and Reformed* (blog), The Gospel Coalition, March 9, 2021, https://www.thegospelcoalition.org/blogs/kevin-deyoung/why-reformed-evangelicalism-has-splintered-four-approaches-to-race-politics-and-gender.

1

The Theological Step
The Sins of Pride and Prejudice

The most effective homileticians start with a question: Why? In comparing the prophetic preaching of Dietrich Bonhoeffer and Martin Luther King Jr., Raphael Gamaliel Warnock asserts:

> Each had wrestled deeply with *proclamation's prior question*: "Why preach in the first place?" In other words, what is it that the preacher presupposes about the gospel and its meaning and what is it that is critically and urgently at stake? Most preachers spend entirely too much time asking, "What shall I preach?" Bonhoeffer and King got it right because, contrary to this question that is too much driven by institutionalism, as theologians in the pulpit and the public square they asked, "Why do we preach?" Moreover, their ministries and martyrdom suggest that, for them, this question regarding the nature of the gospel and its demands upon one's life was itself a matter of life and death.[1]

Why preach? The theological step of this book's homiletical model addresses that question. All gospel proclamation begins with theology, which is the story of the triune God. Every teacher is primarily a theologian who

---

1. Raphael Gamaliel Warnock, "Preaching and Prophetic Witness," in *Bonhoeffer and King: Their Legacies and Import for Christian Social Thought*, ed. Willis Jenkins and Jennifer M. McBride (Minneapolis: Fortress, 2010), 152.

must first comprehend the narrative arc of Scripture correctly before she can communicate it clearly. To this we turn our attention.

A Reconciling Narrative

There are numerous ways to interpret the Bible, including the popular "systematic-theological method (STM), which tends to deal with Scripture topically. . . . *The Bible is about God, sin, the Holy Spirit, the church.*"[2] However, we propose that you interpret the Bible through a *missional meta-narrative*, "one cohesive story revealing the mission of the triune God."[3] This type of approach has been affirmed by the likes of Richard Bauckham,[4] Christopher J. H. Wright,[5] Timothy Keller,[6] Timothy C. Tennent,[7] Scott W. Sunquist,[8] and Craig G. Bartholomew and Michael W. Goheen.[9] More specifically, the reconciling narrative offered here is composed of five movements: Creator, first creation, alienation, reconciliation, and final creation. We contend this reading may prove helpful for preachers because it is "faithful to the nature of the triune God, the Scriptures, Church tradition, and human experience,"[10] it aligns with the plot structure of biblical narratives,[11] and it illuminates how reconciliation is the heart of the gospel and the Christian life and community.

2. Timothy Keller, *Center Church: Doing Balanced, Gospel-Centered Ministry in Your City* (Grand Rapids: Zondervan, 2012), 40.

3. Paul A. Hoffman, *Reconciling Places: How to Bridge the Chasms in Our Communities* (Eugene, OR: Cascade Books, 2020), 50.

4. Richard Bauckham, *Bible and Mission: Christian Witness in a Postmodern World* (Milton Keynes, UK: Paternoster, 2005), 11–12.

5. Christopher J. H. Wright, *The Mission of God: Unlocking the Bible's Grand Narrative* (Downers Grove, IL: InterVarsity, 2006), 8.

6. Keller, *Center Church*, 43.

7. Timothy C. Tennent, *Invitation to World Missions: A Trinitarian Missiology for the Twenty-First Century* (Grand Rapids: Kregel, 2010), 105.

8. Scott W. Sunquist, *Understanding Christian Mission: Participation in Suffering and Glory* (Grand Rapids: Baker Academic, 2013).

9. Craig G. Bartholomew and Michael W. Goheen, *The Drama of Scripture: Finding Our Place in the Biblical Story* (Grand Rapids: Baker Academic, 2004).

10. Hoffman, *Reconciling Places*, 54. Furthermore, this narrative comports with Col. 1:15–23, "a famous text regarding the supremacy of Christ and reconciliation." Hoffman, *Reconciling Places*, 51.

11. Steven D. Mathewson writes, "Plots in Old Testament narrative assume the same basic shape. Generally, they consist of four main stages or elements in the flow of action: exposition, crisis, resolution, and conclusion or denouement." Mathewson, *The Art of Preaching Old Testament Narrative*, 2nd ed. (Grand Rapids: Baker Academic, 2021), 42. In this vein, Creator and first creation fit in the exposition stage, alienation is the crisis, reconciliation is the resolution, and final creation is the conclusion.

A Reconciling Narrative

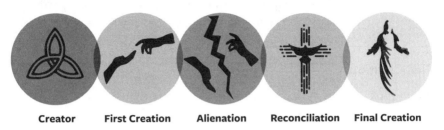

| Creator | First Creation | Alienation | Reconciliation | Final Creation |

Figure 1.1

Creator

The Bible opens with the famous declaration "In the beginning God created . . ." (Gen. 1:1). At the outset of the Scriptures, we are introduced to the Creator God. Yet it must be noted this powerful being predates creation. In his great high priestly prayer, Jesus offers a glimpse into the nature of the Godhead when he entreats, "And now, Father, glorify me in your presence with the glory I had with you before the world began. . . . Father, I want those you have given to me to be with me where I am, and to see my glory, the glory you have given me because you loved me before the creation of the world" (John 17:5, 24). The Christian God is incomparable: he is one being who is "eternal, immortal, invisible" (1 Tim. 1:17) and also exists as three distinct persons. From time immemorial, God the Father, God the Son, and God the Holy Spirit have enjoyed perfect and harmonious communion marked by the mutual sharing of glory and love. When commenting on the "doctrine of the immanent Trinity," Colin Gunton furnishes this insight:

> Because God is, "before" creation took place, already a being-in-relation, there is no need for him to create what is other than himself. He does not need to create, because he is already a *taxis*, order, of loving relations. . . . Overall, the relations of the three are summarised in the concept of love, which involves a dynamic of both giving and receiving. The persons are what they are by virtue of what they give to and receive from each other. . . . The fact that the relations are relations of love entails their freedom, which at least means their non-necessity. . . . [Hence] a trinitarian theology of creation involves the non-necessity of the world. The world does not have to be, because it is the outcome of the free creating act of the God who is already a relational being.[12]

12. Colin E. Gunton, *The Promise of Trinitarian Theology*, 2nd ed. (London: T&T Clark, 1997), 142–44.

Herein lies an astonishing truth: God is self-existent,[13] holy, and majestic (transcendent) as the supreme being, *and* at his core God is so profoundly relational that he creates everything out of the overflow of his love and freedom.

First Creation

That brings us to the second movement in the reconciling narrative: the first creation. The Trinity—as a collective—initiated the formation of all that is, including the heavens and earth. God the Father makes a series of pronouncements, "speaking our world into reality through his son, Jesus Christ, the eternal Word (*logos*) and through the power of the 'hovering' Spirit."[14]

Some themes emerge from the creation account in Genesis 1–2 that we want to accentuate for our purposes here. First, Genesis 1 states seven times that what God created "was good."[15] The word for "good" in Hebrew is *tob*, which conveys the idea of something being "beautiful, pleasant, agreeable, sweet [tasty]."[16] What God produced is empirically attractive, pure in essence, and structurally complete. Second, the world is governed by order and balance: light and dark; day and night; sky, land, and sea; fish and birds; and so on. Interestingly, God institutes a moral architecture: in Genesis 2:17 God commands Adam not to "eat from the tree of the knowledge of good [*tob*] and evil" because to do so will bring death. Within the created order exists a natural set of laws (e.g., day and night, gravity, seasons) and an ethical set of laws (e.g., "right" and "wrong"). Third, the cosmos has integrity; that is, its component parts share a harmonious interrelationship. God, angelic beings, the heavenlies/space, humans, animals, seas, and soil cohabitate within a perfectly interdependent ecosystem.[17] Fourth, the telos or goal of creation is to grow and flourish (cf. Gen. 1:28) for God's enjoyment and glory (cf. Gen. 2:1–3).

13. That is, God "needs nothing outside of himself in order to be fully God. In sum, the God of Scripture is *self-contained* and *self-sufficient*, in no way ontologically correlative to this creation." Robert L. Reymond, *A New Systematic Theology of the Christian Faith* (Nashville: Nelson, 1998), 131.

14. Hoffman, *Reconciling Places*, 52. See Gen. 1:1–26 and John 1:1–5.

15. Gen. 1:4, 10, 12, 18, 21, 25, 31. David A. Dorsey notes "the number *seven* generally represents completeness." Dorsey, *The Literary Structure of the Old Testament: A Commentary on Genesis–Malachi* (Grand Rapids: Baker, 1999), 49.

16. James Strong, *The New Strong's Complete Dictionary of Bible Words* (Nashville: Nelson, 1996), 380.

17. At this point, we are setting aside the sticky wicket of the prehistorical origin of sin, that is, Satan's fall from heaven; cf. Isa. 14; Ezek. 28; Luke 10; and Rev. 12. For a concise explanation, see Louis Berkhof, "Sin Originated in the Angelic World," in *Systematic Theology*, new ed. (Grand Rapids: Eerdmans, 1996), 220–21.

The apex of creation is when God composes human beings, made in "his own image" (Gen. 1:27).[18] The *imago Dei* means both males and females, in a certain way, express the likeness, goodness/purity, intellect/rationality, moral nature, freedom, and immortal spirit (soul) of their Creator.[19] As God's image-bearers, humans have great dignity and are relational and moral creatures. Consequently, they are to enjoy communion with God and with one another. This interconnectedness has a crucial implication: "We are bound up in a delicate network of interdependence" whereby we come to accept "a person is a person through other persons. . . . I belong. I participate, I share."[20] Further, humans are governed by an ethical framework defining "good" and "evil" in social terms. Some attitudes and behaviors promote a fully orbed thriving, while others will inhibit or detract from it. At this point, the world is saturated with the fullness of God's presence, which promotes robust relational bonds. Thus, it is not hyperbolic to assert: "The whole message of the Bible is the story of God's love for and relationship with his creation."[21]

Unfortunately, this idyllic state does not endure—and is quickly shattered.

Alienation

The third movement in our reconciling narrative is found in Genesis 3, which depicts the events precipitating the unraveling of the ties binding everything together. A broad exploration of this pivotal story proves instructive in delineating emblematic themes. The nameless "crafty serpent" slides into the picture and immediately asks a question that distorts God's decree and undermines trust in his character (Gen. 3:1–5). God's prohibition regarding not eating from "the tree of the knowledge of good and evil" was abundantly clear (Gen. 2:16–17). However, rather than swiftly terminating the conversation, the first two humans allow the serpent to entice and manipulate them. He does so masterfully, appealing to their lust and pride (Gen. 3:6). In short order, they disobey God, take and eat the forbidden fruit, and indelibly alter the course of history.

In the first six verses of Genesis 3, then, one can already discern multiple motifs emerging that are related to the fall. These include distrust,

18. See Catherine L. McDowell, *The Image of God in the Garden of Eden* (Winona Lake, IN: Eisenbrauns, 2015).
19. For more on this, see Berkhof, *Systematic Theology*, 202–10.
20. Desmond Tutu, *No Future without Forgiveness* (New York: Doubleday, 1999), 35, 31.
21. Sunquist, *Understanding Christian Mission*, 181.

discontentment, rebellion rooted in lust and pride, passivity, and complicity. Do these faults sound familiar? They are the forces stoking our present divisions.

But that's not all. The story reveals escalating dysfunction and division. Upon discovering they are naked, Adam and Eve cover themselves. When they hear God moving in their vicinity, they hide—perhaps separately.[22] Then God asks Adam why they are taking evasive maneuvers. Called out and cornered, Adam finally speaks up and confesses his fear-based shame: "I heard you. . . . I was afraid" (Gen. 3:10). However, when God's questioning persists, Adam wilts, moves into blame-shifting mode, and swaps the first-person pronoun *I* for the second-person *you* and third-person *she*, effectively casting the responsibility for his sin onto God and his wife: "The woman *you* put here with me—*she* gave me some fruit from the tree, and I ate it" (Gen. 3:12). God turns to Eve and asks for confirmation. Like Adam, she deflects responsibility, asserting, "The serpent deceived me, and I ate" (Gen. 3:13). This small section of the narrative adds to the list of sins fueling polarization and alienation: denial, redirection, justification, rationalization, and scapegoating.

Then God levies just punishments, including "enmity" between Eve and the serpent. Next come a power struggle between husband and wife (Gen. 3:16), difficulty in harvesting food from the land ("painful toil . . . thorns and thistles," 3:17–19), and the introduction of death (imposing itself upon life and relationships; cf. 3:19). Finally, there is the irrevocable expulsion from God's presence when he "banished" and "drove out" the first humans from the garden of Eden (3:21–24).

We now arrive at the crux of sin: "sin in its essence is prideful defiance, rebellion against God, seeking to be God."[23] Louis Berkhof writes, "Adam placed himself in opposition to God, . . . he refused to subject his will to the will of God, to have God determine the course of his life; and . . . he actively attempted to take the matter out of God's hand."[24] At the fall, a seismic event occurred: "The center of authority for man had shifted away from God to himself. Adam and Eve came to believe that they were to be their own authority."[25] Their actions were a foolish attempt to usurp the locus of their

22. This interpretation is contested. Reymond asserts that "the Hebrew literally reads that 'the man hid himself and the woman herself.' It was a case of 'every man for himself.'" Reymond, *New Systematic Theology*, 448.

23. Donald G. Bloesch, *Essentials of Evangelical Theology*, vol. 1, *God, Authority, and Salvation* (New York: HarperCollins, 1978), 108.

24. Berkhof, *Systematic Theology*, 222.

25. Reymond, *New Systematic Theology*, 445.

identity, knowledge, and morality from the only holy and glorious Creator and reserve it for their limited, created selves.[26]

This brings to bear the attending consequences of Genesis 3. Alienation, hostility, and division metastasize in multiple directions, expressed in conflict among various parties, including between God and humans, God and Satan, Satan and humans, men and women, and humans and the land, to name a few. Pastor and reconciler Antoine Rutayisire comments:

> When sin entered the world in Genesis 3, man was separated from God, separated from himself (psychological problems), separated from his neighbour (social problems) and separated from nature (ecological problems). Those four levels of alienation are present wherever you find sin. If we are to preach the message of reconciliation to communities, we need to rediscover that message about sin, for sin is the dividing factor in every situation.[27]

Characteristics of Sin

Although more could be said regarding the repercussions of the fall, it is vital to provide categories delineating the scope of sin so the preacher can better grasp and communicate the realities of human pride and prejudice. Here are some key observations regarding sin.

Sin Is Total and Pervasive

The doctrine of total depravity has been heavily contested throughout church history. Yet we agree with R. C. Sproul's distinction that "total depravity" is not to be confused with "utter depravity." "Total depravity," Sproul writes, "means that I and everyone else are depraved or corrupt in the totality of our being. There is no part of us that is left untouched by sin."[28] This is why Scripture uses the metaphor of yeast, which disperses within and leavens a loaf of bread (see Luke 12:1 and 1 Cor. 5:6–8). Given the scriptural teaching regarding the prevalence of sin, it is not incorrect to assert that sin exists systemically, institutionally, and culturally. We will look at that in more detail below, but here's the key: sin, in all its permutations, stretches its tentacles into every nook and cranny of each family, congregation, city, and nation.

26. For more on the consequences of the fall, see Bruce K. Waltke and Cathi J. Fredricks, *Genesis: A Commentary* (Grand Rapids: Zondervan Academic, 2001).

27. Antoine Rutayisire, "Our Gospel of Reconciliation," in *Christ Our Reconciler: Gospel, Church, World: The Third Lausanne Congress on World Evangelization*, ed. J. E. M. Cameron (Downers Grove, IL: InterVarsity, 2012), 67.

28. R. C. Sproul, *Essential Truths of the Christian Faith* (Wheaton: Tyndale, 1998), 148. Also see Bloesch, *Essentials of Evangelical Theology*, 1:90–92.

On the other hand, we join other theologians in affirming the role of common grace, understood as "the grace of preservation by which man's rapacity is restrained. Indeed, if it were not for common grace, the world would fall into anarchy and disorder."[29]

Sin Is an Act and a State

Sin entails a condition of "separation from God as well as a deliberate violation of his will."[30] Indeed, sin is a *lack of conformity to the moral law of God, either in act, disposition, or state*."[31] It creates a vicious cycle in that it warps human nature in its being, which leads to a corrupt or perverted attitude or orientation toward God, which then fuels sinful actions and habits.

Sin Is Active (Commission) and Passive (Omission or Complicity)

In Genesis 4:7, God warns Cain: "Sin is crouching at your door; it desires to have you, but you must rule over it." Accordingly, sin is "an active opposition to God, and a positive transgression of his law, which constitutes guilt."[32] Scripture also portrays sin as having a passive side: "If anyone, then, knows the good they ought to do and doesn't do it, it is sin for them" (James 4:17). Martin Luther King Jr. cautioned this when preaching to a predominantly Black audience: "We must learn that passively to accept an unjust system is to cooperate with that system, and thereby to become a participant in its evil."[33]

Sin Is Individual and Social

We run across an illustration of individual sin when Cain murders Abel (Gen. 4).[34] Social sin is any sin committed *by more than one* person or sin committed *against more than one person*. For instance, a large collection of people say, "Come, let us build ourselves a city, with a tower that reaches to the heavens, so that we may make a name for ourselves" (Gen. 11:4). Other scriptural examples bear out the prevalence of social depravity on every level: the violence and anarchy displayed in the book of Judges or how prophets like Amos declare God's judgment upon the nations surrounding

---

29. Bloesch, *Essentials of Evangelical Theology*, 1:91.
30. Bloesch, *Essentials of Evangelical Theology*, 1:93.
31. Berkhof, *Systematic Theology*, 233.
32. Berkhof, *Systematic Theology*, 231.
33. Martin Luther King Jr., *Strength to Love* (Minneapolis: Fortress, 2010), 7.
34. See Matthew D. Kim, "Preaching on Race in View of the Image of God," in *Ministers of Reconciliation: Preaching on Race and the Gospel*, ed. Daniel Darling (Bellingham, WA: Lexham, 2021), 4–6.

Israel and upon Israel itself, due to their rampant idolatry and injustice. Dr. King saw it in the exodus narrative: "Egypt symbolized evil in the form of humiliating oppression, ungodly exploitation, and crushing domination."[35] Taking into account the compounding effects of sin, many theologians rightly contend sin is "systemic," in that every society has institutions that "are designed by sinful humans who yield to the authority of Sin."[36] Sin is also a cultural force in that it operates as "*a comprehensive way of being and doing that is embedded in our structures of meaning, morality, language, and memory.*"[37]

Furthermore, we would be remiss if we failed to mention generational sin, which can be defined as "weaknesses or tendencies that are handed down to us through the generations from parents or members of our family. These sins can involve behavioral patterns and ways of thinking that keep us trapped in the past."[38] While passages like Ezekiel 18 indicate each person is responsible for his or her own personal sin, it is clear one generation can negatively influence another one; for instance, Cain and his descendant Lamech commit murder (Gen. 4), and Abraham, Isaac, and Jacob engage in deception (Gen. 12, 26, and 27, respectively).

Sin Enslaves and Degrades Creation

Due to the curse God pronounced on the land (Gen. 3:17–18), "creation was subjected to frustration . . . [and] will be liberated from its bondage to decay" (Rom. 8:20–21). This will continue until God brings it "into the freedom and glory of the children of God" (Rom. 8:21). As will be seen when we explore the fifth movement—final creation—our salvation through Christ culminates in "the renewal of all things" (Matt. 19:28), a glorious new heaven coming down to a new earth (Rev. 21).

---

35. King, *Strength to Love*, 77. King observes, "Pharaoh stubbornly refused to respond to the cry of Moses. . . . This tells us something about evil that we must never forget, namely that evil is recalcitrant and determined, and never voluntarily relinquishes its hold short of a persistent, almost fanatical resistance" (77).

36. Heather Joy Zimmerman, "When Racism Becomes Mundane: Proclaiming a Holistic Hamartiology," *Journal of the Evangelical Homiletics Society* 20, no. 2 (September 2020): 94–103, 99.

37. Duke L. Kwon and Gregory Thompson, *Reparations: A Christian Call for Repentance and Repair* (Grand Rapids: Brazos, 2021), 42. Their definition refers to racism, but it is true of the other *-isms* as well.

38. Nan Brown Self, "What Is a Generational Sin?," *Crosswalk*, July 2, 2018, https://www.crosswalk.com/family/parenting/what-is-a-generational-sin.html. For more information and a list of biblical texts, see Erwin W. Lutzer, "Are There Generational Sins and Curses?," Moody Church Media, https://www.moodymedia.org/articles/are-there-generational-sins-and-curses.

Evil Forces Promote Sin

Although a wide variety of perspectives on spiritual warfare exist across Christian traditions, Scripture makes clear that "the rulers," "authorities," "powers of this dark world," and "spiritual forces of evil in the heavenly realms" (Eph. 6:12) contribute to individual and social sin. The Bible portrays the devil as our "enemy" who "prowls around like a roaring lion looking for someone to devour" (1 Pet. 5:8), "has blinded the minds of unbelievers" toward the gospel (2 Cor. 4:4), and "masquerades as an angel of light" (2 Cor. 11:14). For example, Satan "incited David to take a census of Israel" (1 Chron. 21:1), tries to tempt Jesus to sin (Matt. 4:1–11), and "asked to sift" Simon Peter "as wheat" (Luke 22:31). While human beings are responsible for their sin, we must take the role of spiritual warfare into consideration.[39]

The Four -Isms

The aforementioned categories are concretized in the four -*isms*, which are sins signifying some of America's most prominent and intractable rifts: ethnocentrism, classism, sexism, and partisan-political polarization. The first three have been labeled the "Galatians 3:28 triad" because Galatians 3 pinpoints them as "examples of significant division in the world and the Church, both in the ancient world and at present."[40] Partisan polarization, while not explicitly mentioned in the Scriptures, is covered under the topics of "dissensions [and] factions" (i.e., warring parties; Gal. 5:20)[41] or how "the rulers of the Gentiles lord it [authority] over" their opponents (Matt. 20:25). Keeping all this in mind, here are some definitions.

Ethnocentrism

Ethnocentrism is an idolatrous form of social sin in which one person or group holds an attitude of suspicion or superiority against another person

---

39. In our opinion, Eastern and majority-world cultures tend to have more sensitivity to spiritual warfare than we do in the West.

40. Hoffman, *Reconciling Places*, 29. See also Michelle Lee-Barnewall, *Neither Complementarian nor Egalitarian: A Kingdom Corrective to the Evangelical Gender Debate* (Grand Rapids: Baker Academic, 2016), 87–88; Timothy George, *Galatians: An Exegetical and Theological Exposition of Holy Scripture*, New American Commentary 30 (Nashville: Holman, 1994), 284–85.

41. The Greek word for "factions," *hairesis*, is used in Acts 5:17 to describe the Sadducees as a sect and in Acts 15:5 to describe the Pharisees as a sect. Both groups intermixed religion with political power to separate themselves from others in first-century Israel.

or group specifically due to their real or perceived ethnicity.[42] This posture commonly leads to expressions of exclusion, derision, scapegoating, violence, and systematic injustice, which are an affront to the holy Creator and his image-bearers. Among many scriptural examples that could be cited is the apostle Paul recounting how he rebuked Peter for his cowardice and hypocrisy in refusing to eat with gentiles (Gal. 2:11–21) after God's will had been articulated in Acts 10–11.[43]

Classism

Classism is an idolatrous form of social sin in which one person or group holds an attitude of suspicion or superiority against another person or group specifically due to their real or perceived socioeconomic status or identity.[44] This includes elements such as "privilege, immigration or citizenship status, wealth, poverty, geography, education, socialization, and cultural factors."[45] This posture commonly leads to expressions of exclusion, derision, scapegoating, violence, and systematic marginalization, which violate God's character and that of his image-bearers. Scriptural illustrations include James 2, 1 Corinthians 11, and Philemon, in which the apostle Paul challenges Philemon "to receive Onesimus back, not as a runaway slave, but as a 'dear brother in the Lord' (v. 16) . . . [because] the gospel has changed the nature of their relationship: their mutual bond in Christ now transcends their sociocultural identities of slave and master."[46]

Sexism

Sexism is an idolatrous form of social sin in which members of one sex hold an attitude of suspicion or condescension against members of the opposite

42. Here I (Paul) am building upon the definition provided by my coauthor: see Matthew D. Kim, *Preaching with Cultural Intelligence: Understanding the People Who Hear Our Sermons* (Grand Rapids: Baker Academic, 2017), 97.

43. Paul A. Hoffman, "Galatians," in *The Big Idea Companion for Preaching and Teaching: A Guide from Genesis to Revelation*, ed. Matthew D. Kim and Scott M. Gibson (Grand Rapids: Baker Academic, 2021), 499–505.

44. We do not believe classism should be summarily dismissed as a Marxist concept. Scripture predates Marxism and contains hundreds of passages admonishing those with wealth and power to treat those who are economically and socially disadvantaged with justice and generosity. For more on this, see appendix F.

45. Hoffman, *Reconciling Places*, 31. As will be shown in the next chapter, ethnicity and class are intertwined.

46. Paul A. Hoffman, "Philemon," in *The Big Idea Companion for Preaching and Teaching: A Guide from Genesis to Revelation*, ed. Matthew D. Kim and Scott M. Gibson (Grand Rapids: Baker Academic, 2021), 553.

sex—real or perceived. This stance commonly leads to expressions of exclusion, derision, and scapegoating, and intentional forms of intimidation, targeting, and even violence. This contradicts the righteousness of God and demeans his image-bearers. In this book, our discussion of sexism will be limited to male/female issues of church leadership, but we acknowledge that sexism can be a dimension of cultural clashes regarding gender identity: transgenderism, LGBTQ+, intersex, and other hot-button issues related to human sexuality. One text that addresses sexism is the apostle James commanding Christians "to look after orphans and widows in their distress" (James 1:27).[47]

Partisan Polarization

Partisan polarization is an idolatrous form of social sin called a "megaidentity,"[48] in which members of one political group hold an attitude of suspicion or superiority specifically against members of another party—real or perceived. This posture commonly leads to expressions of exclusion ("negative sorting"), derision, scapegoating, and methodical retribution, which dishonor the almighty God and his image-bearers. One scriptural example is the tribal warring and posturing between the leaders (and their followers) within the church in Corinth (1 Cor. 1:10–17).

Summarizing Sin

Let's be clear: it is our opinion that teachers and preachers cannot constructively address our divisions unless they tackle sin in a robust way. One of the criticisms of the evangelical movement—one that we affirm—is that all too often it has downplayed or minimized the effects of sin generally, and social sin specifically. There can be no true and lasting healing apart from an honest analysis and diagnosis of what ails us.

Alienation, however, is not the final movement in God's story. Amid God's response to sin (cf. Gen. 3:14–19) is a crucial promise: Eve's "offspring" (or "seed") "will crush" Satan (Gen. 3:15, cf. Rom. 16:20). Numerous scholars detect a foreshadowing of the gospel here. Eve's descendant Jesus Christ will indeed "destroy the devil's work" (1 John 3:8). Next, God doesn't give the first sinners the full punishment they deserve—immediate death. He allows

47. Craig Keener notes, "True religion involves defending the socially powerless (Exod. 22:20–24; Ps. 146:9; Isa. 1:17). . . . Orphans and widows had neither direct means of support nor automatic legal defenders in that society." Keener, *The IVP Bible Background Commentary: New Testament* (Downers Grove, IL: InterVarsity, 1993), 693.

48. Lilliana Mason, *Uncivil Agreement: How Politics Became Our Identity* (Chicago: University of Chicago Press, 2018), 14.

them to experience consequences, but not the full brunt. Significantly, God ejects them from the garden and so removes the opportunity to engage in the self-salvation project. That is, Adam and Eve are denied the chance to partake of "the tree of life," which would rectify their rebellion and enable them to "eat, and live forever" (Gen. 3:22). Last, God clothes the first humans, which prefigures the future justifying work of Jesus Christ.

That brings us to the fourth movement: reconciliation.

Reconciliation

There is good news. "The Godhead initiates a rescue operation where the entire cosmos is to be redeemed and healed."[49] It commences openly when God invites Abraham into his reconciling mission through the formation of a special community, Israel, Yahweh's "light for the Gentiles" (Isa. 49:1–7). Later, God sends Abraham's promised descendant, Jesus Christ, to our desperate and bleak planet. According to Matthew 1:23, he is "'Immanuel' (which means 'God with us')." He is absolutely unique: God "was pleased to have all his fullness dwell in him, and through him to reconcile to himself all things . . . by making peace through his blood, shed on the cross" (Col. 1:19–20). God's "purpose" was to form "one new humanity" by having Jesus tear down "the dividing wall of hostility" between Jews and gentiles and so "to reconcile both of them to God through the cross" (Eph. 2:14–16).[50] God's "new creation"—his body, the church—has been granted "the ministry of reconciliation," which includes spreading "the message of reconciliation" and serving as "Christ's ambassadors" (2 Cor. 5:17–20).

Now, how does this relate to our divisions, and specifically, to the sins of ethnocentrism, classism, sexism, and partisan polarization? This brings to bear ecclesial life (ecclesiology). As Lesslie Newbigin asserts, each local church can serve as a "Hermeneutic of the Gospel."[51] Christ's church is not an artifact, relic, or totem but rather "a living, dynamic, and diverse witness, a performative sign of God's love."[52] We exist to reflect Christ's image,

49. Hoffman, *Reconciling Places*, 53.

50. As it relates to Israel, we are not advocating for what is sometimes called "replacement theology." Instead, we concur with Michael Goheen's sentiments: "It is not that the church is displacing Israel. Jesus is not founding a brand-new community. Rather, Israel itself is being purified and reconstituted. . . . Later, after the death and resurrection of Jesus, gentiles are incorporated into the history and life of Israel, and this becomes the new covenant community." Goheen, *A Light to the Nations: The Missional Church and the Biblical Story* (Grand Rapids: Baker Academic, 2011), 84.

51. Lesslie Newbigin, *The Gospel in a Pluralist Society* (Grand Rapids: Eerdmans, 1989), 222.

52. Hoffman, *Reconciling Places*, 58.

which is "the hope of glory" (Col. 1:27). Because the body of Christ exists as a reconciled community who represent the kingdom of the triune God to the world, we must embody and proclaim the gospel of reconciliation first internally, then externally. That is, we must prioritize seeking to own this identity as a counterculture within the wider culture. It is unattainable to do this sinlessly, but we can strive to do it consistently. If we cannot, we have nothing to offer the outside world but a hypocritical, dysfunctional witness—which is no witness at all. It seems to us that too many congregations and Christians are devoting too much effort to policing (at its best, humbly critiquing, and at its worst, self-righteously haranguing) those outside the church—people who do not publicly identify as practicing Christ-followers—and not devoting enough effort to developing a thriving, wholistic culture marked by diversity within unity. How can the church call the world to surrender to the Prince of Peace while our congregations remain roiled by infighting and disunity? We must work hard to first eliminate the *-isms* plank from our own eye, so we may have clear enough vision to observe the speck in the world's eye (cf. Matt. 7:3–5). The reconciled and reconciling "one new humanity," however, would be wise to heed Dietrich Bonhoeffer's challenge to temper our expectations:

> *Christian brotherhood is not an ideal, but a divine reality.* . . . By sheer grace, God will not permit us to live even for a brief period in a dream world. . . . He who loves his dream of a community more than the Christian community itself becomes a destroyer of the latter. . . . Because God has bound us together in one body with other Christians in Jesus Christ . . . we enter into that common life not as demanders but as thankful recipients.[53]

Ultimately, the church's reconciling mission must be rooted in proclaiming the cross of Jesus and grounded in the tenacious and practical love we corporately share in the Spirit (Col. 1:8). Thus, when it comes to preaching reconciliation, we must preach Christ—he is our mandate. And to preach Christ properly, we must ensure we live *in* him and *for* him, concretely, *now* and *together*. This is how the world will comprehend the gospel—God's reconciling work through his Son in the power of the Spirit—until Jesus comes again.

Final Creation

The fifth movement in the reconciling narrative presented here is the final creation. God's story climaxes with the restoration of communion between

---

53. Dietrich Bonhoeffer, *Life Together* (San Francisco: Harper San Francisco, 1954), 26–28.

God, his people, and creation. All is reconciled: fully connected to and reflecting once again the life of the Trinity.[54] This means salvation is fully social and material: the Bible concludes with the new Jerusalem, a resplendent garden-city that has been "cleansed of all suffering, tears, injustice, evil, and sin. . . . [It] will not only contain saved individuals—it will have a new humanity without violence and conflict, war and injustice."[55] How will this happen? God will bring about "the regeneration of the world. . . . The universe is not going to be destroyed, but rather liberated, transformed and suffused with the glory of God."[56]

And who occupies the final creation? Revelation 7:9 sketches a stunning portrait of a "great multitude" of worshipers "from every nation, tribe, people and language, standing before the throne and before the Lamb" (Rev. 7:9). Fascinatingly, the redeemed maintain their ethnicity: God does not whitewash them like eggs in a carton. Furthermore, presumably these are men and women who represented on earth a diversity of classes and socioeconomic statuses along with various political positions. Yet the focal point of this scene is our great Reconciler, Jesus Christ. Unity, not division, is God's final word.

Implications and Definitions

It is paramount to underscore some implications of the reconciling narrative presented in this chapter. The purpose of preaching is not simply to identify our divisions but also to communicate the Scriptures in a way that cultivates reconciliation and unity. What are reconciliation and unity? To reconcile is to repair or mend a broken relationship, and it has two axes or horizons: the vertical and the horizontal. In the vertical or divine horizon, reconciliation is the gospel: it is the heart of the triune God's story and plan to redeem and restore "all things" (Matt. 19:28). As for the horizontal or social axis, it occurs when Christians bring forgiveness, healing, and justice into a situation marked by alienation and brokenness. While the primary agent of reconciliation is God, in his grace and wisdom, he calls his people to join him on his mission.[57] And we are convinced that reconciliation fosters unity. Unity is

---

54. Some have termed it the "Beatific Vision," where God's people "can look beyond the veil and gaze directly upon the purity of God's splendor." Sproul, *Essential Truths of the Christian Faith*, 282.

55. Timothy Keller, "The Sin of Racism," *Life in the Gospel*, June 2020, https://quarterly .gospelinlife.com/the-sin-of-racism.

56. John Stott, *Romans: God's Good News for the World* (Downers Grove, IL: InterVarsity, 1994), 241.

57. For more on agency, see Hoffman, *Reconciling Places*, 54–55.

many diverse parts interconnected to form one body (1 Cor. 12) established by the cross (Eph. 2:11–22) through the power of the Holy Spirit (1 Cor. 12:12–14).[58] Unity is nourished and maintained through connection to Jesus, "the true vine" (John 15:1). Here's the crux: unity is a reality that must be lived out for the world to see. Faithful heralds proclaim the gospel in order to produce this fruit.

This raises a second implication: to promote reconciliation and unity, preachers and teachers will take pains to proclaim the "four great equalizers" related to the reconciling narrative we presented above: the *imago Dei*, human sinfulness, the vast atoning love of Jesus Christ, and the final judgment.[59] Theologically speaking, these four biblical truths demonstrate that all humans are equal in God's sight, and thus why "God does not show favoritism" (Rom. 2:11), and hence why Christians "must not show favoritism" (James 2:1). If God's people will embrace these equalizers and allow them to animate their witness, they will exemplify Christlike attitudes, such as humility, social inclusion (or hospitality), identification, and mutuality, to name a few.[60] Imagine what it would look like if God's holy and chosen people embodied these values and postures and reflected them to our strife-ridden world!

Conclusion

We started this chapter with a question: Why *preach*? The answer lies in the theological dimension of our model. If the preacher fails to adequately engage theology—the story of God—he may produce shallow and ineffective sermons, ones that will not meaningfully address the sins of pride and prejudice feeding our divisions. This chapter has proffered grist for the mill by presenting a five-part reconciling narrative for understanding Scripture: Creator, first creation, alienation, reconciliation, and final creation. Without the Creator movement, neither preacher nor parishioners will comprehend the ultimate standard of reality: the harmonious relationality of the triune Godhead. Without the first creation stage, God's purpose for the cosmos and humanity is unclear. Without the alienation movement, the communicator lacks the insight to identify and analyze the sins afflicting and polarizing

---

58. Theologians label the supernatural and ontological connection Christians share "theosis." Ross Hastings explains: "This is the miracle of theosis, the union of Christ with his church. Note that this is a communal or specifically ecclesial reality, though it also related to each individual person in the community." Hastings, *Missional God, Missional Church: Hope for Re-Evangelizing the West* (Downers Grove, IL: IVP Academic, 2012), 82.

59. See Hoffman, *Reconciling Places*, 84–89. More on this in chapter 7 below.

60. See Hoffman, *Reconciling Places*, 89–91.

humanity. Without reconciliation, listeners are left in despair as the problem eclipses the solution—when in fact, God's grace superabounds (Rom. 5:17) and is our only hope. And without the final creation element of the story, the homiletician forfeits giving her audience the perspective and motivation our guaranteed future imparts.

Yet theological exposition is only part of the paradigm. It must be accompanied by contextualization. A mature preacher will develop multiple intelligences—that is, learn to skillfully exegete the history, culture, and lived experience surrounding the congregation. Consequently, in the next chapter we will shift our attention from *God's story* to the *emplaced stories* of his people.

Questions for Reflection

1. Is there a particular hermeneutical framework (e.g., historical-grammatical, systematic-theological, redemptive-historical, Christocentric) you use to interpret the Scriptures? If so, where does it come from? How has it served you?

2. Reflect on the reconciling narrative presented here. What are its strengths and weaknesses? How would you modify it? How might it sharpen your preaching when it comes to addressing our divisions, reconciliation, and unity?

3. In what ways do you agree with the definitions of the four *-isms* (ethnocentrism, classism, sexism, and partisanism) presented in this chapter? How do you disagree?

Practical Next Steps

1. Review the sermons you delivered over the last six to twelve months. From a thematic standpoint, which topics do you tend to accentuate or lean toward: God's nature, creation, the fall/sin, redemption, heaven? Which themes are underrepresented in your sermons? What passages or books (from the Old or New Testaments) have you preached from over the past six months to a year?

2. Consider sketching a five-part sermon series employing the reconciling narrative. What biblical texts would you use?

2

The Contextual Step

America's Past and Present Reality

In chapter 1, the theological step of the homiletical process responded to the question, Why preach? This chapter will explore the contextual step by asking, *How* do we preach the gospel so it addresses *this time in this place*?

This is no small task, because it involves engaging two intersecting planes. First, the preacher is attuned to the particular exigencies of our current moment. At the same time, she recognizes the history of the United States is complicated, contradictory, and in numerous cases even deplorable. America's checkered past of sinful oppression is revealed through the diagnostic *-isms* related to ethnicity, class, gender, and politics. The *-isms* bedeviling us at present are nothing new. The ugly reality is that individual and corporate sins have been left to their own devices—seldom addressed or confronted by Christian leaders, pastors, and preachers. A homiletician who exegetes the Scripture text alone, without also exegeting the culture, cannot expect transformational results that address this time and place.

To accomplish this goal, preachers should cultivate multiple intelligences: cultural, emotional, and historical intelligence. This chapter focuses on historical intelligence. A community's collective memory and spiritual condition are an integral part of the homiletical moment. Until the preacher comprehends the significance of our unresolved sins—familial/generational, historical, local, and national—embedded in his congregation, it will prove difficult to bridge these four diagnostic chasms.

A Taxonomy of Intelligences

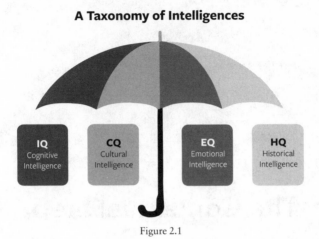

Figure 2.1

How do we preach, then? Twenty-first-century preachers must develop multiple intelligences and deploy them in their preaching. (Of course, the social location of your specific congregation will determine which intelligence should be emphasized.)

This chapter will introduce terms and concepts that will later be employed in chapter 5 as part of the methodological step. It begins below with a brief taxonomy of the three major types of intelligence mentioned above (see fig. 2.1). The preacher will be wise to place them in his homiletical tool kit, to support his role as a contextual theologian. The focus of this chapter is twofold: to introduce the reader to these concepts and to explain and apply historical intelligence to our divided times.

Developing Multiple Intelligences

Almost everyone is familiar with the concept of intelligence quotient, or IQ, developed by psychologist Alfred Binet (circa 1900) in Paris. IQ was based on a standardized test that supposedly measured a person's cognitive abilities and generated a score by this formula: "mental age divided by chronological age and multiplied by 100."[1] However, according to scholar Howard Gardner, author of the seminal book *Multiple Intelligences*, intelligence is not so one-dimensional or merely a fixed numeric measurement

---

1. Howard Gardner, *Multiple Intelligences: New Horizons in Theory and Practice*, rev. and exp. ed. (New York: Basic Books, 2006), 3.

(e.g., saying that a person has an IQ of 90, 120, or 150). Gardner contends that "human cognitive competence is better described in terms of a set of abilities, talents, or mental skills, which I call *intelligences*."[2] These multiple intelligences broaden the definition of cognitive intelligence to include all types of intelligence: musical, artistic, craft/trade, science, math, languages, writing ability, sports, and more. Every person is endowed with different intelligences—including cultural, emotional, historical, institutional,[3] and spiritual intelligence[4]—and has the capacity to expand and strengthen them. Due to space limitations, we will focus on cultural, emotional, and historical intelligence.

Cultural Intelligence

As conceptualized by business professors P. Christopher Earley and Soon Ang and more recently popularized by David A. Livermore, cultural intelligence quotient (CQ) represents "the capability to deal effectively with other people with whom the person does not share a common cultural background and understanding."[5] To develop awareness of one's own or another cultural background, one can explore a culture's particular aspects, such as

> language, fashion, social media, trends, worldviews, musical tastes, news, values, politics, race, ethnicity, cuisine, beliefs, gender issues, mores, human sexuality, blue collar, white collar, religious preferences, the arts, sports, hip-hop, church traditions, evangelical, mainline, progressive, liberal, conservative, Baptist, Presbyterian, Anglican, Methodist, R-rated, PG-rated, and so on.[6]

In today's high-tech world, pastors and preachers must navigate another cultural reality, social media. According to Douglas S. Bursch, "Our online existence is turning us into angry, dehumanizing, polarizing people."[7] Although the genesis of CQ came in the business community, preachers would

2. Gardner, *Multiple Intelligences*, 6.
3. See Gordon T. Smith, *Institutional Intelligence: How to Build an Effective Organization* (Downers Grove, IL: InterVarsity, 2017).
4. See Kris Vallotton, *Spiritual Intelligence: The Art of Thinking Like God* (Minneapolis: Chosen, 2020).
5. See P. Christopher Earley and Soon Ang, *Cultural Intelligence: Individual Interactions across Cultures* (Stanford, CA: Stanford University Press, 2003), 12.
6. Matthew D. Kim, *Preaching with Cultural Intelligence: Understanding the People Who Hear Our Sermons* (Grand Rapids: Baker Academic, 2017), 4.
7. Douglas S. Bursch, *Posting Peace: Why Social Media Divides Us and What We Can Do about It* (Downers Grove, IL: InterVarsity, 2021), 2.

benefit from growing in cultural intelligence to sharpen their skills for general pastoral ministry and for the pulpit.

As it pertains to preaching to a fractured country, cultural intelligence may have varied expressions. First, the astute preacher studies his or her congregation demographically. He or she must understand who the listeners are and what their beliefs, values, and worldviews are, especially regarding our diagnostics of ethnicity, gender, class, and politics. As one can imagine, the spectrum of divergent views represented in a given church context can be broad. It might be advantageous to assess the range of perspectives by taking a survey of the congregants on these -*isms* and other matters. While surveys may offer only a panoramic view, they will still provide the preacher with valuable background on who is listening out there. Consider exploring the cultural intelligence tools presented in *Preaching with Cultural Intelligence: Understanding the People Who Hear Our Sermons*.

Second, to go deeper, culturally intelligent preachers will spend time with listeners who hold different perspectives to learn what they believe and how they came to hold those beliefs. Rather than get defensive, preachers will open their ears and minds for new theories and ideas. They will not immediately view counterarguments as threats. They will ask open-ended questions and listen to their church members without interrupting them, pushing back, or attempting to persuade them toward the preacher's personal views. In most cases, listeners have adopted a position based on years of exploration and rumination. Our initial task is to actively listen and ask how they came to that conclusion.

Emotional Intelligence

Preaching to a divided nation will also require greater emotional intelligence. Daniel Goleman introduced the concept of emotional intelligence, or EQ, which he defined as "the capacity for recognizing our own feelings and those of others, for motivating ourselves, and for managing emotions well in ourselves and in our relationships."[8] EQ involves five areas of relational intelligence: "(1) self-awareness, (2) self-regulation, (3) motivation, (4) empathy, and (5) social skill."[9] It goes beyond mere social or relational skills; it relates to the ability to empathize with others as embodied beings who live in a particular social/cultural location.

8. Daniel Goleman, *Working with Emotional Intelligence* (New York: Bantam Books, 1998), 317.
9. Lori Ciccarelli Stotko, "Emotional Intelligence for Effective Ministry," *Ministry*, March 2020, https://www.ministrymagazine.org/archive/2020/03/Emotional-intelligence-for-effective-ministry.

EQ can be lacking in our culture today, and perhaps even in our pulpits.[10] When preachers lack emotional intelligence, their sermons lack empathy for those who sit silently and listen (despite their feelings and emotional state being unacknowledged). Sermons that are primarily left-brained, cognitive, linear or lecture-styled, and express little consideration of the preacher's or listeners' emotional state or relational context, indicate a low EQ.

What is the litmus test, then, of whether a preacher possesses emotional intelligence? We start by posing the antithesis, what Peter Scazzero calls the "emotionally unhealthy leader." He defines it this way:

> The emotionally unhealthy leader is someone who operates in a continuous state of emotional and spiritual deficit, lacking emotional maturity and a "being *with* God" sufficient to sustain their "doing *for* God." . . . Emotional deficits are manifested primarily by a pervasive lack of awareness. Unhealthy leaders lack, for example, awareness of their feelings, their weaknesses and limits, how their past impacts their present, and how others experience them.[11]

Since people whose emotional intelligence is underdeveloped lack self-awareness, they have difficulty navigating the emotional condition of others. Thus, preachers whose EQ is low may preach with a harsh or hostile tone—accusatory, self-righteous, and devoid of compassion. Their sermons may not consider or acknowledge multiple perspectives on a given issue. They may fail to address questions that their listeners are asking.[12] This amounts to usurping God's message for Israel as our own: "My thoughts are not your thoughts" (Isa. 55:8). In essence, it's preaching devoid of love and full of detached condescension.

Preaching with emotional intelligence, on the other hand, looks quite different. With emotional feelers extended, the preacher scans the congregation throughout the sermon looking for visible cues such as body language and establishing eye contact to monitor listeners' emotional responses to the preached Word. He chooses his words carefully with sensitivity and grace. He communicates even hard truths winsomely and irenically. He doesn't exploit the congregation as a punching bag to offload his own ministerial stress, anger, or frustration.

"Empathy," Lenny Luchetti maintains, "gives preachers the capacity, the grace really, to slip their feet into the shoes of their congregants so that they

---

10. Stotko, "Emotional Intelligence for Effective Ministry." See also Matthew D. Kim, *Preaching to People in Pain: How Suffering Can Shape Your Sermons and Connect with Your Congregation* (Grand Rapids: Baker Academic, 2021).

11. Peter Scazzero, *The Emotionally Healthy Leader: How Transforming Your Inner Life Will Deeply Transform Your Church, Team, and the World* (Grand Rapids: Zondervan, 2015), 25.

12. See, for example, Meirwyn Walters, *Intentional Preaching: A View from the Pew* (Peabody, MA: Hendrickson, 2020).

think and feel what their people think and feel. . . . Without empathy, preachers cannot begin to fully know and love the people to whom they preach."[13] As preachers who want to assess our own EQ, we might ask ourselves some questions: Am I aware of the varied emotions represented in the congregation? How is my congregation reacting to recent events in our congregation, community, or nation? What emotions might be triggered by the content of the text I'm preaching on today? How do I need to prepare my listeners for experiencing those emotions in the preaching moment? And how do I meet them in the midst of these emotions?[14] The high-EQ preacher is an empathetic pastoral leader who knows how to encourage, inspire, and bring hope to a broken congregation that has encountered another war-torn week living in a divided community, a divided state, a divided nation, and a divided world, and perhaps even in a divided family.

Historical Intelligence

Finally, we come to historical intelligence. In *A New Archetype for Competitive Intelligence*, John J. McGonagle Jr. and Carolyn M. Vella mention the term in the context of business intelligence and management information systems.[15] In business, historical intelligence relates to collection and analysis of data from the past (such as "production capacity, budgets, and long-range plans of key targets"[16]) used to compare with current data. Taking a different angle on the concept, we would like to posit this working theory of historical intelligence: Historical intelligence (HQ) is knowledge of past events, issues, ideas, or actions that in some measurable way influences—whether positively, negatively, or neutrally—the present and future reality of society, its powers, and its structures. Furthermore, HQ recognizes that history is captured, codified, and distributed through the vehicle of narrative. Stories are transmitted via multiple channels, including oral, visual (art), and script (writing or texts).[17] Last, it should be noted that while history is ultimately governed by the triune God, it is also true that "it is the victor who writes the history and counts the dead."[18]

13. Lenny Luchetti, *Preaching with Empathy: Crafting Sermons in a Callous Culture* (Nashville: Abingdon, 2018), xiii.

14. Thanks to Heather Joy Zimmerman for these important insights.

15. John J. McGonagle Jr. and Carolyn M. Vella, *A New Archetype for Competitive Intelligence* (Westport, CT: Quorum Books, 1996). We are unaware of other uses of the term *historical intelligence* and McGonagle and Vella do not define the term in their book.

16. McGonagle and Vella, *New Archetype*, 185.

17. The study of historians and the ways history is composed is called *historiography*.

18. Sir William Francis Butler, *Charles George Gordon* (London: MacMillan and Co., 1892), 6.

In the context of the local church, we will want to grow in historical intelligence by learning about our congregation's past. Why? History not only repeats itself but is something that cannot be completely forgotten in institutional memory. Its impact continues in every sphere of life. What is your church's history? What have been the most significant historic doctrines of your church? What theological hills were your church members willing to die on?[19] What types of conflict has your church experienced externally (in the community) and internally (within their local body of Christ)? What has been a dominant identity or image for your church—that is, what does your congregation want the church to be known for? What do you know already about your church? What do you not yet know? What have you not bothered to ask?

I (Paul) am continuously reminded of the history of the congregation I serve. How? On the wall of the church office is a framed chronology of all the pastors who have shepherded the flock, going back to 1966 (that founding pastor built our facility and moved the congregation to our current location in 1972). Due to God's grace operating through a handful of our oldest members who've reminisced candidly with me, I know the stories of all those pastors and the characteristics of their tenure. It is humbling to ponder the previous struggles and triumphs and to know I am but one link in a long chain.

The examples above of multiple intelligences testify that preaching is not a linear, one-dimensional theological discipline or ministry activity. Preaching is an art and a craft, a multidisciplinary task that requires some measure of dexterity in numerous disciplines: biblical exegesis, biblical theology, systematic theology, church history, counseling, psychology, anthropology, sociology, cultural exegesis, communication, and more.[20] For this reason, the astute preacher cultivates skills not only in scriptural interpretation but also with regard to cultural intelligence, emotional/relational intelligence, and historical intelligence. Each type helps the preacher communicate across various divides.

Now that we have described how multiple intelligences relate to the homiletical process, we want to recollect our multiple histories as a nation called the United States of America.

19. See Gavin Ortlund, *Finding the Right Hills to Die On: The Case for Theological Triage* (Wheaton: Crossway, 2020).
20. See Matthew D. Kim, *A Little Book for New Preachers: Why and How to Study Homiletics* (Downers Grove, IL: IVP Academic, 2020), 29.

Remembering Multiple Histories

Born in Chicago and raised in the suburbs, I (Matt) spent my entire childhood learning in the American educational system. As I moved along annually from kindergarten through high school, I don't believe my teachers even once assigned a textbook, or any literature, that was not written by a white author. Most of the people lauded in my history books were white men—national government leaders and presidents such as George Washington, Abraham Lincoln, and John F. Kennedy, and on rare occasions white women like Helen Keller, Amelia Earhart, and Clara Barton. Moreover, I don't recall hearing a single story—positive or negative—about a person of Asian descent. It was as if my entire ethnic/racial group did not exist, at least not in American textbooks.[21] Celebrated figures in US history like Christopher Columbus and the dynamic duo explorers Lewis and Clark were revered for their courage in exploring a strange land, with no mention of the fact that these lands were inhabited by Indigenous peoples.[22] Their lands were taken from them by force, and sometimes execution. It is a sordid tale, but one that must be acknowledged.

A major contributor to the cycle of systemic sin in our nation stems from existing educational, pedagogical, and scholarly structures. We must ask, Who's writing the history? Who controls the narrative? Whose perspective on history are we receiving, and is it a balanced and others-encompassing retelling of historic events?

Our goal regarding historical intelligence is to challenge preachers to read and explore non-white and non-Western authors who provide a perspective beyond a "white normative" (defined later in this chapter) view of history. Ethnic minorities' narratives compose a significant part of US history. Similarly, the Scriptures regularly portray history through the experiences and points of view of people on the margins of society, such as the stories found in Exodus, Ruth, Nehemiah, Esther, and Daniel, and that of the Ethiopian eunuch, Onesimus, and many more.

Historic Sins of Idolatry

How can we develop historical intelligence to aid our preaching? Let's begin this section by identifying historic sins of idolatry in the US that are

---

21. See Deepa Shivaram, "Illinois Has Become the First State to Require the Teaching of Asian American History," NPR, July 13, 2021, https://www.npr.org/2021/07/13/1015596570/illinois-has-become-the-first-state-to-require-the-teaching-of-asian-american-hi.

22. Mark Charles and Soong-Chan Rah, *Unsettling Truths: The Ongoing, Dehumanizing Legacy of the Doctrine of Discovery* (Downers Grove, IL: InterVarsity, 2019), 13.

related to pride and "being right." We might call the latter *rightness*, or the need to be right, which has been defined as "the state of being morally or legally correct."[23] Obviously, the antithesis of and antidote to pride is humility—a virtue that is sorely lacking in our self-important society (as we will go into in chap. 5).[24] There are various ways to investigate historical intelligence. We will briefly explore the concept through the lens of idolatry: familial/generational idols, local idols, congregational idols, and national idols. What might familial or generational idolatry look like for preachers and listeners?

Familial/Generational Idols

As mentioned in chapter 1, the Bible is clear about the existence of generational sin. As we get to know the oral history of the family members in our churches and the oral history of our congregations, we will discover patterns of sin and idolatry. This is not new; it goes back to the third commandment in Exodus 20:5–6: "You shall not bow down to them [idols] or worship them; for I, the LORD your God, am a jealous God, punishing the children for the sin of the parents to the third and fourth generation of those who hate me, but showing love to a thousand generations of those who love me and keep my commandments."

This concern regarding the impacts of generational sin is repeated in the New Testament. In John 9:1–3, the Gospel author records: "As he went along, he saw a man blind from birth. His disciples asked him, 'Rabbi, who sinned, this man or his parents, that he was born blind?' 'Neither this man nor his parents sinned,' said Jesus, 'but this happened so that the works of God might be displayed in him.'" Common generational sins include adultery and fornication; sexual, verbal, and physical abuse; bullying, neglect, and abandonment; addiction to drugs and alcohol; pride, gossip, and slander, and more. How are ethnocentrism, classism, sexism, and partisanism perpetuated? Oftentimes, it's through the virus of generational sin spread through one conversation, one judgment, one slanderous comment, one teaching moment at a time.

For our purposes, we will look at the dominant sin infecting all of our *-isms*: the idol of pride, especially through the lens of needing to be right.

23. See https://dictionary.cambridge.org/us/dictionary/english/rightness.
24. Recent books emphasizing humility include Justin A. Irving and Mark L. Strauss, *Leadership in Christian Perspective: Biblical Foundations and Contemporary Practices for Servant Leaders* (Grand Rapids: Baker Academic, 2019); and John Dickson, *Humilitas: A Lost Key to Life, Love, and Leadership* (Grand Rapids: Zondervan, 2018).

Regarding our current Christian culture, Tara Beth Leach observes: "Instead of falling to our knees, we took to larger platforms and louder megaphones to make our views known. We took to Twitter with hateful words and memes. Instead of peacemaking, we took to dividing and violent speech. We were more interested in being right than unified, so we drew harder lines in the sand and pushed the weak, marginalized, and hurting away."[25]

Identifying the problem of sinful pride is merely the beginning of the journey. Historical intelligence also includes distinguishing the various idols fed by pride, and deconstructing them.

Local Idols of Pride and of Rightness

What do pride and rightness look like locally? Hometown heroes and celebrities provide a lighthearted example. Take, for instance, Jim Schwantz, the pride of William Fremd High School in Palatine, Illinois, where I (Matt) graduated from. Schwantz, a star athlete in football and baseball, was hallowed in Fremd's hallways and locker room by coaches and students alike. He received a football scholarship to attend Purdue University and became a linebacker for the Chicago Bears—any local aspiring football player's dream come true.[26] Who is that homegrown person/celebrity in your town, whether in the arena of sports or some other specialty?

Local idols can express themselves through rightness based on local mores and cultural values. Perhaps in your town or community, it's frowned upon to dance, drink alcohol, play the lottery, vote for a particular political candidate or party, and more—or maybe those very same things are touted and encouraged. If you believe the contrary, or behave on the contrary, you are seen as an outlier; this can be particularly true of transplants who move to a new town and don't know the "local rules." Local idols of pride and rightness can be found in every community.

What are the predominant opinions and behaviors regarding ethnocentrism, classism, sexism, and political division where you live and work? How do your views intersect with the locals'? Researching your community will sharpen the quality of your preaching.[27]

25. Tara Beth Leach, *Radiant Church: Restoring the Credibility of Our Witness* (Downers Grove, IL: IVP, 2021), 17.

26. See http://vonsydowsmoving.com/about-vonsdow/jim-schwantz.html for an example of a local company celebrating Jim Schwantz as a hometown hero.

27. For the practical steps of such research, see Paul A. Hoffman, *Reconciling Places: How to Bridge the Chasms in Our Communities* (Eugene, OR: Cascade Books, 2020), 12–47, which offers "the four facets" of place: "the concrete, interactive, sacramental, and eschatological" (27).

Congregational Idols of Pride and of Rightness

Churches, too, internalize and exude sins of pride and of rightness, with or without their knowledge. Leonora Tubbs Tisdale asserts congregations take on "personas" or "self-images" and can pride themselves on being a certain type of church. For instance, she identifies five major congregational identities churches adopt and project to the world:

- Survivor Church (reactive to the crises of an overwhelming world)
- Crusader Church (proactive in seeking out issues and championing causes)
- Pillar Church (anchored in its community and taking responsibility for the community's well-being)
- Pilgrim Church (caring for immigrants with ethnic, national, or racial roots)
- Servant Church (caring for and supporting individuals in need)[28]

To Tisdale's list we add the following:

- Evangelistic Church (reaching the spiritually lost)
- Cool Church (hip and relevant in dress, presentation, and use of technology)
- Hyper-Spiritual Church (strongly emphasizes the spiritual gifts in 1 Corinthians 12)
- Doctrinal Church (highly emphasizes the cognitive side of faith and secondary matters)

If these self-images become idols, they may inflict internal harm on a congregation, or hurt others outside that church when the congregation's identity is threatened. (For more, see the discussion of bounded sets in chap. 5.)

Congregational rightness usually exposes itself as theological superiority. A church's self-perception is predicated upon what they believe to be the right doctrines; everyone else is regarded as heretical or less-than. Considering all the stances of rightness on biblical, theological, denominational, and congregational grounds, it's no surprise that there are approximately forty-five thousand different denominations splitting hairs over the minutiae of theology and ministry philosophy.[29]

28. Leonora Tubbs Tisdale, *Preaching as Local Theology and Folk Art* (Minneapolis: Fortress, 1997), 84.
29. Todd M. Johnson, "Christianity Is Fragmented—Why?," Gordon Conwell Theological Seminary, November 6, 2019, https://www.gordonconwell.edu/blog/christianity-is-fragmented-why. See also Kim, *Preaching with Cultural Intelligence*, 65.

So what are the idols of rightness in your local church? When does "correct" theology or biblical interpretation over nonessential doctrines prevent you from worshiping and fellowshipping with other pastors and churches? The desire to be right is a Christian malady that we fail to address enough. When theological pride and the idol of being right eclipse the biblical command to love our neighbors, it is time to provide a corrective (see appendix C).

Idol of National Identity above Christian Identity

What are some national idols that afflict your particular area? Can you name them? And will you have the boldness to confront them in your congregation? Throughout US history, whether promoted by the news media, Hollywood, or politicians, being American has been represented not only as synonymous with being Christian but often as more important. Thus, we are staring at an idol of national identity as superior to one's Christian identity. As Jared E. Alcántara warns, "A fine line exists between healthy patriotism and blind nationalism."[30] For example, when politicians misuse Scripture in an attempt to deify America as a nation, they are promoting nationalism over Christian orthodoxy and orthopraxy.[31] Those who have bought into hypernationalism may commit similar sins of proclamation from the pulpit. Preaching to a divided nation means speaking truth to power and addressing hypernationalistic and ethnocentric tendencies. (For more on Christian nationalism, we offer some sources in appendix F.)

Three Disclaimers on the Use of Historical Intelligence

When considering using historical intelligence, keep in mind a few disclaimers to weigh as you continue reading this book. The subject can be highly charged, and immediate, gut-level reactions may come to the surface.

First, the complicated and contentious issues surrounding America's racialized history[32] and its corollaries "white normative standard" and "white

---

30. Jared E. Alcántara, "Preaching That Destroys the Gods" (presentation, Annual Meeting of the Evangelical Homiletics Society, online, October 15, 2020), 10.

31. Here are two examples from President Joe Biden and former Vice President Mike Pence: Samuel Goldman, "Biden Chooses the Wrong Bible verse," *The Week*, August 27, 2021, https://theweek.com/afghanistan/1004234/biden-bible-verse; Jack Jenkins and Emily McFarlan Miller, "Pence Altered a Biblical Reference, Changing 'Jesus' to the American Flag in His Convention Speech," *Washington Post*, August 27, 2020, https://www.washingtonpost.com/religion/2020/08/27/pence-bible-rnc-jesus-flag.

32. See Jemar Tisby, *The Color of Compromise: The Truth about the American Church's Complicity in Racism* (Grand Rapids: Zondervan, 2019), chap. 2.

advantage" cannot be ignored. White normativity, or the white normative standard, "means that whiteness became and was ingrained as the bar or canon by which things were evaluated or contrasted. Whiteness became the racial category by which all others were evaluated."[33] White advantage connotes that by virtue of being white, a person in Western cultures often benefits from an inherent advantage over other racial/ethnic groups in society (while simultaneously being disadvantaged in other contexts).[34] On the other hand, we recognize whites are not universally advantaged: there are impoverished, largely white areas of our nation, such as those described in *Hillbilly Elegy*[35] and *The Left Behind*.[36] Moreover, being white does not automatically mean that every white person has escaped the hardships of suffering and injustice.

The concept of white normativity may be new to some readers, controversial to others, and perhaps even rejected by more than a few. We grant there is a spectrum of opinions here. Reflexively, I (Paul) recognize that as a white male, I am connected, consciously or not, to a larger cluster who have benefited from and perpetuated their position at the top of America's social and economic hierarchy. I grieve this reality and wrestle to understand it, to accept it, to even know how to respond. Thus, my posture is one of humility, listening, growth, and—whenever it's called for—repentance.

Second, we reject the notion that addressing the ugly blemishes of racism and white advantage should be immediately and pejoratively labeled and summarily dismissed as critical race theory (CRT). Consider suspending judgment until you hear a person's perspective and argument. Further, we concur with Rasool Berry's claim that "while every critical race theorist sees systemic racism as a problem to confront, *not everyone who sees systemic racism as a problem to confront is a critical race theorist.*"[37] (For a definition of CRT and some reflections on it, see appendix A.)

Third, to be clear, we are not suggesting that white people (as a group of human beings made in God's image) are ipso facto malicious or oppressive, or that American history *should only or exclusively* be interpreted through the

---

33. Ken Wytsma, *The Myth of Equality: Uncovering the Roots of Injustice and Privilege* (Downers Grove, IL: InterVarsity, 2019), 20.

34. See Stephen J. Aguilar, "The Language of 'Privilege' Doesn't Work," InsideHigherEd.com, November 15, 2016, https://www.insidehighered.com/views/2016/11/15/why-its-better-talk-about-advantage-rather-privilege-essay.

35. J. D. Vance, *Hillbilly Elegy: A Memoir of a Family and Culture in Crisis* (New York: Harper, 2016).

36. Robert Wuthnow, *The Left Behind: Decline and Rage in Small-Town America* (Princeton: Princeton University Press, 2019).

37. Rasool Berry, "Critical [G]race Theory: The Promise and Perils of CRT," *P2C Students* (blog), February 16, 2021, https://p2c.com/students/articles/critical-grace-theory-the-promise-and-perils-of-crt.

lenses of power, economic and class disparities, or systemic racism. However, we maintain that until recent decades the impact of these destructive forces have been ignored or downplayed in national and Christian environs. The current focus on white advantage, then, is a long overdue corrective to a lacuna in America's history. Frankly, it is a consequence of the failure of numerous Christians to confront our pervasive prejudices with the gospel of grace, justice, and righteousness.[38] While we may disagree on these terms, preaching to a divided nation necessitates a level of open-mindedness to interact with those with whom we may disagree and not shy away from difficult conversations.

Conclusion: Feeding the Enemy-Making Machine

In his challenging book, *The Church of Us vs. Them*, David E. Fitch underscores the myriad ways American Christians have become pitted against each other. He comments: "Evangelicals have allowed these fundamental convictions [his examples are politics, nationalism, race, and sexuality] to become the source of division, anger, and antagonism among us and between us and the people around us. In the process we've become the church of us vs. them."[39] Fitch observes that these and other identity markers have redirected the church's vision away from Jesus and simultaneously discredited our faith: "Our witness, as a people, to the life, death, and resurrection of Jesus Christ has become tainted with the ugliness of enemy making."[40] Living to promote one issue, one doctrine, one belief, one ideology has led us to poison and denigrate ourselves. Rather than uniting around our common faith in the person and work of Jesus, we have partitioned ourselves over biblical, theological, and cultural minutiae. When we engage in this phenomenon, we feed the "enemy-making machine."[41] Every time Christians value various quarrels above the centrality of the gospel, we feed another meal to the schism-making machine. We can and must do better. Let's harness our multiple intelligences to change this trend and write a better story, one that aligns with the gospel.

To summarize: in this chapter, we have explored the theory of multiple intelligences, zeroing in on historical intelligence. Since history does not simply remain in the past but shapes the present and the future, the effective preacher will dedicate time and attention to learning about his or her context—the

---

38. Berry states, "Critical race theory exists because the church in America ignored the inherent biblical critique of systemic racism in America." Berry, "Critical [G]race Theory."

39. David E. Fitch, *The Church of Us vs. Them: Freedom from a Faith That Feeds on Making Enemies* (Grand Rapids: Brazos, 2020), ix, 3.

40. Fitch, *Church of Us vs. Them*, 8–9.

41. Fitch, *Church of Us vs. Them*, 29.

historical, cultural, and social locale. Though our congregations may be split over each of the four -*isms*, our aim is a peaceful church amid a plurality of perspectives. With the Holy Spirit's help, we can promote reconciliation and unity within a divided body of Christ. Looking forward, the intelligences outlined here will facilitate our conversation in chapter 5 about developing a homiletic for our times. But before that, we will turn our attention to the third step of our homiletical model.

Questions for Reflection

1. How are you currently exercising your multiple intelligences—in particular, your cultural and historical intelligences?
2. What are some intelligences that you or your congregation could be more intentional in developing and employing?
3. What are some of the obstacles preventing your church from exploring and combating the four -*isms*?

Practical Next Steps

1. For the next several weeks, read the local newspaper or the local news online. What trends do you see with regard to our four -*isms*? How do local news reporters frame the issues? Do you agree or disagree with them?
2. Determine and write down three to five especially prominent local idols in your city, town, or community. How do they creep into your church's self-image?
3. Read a historical book about your state, city, or town. Write down some observations and share them with your church's leadership.

3

The Personal Step
Facing Our Sin and Acknowledging Our Prejudices

We now arrive at the personal step of our paradigm. Mature preachers make tending their own souls a nonnegotiable priority. To speak with humility, vulnerability, and holiness, we must be willing to examine our hearts, face our prejudices, and allow the Holy Scriptures and the presence of God and others to expose our blind spots, so we can confess our sin to God and safe friends or accountability partners. Otherwise, our unexamined shadow side, tainted by partiality, will make our preaching more hypocritical than healing and more condescending than authentic and transformational. To foster reconciliation and unity, then, communicators must be coherent internally and interconnected externally—that is, demonstrate integrity of heart and consistently righteous social relations. But what does that look like, and how does the preacher cultivate it?

The answer is that homiletical renewal animates homiletical maturity. Figure 3.1 illustrates this framework. We will spend the rest of the chapter elucidating and applying this template.

Psalm 51: The Prototype for Homiletical Renewal

In this book we are not formulating a new paradigm as much as unearthing an extant one found in Psalm 51. Many commentators would agree that Psalm 51

Homiletical Renewal

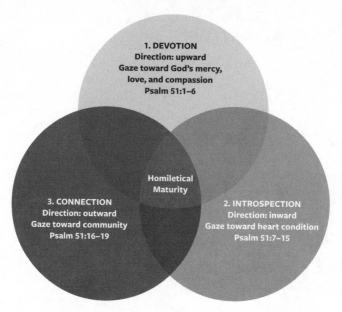

Figure 3.1

"is the fourth, and surely the greatest, of the seven 'penitential psalms.'"[1] King David composed this psalm after the prophet Nathan confronted him about his gross sexual sin with Bathsheba[2] and his arranging of the murder of her husband, Uriah (see 2 Sam. 11–12).

At times, this psalm has been interpreted in an overly individualistic and pietistic way, reducing it to one person's private repentance before God. David's prayer, however, also reveals the social and public implications of sin, repentance, and restoration. Scholars J. A. Motyer and Willem A. VanGemeren bring to bear these broader themes in their outlines of the psalm. Motyer presents a tripartite structure:

1. Derek Kidner, *Psalms 1–72*, Kidner Classic Commentaries (Downers Grove, IL: IVP Academic, 1973), 206. He labels Psalms 6, 32, 38, 51, 102, 130, and 143 as penitential psalms. See Kidner, *Psalms 1–72*, 77.

2. As numerous scholars have pointed out, David's sexual encounter with Bathsheba is less a consensual, adulterous affair than a coercive event that could be considered rape. For more information, see "David's Rape of Bathsheba and Murder of Uriah (2 Samuel 11–12)," *The Theology of Work Project*, https://www.theologyofwork.org/old-testament/samuel-kings-chronicles-and -work/the-golden-age-of-the-monarchy-2-samuel-1-24-1-kings-1-11-1-chronicles-21-2/davids -successes-and-failures-as-king-2-samuel-1-24/davids-rape-of-bathsheba-and-murder-of-uriah -2-samuel-11-12.

1. God and the individual: repentance and forgiveness (51:1–6)

2. The dimensions of true repentance (51:7–15)

3. God and the community: what pleases the Lord (51:16–19)[3]

He avers that David's "sin threatened the fabric of public life. Consequently, he would be as anxious for the building up of Jerusalem (18) as for his own restoration."[4] VanGemeren organizes Psalm 51 this way:

1. Prayer for individual restoration (51:1–2)

2. Confession and contrition (51:3–6)

3. Prayer for restoration (51:7–12)

4. Thanksgiving (51:13–17)

5. Prayer for national restoration (51:18–19)[5]

Insightfully, VanGemeren points out how this psalm underscores the communal ramifications of the king's iniquity when the psalmist asks God to help him "be instrumental in restoring sinners to the 'ways' of the Lord" (v. 13). The "significance of these verses [18–19] lies in the community identification with David's sin, the need for grace, and the anticipation of divinely bestowed joy."[6]

Derek Kidner sheds additional light on the communal implications of Psalm 51. He remarks that in verse 8, "David seems to picture the outcast's return into society, greeted by the sounds of welcome and festivity."[7] Later on, Kidner rightly observes, "The last two verses show that the nation, in its own darkest hour, found words here for its own confession and its rekindling of hope."[8]

In summary, all sin—including individual sin—impacts the community, and thus public repentance, reconciliation, and renewal leading to holiness are called for. The corporate body also enjoins the sinner and his penitent prayer, as some measure of communal liability is recognized. Accordingly, preachers refuse to separate the part from the whole, the person from the

3. J. A. Motyer, "The Psalms," in *New Bible Commentary*, 21st-century ed., ed. G. J. Wenham, J. A. Motyer, D. A. Carson, and R. T. France (Leicester, UK: Inter-Varsity, 1994), 518–19.

4. Motyer, "The Psalms," 518.

5. Willem A. VanGemeren, "Psalms," in *NIV Bible Commentary*, ed. Kenneth L. Barker and John Kohlenberger III, vol. 1, *Old Testament* (Grand Rapids: Zondervan, 1994), 853–54.

6. VanGemeren, "Psalms," 854.

7. Kidner, *Psalms 1–72*, 209.

8. Kidner, *Psalms 1–72*, 206–7. He adds that Psalm 51 "has shown generations of sinners the way home, long after they had thought themselves beyond recall" (210).

nation. This is one aspect of God's ultimate goal for preachers—a Christlike maturity. We define that below.

The Target: Homiletical Maturity

Jesus taught that it is God's will for both individual Christians and the body of Christ to "be perfect, therefore, as your heavenly Father is perfect" (Matt. 5:48). *Perfect* is not necessarily equivalent to *sinless*. The Greek word is *teleioi*, which means "completeness," "consummate (in character)" or "maturity."[9] God's aim for the preacher and congregation is that they would become, ontologically speaking, as mature or complete as possible in this life. This includes integrity or wholeness due to the formation of Christ in us. Theologians refer to this process as *sanctification*, our purification leading to maturation. And while it is our conviction that our sanctification will not be finalized until Christians are *glorified*, we are to eagerly and actively join God in this necessary work.

So, then, what does "perfection" look like? In Colossians 1:28, the apostle Paul declares, "He [Christ] is the one we proclaim, admonishing and teaching everyone with all wisdom, so that we may present everyone fully mature [*teleioi*] *in Christ*." We become more complete as, through the Spirit of Christ, Jesus possesses and reigns over every area of our lives: our spirits, minds, attitudes, habits, relationships, physical bodies, finances, vocation, sexuality, and so forth. The Spirit will not cohabitate with our sin, so along this journey the Spirit increasingly crucifies and disposes of all forms of pride and prejudice within us. The zenith of this journey is a renewed *imago Dei*: "And we all, who with unveiled faces contemplate [or reflect] the Lord's glory, are being transformed *into his image* with ever-increasing glory" (2 Cor. 3:18). For a Christian, perfection is having all of one's internal impurities and external blemishes removed so as to flawlessly reflect the image of Jesus Christ to his saints and the world. For the collective people of God, perfection is reaching a state of being "filled to the measure of all the fullness of God" (Eph. 3:19) so as to become the "holy" and "radiant" bride of Christ (Eph. 5:26–27). For a preacher, a notable consequence of this transformation is God steadily closing any gaps between the affections ensconced in the communicator's heart, the thoughts and attitudes curated and indexed within her mind, and the truths uttered in public before the congregation and the heavenly host.

9. James Strong, *The New Strong's Complete Dictionary of Bible Words* (Nashville: Nelson, 1996), 711.

Reflexivity

We propose that maturity is influenced by a deep form of reflection some-times called *reflexivity*.[10] At its core, reflexivity is "an acknowledgement of the significance of the self in forming an understanding of the world. . . . [It is] the concern to understand more deeply the ways of the self, positioned within the networks of society."[11] Expressed differently, it is "the exercise of recognizing how aspects of one's identity or social location can affect one's vision of the social world."[12] The goal, by God's grace, is to help scholars and homileticians identify and remove their "hidden and unexamined prenotions"[13] (cf. Ps. 139:23–24).

Reflexivity possesses three traits that merit accentuation here. First, it is more a voyage than arrival, more a posture than achievement. That is why it is sometimes called a "disposition" or "reflex."[14] It is a muscle that can be trained or a discipline that can be nurtured with proper attention and effort.

Second, at its best, it is a collaborative, cumulative form of social wisdom, and so "must be conceived and practiced as an eminently collective under-taking, one to be engaged in on an ongoing basis by the scientific field as a whole. It is a process that, in principle, is never complete; it builds continually and necessarily on the accomplishments of past reflexivity."[15] Reflexivity, then, is not isolationist, protectionist, or static. Rather, it is profoundly participa-tory: the health and integrity of the community and its contribution are stewarded by its members, who grasp that the whole is indeed greater than its constituent parts.

Third, John Swinton and Harriet Mowat assert that reflexivity is both per-sonal and epistemological. The personal aspect "urges us to take seriously the suggestion that all research [or preaching] is, to an extent, autobiography."[16] This includes acknowledging how, precisely, "our own values, experiences, interests, beliefs, political commitments, wider aims in life and social identities

---

10. Reflexivity originates in the social sciences and has some affiliation with critical race theory (CRT). This may raise the antennae of some readers. Please weigh our ideas on their merits and see appendix A for a few reflections on CRT.

11. Elaine Graham, Heather Walton, and Frances Ward, *Theological Reflection: Methods* (London: SCM, 2005), 19–20.

12. Mustafa Emirbayer and Matthew Desmond, "Race and Reflexivity," *Ethnic and Racial Studies* 35, no. 4 (April 2012): 577.

13. Emirbayer and Desmond, "Race and Reflexivity," 585.

14. Emirbayer and Desmond, "Race and Reflexivity," 591.

15. Emirbayer and Desmond, "Race and Reflexivity," 591.

16. John Swinton and Harriet Mowat, *Practical Theology and Qualitative Research* (London: SCM, 2006), 60.

have shaped the research."[17] Additionally, the epistemological aspect "encourages us to reflect upon the assumptions (about the world and about the nature of knowledge) that we have made in the course of the research"[18] (or sermon preparation). This type of reflection enables a communicator to recognize her lenses epistemologically (in general), hermeneutically (the text), and homiletically (the preaching event). Here's the nub: all of us have lenses, and those lenses have limitations and blind spots we want God to purify.[19] What does that look like, practically speaking? We hope the illustrations below offer some clarity.

Maturity: Two Stories

When I (Matt) was in elementary school, one searing event ruptured my epistemology and sense of identity, shifting me from a white and majority (or insider) self-understanding to a Korean and Other (outsider) status. In other words, my interpretive framework was altered, tilting away from innocence, acceptance, and inclusion, toward shame, rejection, and alienation. What happened? I, an American-born citizen of second-generation Korean American heritage and a native English-speaker, was asked by my well-intentioned teacher to help two Korean immigrants—with minimal English-language skills—assimilate to our school, where English was the dominant language. On the surface, this might appear to many whites as a normal or reasonable request. Yet, however well-meaning the intent, the repercussions were significant and disruptive, shoving me from stasis into liminality. I'll borrow here from one of my earlier books to recall my reflexive musing:

> Up until that time, I had always viewed myself only as American and even as white. Seeing these Korean adoptees became a painful reminder of my Other ethnicity, which at the time I was ashamed of. I resented that my teacher had placed me in the Other category. This life event altered my existence, forcing me to understand that American society would never see me as white. . . . While

17. Carla Willig, quoted in Swinton and Mowat, *Practical Theology and Qualitative Research*, 59–60.

18. Swinton and Mowat, *Practical Theology and Qualitative Research*, 60.

19. For an example, see the "white evangelical tool kit" (which often hampers reconciliation) in Michael O. Emerson and Christian Smith, *Divided by Faith: Evangelical Religion and the Problem of Race in America* (Oxford: Oxford University Press, 2000), 76. Ironically, it seems Black evangelicals possess a contrasting lens, almost point-by-point. See David K. Ryden, "Evangelicals and the Elusive Goal of Racial Reconciliation: The Role of Culture, Politics, and Public Policy," in *Is the Good Book Good Enough? Evangelical Perspectives on Public Policy*, ed. David K. Ryden (Lanham, MD: Lexington, 2011), 205–24.

much progress has been made internally coming to terms with my Korean and American identity, I still experience the shame of being seen as different from the majority culture.[20]

More recently, my son Aidan, who was in third grade at the time, told us what happened during a class "spirit week." His teacher had asked students to wear clothing from a place they would like to visit. My son, who loves basketball and was eager to watch a game firsthand at the United Center where the legendary Michael Jordan played, wore a Chicago Bulls jersey. The mother of one of the students, who was listening in on the class remotely, chimed in, "Aidan, why didn't you wear something from Korea?" This question didn't make sense to Aidan, who is a third-generation American (I was born in Chicago, my wife was born in upstate New York, and he was born in Denver and raised in the Boston suburbs). You may be asking: what's the big deal? Instead of letting the incident go (as has been the unfortunate response of many Asian Americans), I'm proud to say that Sarah (my wife) sent an email to the teacher and to this student's mother. While the teacher apologized and thanked her for sharing Aidan's confusion because she said she felt uncomfortable too, the mother was indignant as she meant nothing offensive by it. She even claimed that her comment wasn't racist because she loves people of all cultures. She boasted in her email that she wanted Aidan to show off his culture. And yet, we want to ask: What does she mean by "his culture"? Why does she assume that he isn't American? Why didn't this woman ask any Caucasian students why they didn't wear clothing from Poland, Germany, or Ireland (from any other ethnic heritage)? Aidan was singled out because he's a visible ethnic minority. My third-generation American son should not be subjected to such discrimination. We are in the twenty-first century, and yet many still think or assume that second, third, fourth, fifth, and sixth-generation Americans of Asian descent are not American. Her seemingly innocent question had triggered something in my son, enough for him to bring it up.

This privilege of self-preservation and denying one's culpability or complicity with prejudice is a byproduct of being part of the majority culture. The woman could exhibit bias and yet claim innocence. The fact that Aidan's teacher later apologized and admitted her uncertainty of how to handle the situation went a long way. She later asked questions and took a posture of wanting to learn more. Her behavior shows that some are willing to engage and grow while others double down to justify their actions. To begin to break down our varied -isms will require the much-appreciated attitude of

20. Matthew D. Kim, *Preaching with Cultural Intelligence: Understanding the People Who Hear Our Sermons* (Grand Rapids: Baker Academic, 2017), 53.

Aidan's teacher: one of humility, curiosity, and repentance. If our questions and comments cause confusion or hurt in any way (even if unintentionally), we acknowledge, confess, and ask for forgiveness.

Almost every homiletician has stories of discombobulating wounds that must be explored, for their ramifications shape our calling and craft, for ill or good. Indeed, if our heartaches are not handled in a redemptive way, they can compound into pain, or worse. The old truism "hurt people hurt people" is one we sorrowfully confess to participating in at times, while also watching it unfold in the ministries of countless others. On the other hand, if we are willing to embrace our brokenness and invite the Holy Spirit, and mature friends, to show us how it fits into God's story and activity in renewing and reconciling all things to himself, we come to see *how* our suffering advances God's purposes while also deepening us as Christians and communicators.[21] That brings us to our model of homiletical renewal.

Homiletical Renewal: A Tripartite Model

Three movements are required for a robust homiletical renewal to occur: devotion, introspection, and connection. These movements interact in a dynamic way: they are sometimes sequential but perhaps more often overlapping and simultaneous. Without the Godward gaze, homiletical renewal lacks its animating force and source: the worship of the triune God. Without the inward gaze, there is no internal reflection upon the herald's heart condition and thus no true repentance leading to transformation (like that found in Rom. 12:1–2). And without the outward gaze toward community (e.g., spiritual friendships and accountable relationships) the herald or messenger lacks the necessary infrastructure or ecosystem to support lasting growth and development, leading to a thin and isolated—even anemic—faith. With that in mind, let's explore how the model operates.

Devotion

Regarding devotion, the direction is upward and the emphasis is on worshiping the God of mercy, love, and compassion (cf. Ps. 51:1–6). In recent decades, in the West the devotional life has increasingly been framed through the development of spiritual disciplines. The classic text is Richard Foster's

---

21. This is true of the authors. Matt's experiences led him to teach about the importance of cultural intelligence, while I (Paul) have become a proponent of reconciliation as a result of some formative events in my life. For examples, see the introduction to Paul A. Hoffman, *Reconciling Places: How to Bridge the Chasms in Our Communities* (Eugene, OR: Cascade Books, 2020).

Celebration of Discipline, but there are many others.[22] Practices vary widely depending on one's theological tradition or convictions, ecclesiology, ethnicity, and location, and so it's unhelpful to be overly prescriptive. That said, consistent—even daily—prayer and the study of Scripture are crucial if the preacher hopes to develop an upward-facing devotional life. Let's investigate these two practices.

Prayer: Adoring, Confessing, and Interceding

Prayer is communion with God the Father (Matt. 6:9) through the Son (in Jesus's name; cf. Acts 4:10), in the power of the indwelling Spirit (Rom. 8:26–27). It includes speaking and listening, praise and silence, intercession and journaling—broad and dynamic indeed. Nevertheless, despite this panoply of portals into the heart of the Trinity, our aim is to accentuate three thrusts in the arena of prayer: adoring, confessing, and interceding.

In Psalm 51:1, David appeals to three of God's attributes: "mercy," "unfailing love," and "great compassion." After the inscription, the second word in the English text of this psalm is "mercy" (*hanan*), which means "to *bend* or *stoop* in kindness to an inferior."[23] Right out of the gate, David recognizes he is a broken man who approaches an all-holy and superior Being. There are no delusions of grandeur—he is unworthy to be in God's presence and call upon his name. God's dealing with David is totally due to God showing him compassion by stooping down to him. God demonstrates mercy because of his "unfailing love." In the Hebrew text the first word in verse 1 is *hesed*, which refers to God's "favour, loving-kindness,"[24] and his loyal, covenantal love toward his people. "Great compassion" (*raham*) means "bowels . . . tender love, (great, tender) mercy, pity, womb."[25] God's depth of care for his people originates in the most intimate place within him, similar to the human small intestine (or bowels) or the womb of a woman.

Why do these details matter? This renowned penitential psalm commences with a declaration of worship directed toward God; before David repents of

22. Richard Foster, *Celebration of Discipline: The Path to Spiritual Growth*, special anniv. ed. (New York: HarperOne, 2018). A full explication of pastoral spiritual disciplines is beyond the scope of this book, so in addition to Foster's book we recommend the following as other good starting points: Peter Scazzero, *The Emotionally Healthy Leader: How Transforming Your Inner Life Will Deeply Transform Your Church, Team, and the World* (Grand Rapids: Zondervan, 2015); and Scott M. Gibson, "The Preacher's Personal World," in *The Worlds of the Preacher: Navigating Biblical, Cultural, and Personal Contexts*, ed. Scott M. Gibson (Grand Rapids: Baker Academic, 2018), 57–64.

23. Strong, *New Strong's Complete Dictionary of Bible Words*, 371.

24. Strong, *New Strong's Complete Dictionary of Bible Words*, 372.

25. Strong, *New Strong's Complete Dictionary of Bible Words*, 518.

his sin, he recognizes the majesty of the one he is approaching. We see praise preceding petition numerous times in Scripture. Daniel Henderson observes regarding the Lord's Prayer: "The first part of the prayer is God-ward while the second part is man-ward. I like to describe it this way: 'He is worthy. I am needy.' . . . The more we seek the Lord, with a passion for His worthiness, the more we are gripped with our neediness. Adoration cultivates desperation."[26] Additionally, one can look to Acts 4:24–30, the first and longest prayer recorded in that book. H. B. Charles Jr. notes that the first five verses are devoted to "invocation" (vv. 24–28) while the final two verses are "supplication" (vv. 29–30).[27] In the final analysis, praise and celebration fuel not only homiletical renewal but all of life: "The secret of spiritual living is the power of praise. Praise is the harvest of love. . . . Celebration is an act of expressing respect or reverence for that which one needs or honors."[28]

Worship not only glorifies God; it also engages the preacher's heart in affectional formation. When revering God, we "taste and see that the Lord is good" (Ps. 34:8) and realize anew "how lovely is your dwelling place, Lord Almighty! My soul yearns, even faints, for the courts of the Lord" (Ps. 84:1–2). Adoration is crucial to our discipleship because it immerses us in God's presence and directs us toward his character, which inevitably purifies our desires: "Jesus's command to follow him is a command to align our loves and longings with his—to want what God wants, to desire what God desires, to hunger and thirst after God and crave a world where he is all in all."[29]

Having said that, it is far easier said than done. I (Paul) have long struggled to establish a consistent practice of prayer, and particularly worshipful prayer. Time and again, I've been helped by praying through the Psalms, God's divinely inspired book of prayer and worship. In my weakness, I've come to acknowledge I cannot do better than to pray God's thoughts after him, drawing from the book that taught Israel, Jesus, the early church, and countless Christians how to bless our heavenly Father. During numerous seasons of listless prayer, I could always open the psalter and simply read one psalm out loud in a meditative fashion. Yes, this is prayer. If you find yourself in a dry or inconsistent period, start there: every day read one psalm (quietly or aloud) and then write down, in your own words, a prayer based on that psalm. If you

26. Daniel Henderson, *Old Paths, New Power: Awakening Your Church through Prayer and the Ministry of the Word* (Chicago: Moody, 2016), 102.

27. H. B. Charles Jr., "Why Prayer Is Necessary for Revival" (sermon, The Gospel Coalition 2019 Arizona Regional Conference, Gilbert, AZ, February 23, 2021), available at https://www.thegospelcoalition.org/podcasts/tgc-podcast/why-prayer-is-necessary-for-revival.

28. Abraham J. Heschel, *Who Is Man?* (Stanford, CA: Stanford University Press, 1965), 116–17.

29. James K. A. Smith, *You Are What You Love: The Spiritual Power of Habit* (Grand Rapids: Brazos, 2016), 2.

are really stuck, consider using a devotional based on the psalms,[30] following the daily office or *Book of Common Prayer*, or even praying through the Puritan-authored book of prayers, *The Valley of Vision*.[31] In the "Connection" section of this chapter we will highlight the importance of communal prayer.

The second form of prayer is confession. In Psalm 51:1–5, David confesses his sin without rationalization or equivocation. He pleads with God: "blot out my transgressions" (v. 1) and "wash away all my inequity and cleanse me from my sin" (v. 2). Next, he plaintively states, "I know my transgressions, and my sin is always before me. Against you, you only, have I sinned and done what is evil in your sight" (vv. 3–4). Preachers can do no less than this. Before we become proficient proclaimers, we must become genuine and regular repenters, agreeing with God that we have sinned and are desperate for his purifying touch (cf. 1 John 1:9).

The third form of prayer accentuated here is intercessory prayer. The noun used in 1 Timothy 2:1, *intercession*, is a technical term denoting the concept of "approaching the King of all kings and making a specific appeal that he will intervene and deliver a particular outcome."[32] The communicator asks God to soften all hearts (including hers) involved in the exhortatory event; to pierce the carapace of pride within the listeners with the gospel of grace, reconciliation, and unity; and to prune all prejudice and *-isms* from herself and the congregation. E. M. Bounds's stirring avowal says it best:

> The character of our praying will determine the character of our preaching. Light praying will make light preaching. Prayer makes preaching strong, gives it unction, and makes it stick. . . . No learning can make up for the failure to pray. No earnestness, no diligence, no study, no gifts will supply its lack. Talking to men about God is a great thing, but talking to God for men is greater still. He will never talk well and with real success to men for God who has not learned well how to talk to God for men.[33]

Beholding Scripture So It Holds the Messenger

Prayer must be coupled with the diligent and devotional study of the Holy Scriptures, which sculpts the homiletician's heart and desires, directs her field of vision, and animates her imagination. The faithful communicator allows

30. Two suggestions: Timothy Keller and Kathy Keller, *The Songs of Jesus: A Year of Daily Devotions in the Psalms* (New York: Viking, 2015); and Daniel Henderson, ed., *Praying the Psalms*, vol. 1, *Psalms 1–41* (Denver: 64PRESS, 2021).

31. Arthur Bennett, ed., *The Valley of Vision: A Collection of Puritan Prayers and Devotions* (Edinburgh: Banner of Truth, 1975).

32. Hoffman, *Reconciling Places*, 114.

33. E. M. Bounds, *Power through Prayer* (Grand Rapids: Baker, 1982), 31.

God's words to form him before they inform the congregation. That is, God must speak *to* before speaking *through*. In Psalm 51, David declares, "You taught me wisdom in that secret place" (v. 6) before later promising, "I will teach transgressors your ways, so that sinners will turn back to you" (v. 13). VanGemeren remarks, "Only by receiving revelation from the outside ('you teach me') can the inside become whole."[34] If God's loving and transformative wisdom is not implanted within the preacher's heart, then he will be in danger of entering the pulpit as "a clanging cymbal" (1 Cor. 13:1) or a vacuous marionette devoid of the Spirit's sacred fire.

So then, how can the teacher faithfully ingest (cf. Ps. 119:103) the nourishment that is God's Word? Again, approaches vary. Some preachers prefer to spend time praying through and contemplating the sermon text as part of their personal practice, while others focus on nurturing a scriptural-devotional life apart from the sermon calendar. Still others deftly combine both. The key is beholding the Bible so it holds you.

With that in mind, here are some suggestions:

- *Read a one-year Bible*, or read the Old Testament or New Testament in one year.
- *Do a topical study.* For instance, I (Paul) once studied every reference to the Holy Spirit in the New Testament.
- *Soak in a Scripture passage.* Memorize and ponder one text—like Romans 8—holding it to the light and slowly examining and enjoying each facet. I (Paul) spent my recent nine-week sabbatical reflecting on Psalm 23.
- *Join a group study (preferably one you don't have to lead!).* During the writing of this book, I (Paul) devoted eight months (via Bible Study Fellowship on Zoom) to exploring Genesis. It was a rich season.

Let's get practical: how does the devotional step crucify ethnocentrism, classism, sexism, and partisan polarization in the preacher? If the teacher reflects on Galatians 3:26–29, she will glean that her primary identity is as an adopted child of God and heir because "the gospel transcends the importance of one's ethnicity, class, and sex."[35] While adoption does not eliminate secondary and tertiary identities, it does reprioritize them under our supreme

34. VanGemeren, "Psalms," 854.
35. Paul A. Hoffman, "Galatians," in *The Big Idea Companion for Preaching and Teaching: A Guide from Genesis to Revelation*, ed. Matthew D. Kim and Scott M. Gibson (Grand Rapids: Baker Academic, 2021), 505.

identity as children of our heavenly Father, the Creator King.[36] Because God has justified us, through *theosis*—our union with Christ ("baptized into Christ," Gal. 3:27)—our secondary identities can be properly appreciated as God-given differences, rather than bearing the crushing weight of defining our sense of self, meaning, and existence. The gospel is the antibiotic that kills the infection of idolatrous identities (e.g., nationalism: "I am an American before I am a Christian; I thus consider immigrants inferior, even if we share the same faith"). Moreover, the truth that we "are all one in Christ Jesus" (Gal. 3:28) motivates the communicator to foster reconciliation and unity, as we will discuss in chapter 5.

In summary, although devotion is critical to catalyzing homiletical renewal in the herald, it is insufficient by itself. That brings us to the second section in our tripartite model.

Introspection

After the upward gaze comes the inward gaze and its emphasis on reflection leading to true repentance (cf. Ps. 51:7–15). Worship and truth must be internalized—woven into the fabric of the communicator's redemptive story and ministry practice—and thus fully integrated into his or her lived experience. This step is the obedient response to "examine" and "test" (2 Cor. 13:5) the herald's heart by inviting the Holy Spirit to reveal the vices (*-isms*) and virtues traced to unresolved plot twists and developments in her life. The mature communicator is wise to recognize and chart the inflection points, the places where God's story has intersected with her story and brought reconciliation. Wounded healers, having repeatedly received and savored God's merciful restoration, can dispense it to others. Candid self-awareness brings about genuine repentance, first in the communicator and then in the congregation.

Psalm 51:7–15 demonstrates this point. As mentioned earlier, Motyer labels this unit "the dimensions of true repentance."[37] Here, David begs God to initiate deep change within him: to "cleanse" him (v. 7),[38] "wash" him (v. 7), "create in [him] a pure heart" (v. 10), and "restore to [him] the joy of your salvation and grant [him] a willing spirit, to sustain [him]" (v. 12). The king "looks for no half-hearted help. . . . With the word *Create* he asks for nothing less than a

---

36. For more on this, see Paul A. Hoffman, "The Identity Imperative: Three Keys to Preaching on Identity in an Era Marked by Identity Confusion and Construction," *Preaching* 36, no. 3 (Spring 2021): 10–13.

37. Motyer, "The Psalms," 519.

38. This is a technical word that means "purge" or "de-sin." Kidner, *Psalms 1–72*, 209.

miracle."[39] David has stared at the ugly deformities scarring his soul and finds them revulsive. His heinous sin prompted him to make an unsparing appraisal.

This kind of repentant reflection is indispensable for preachers. But where do we begin? First, if you have never done so, consider taking a personality profile indicator like the Myers-Briggs Type Indicator, the DiSC® Profile, or the Enneagram.[40] Keep in mind these tests are meant to be more descriptive than prescriptive. The purpose is to discover how you interpret the world, your motivations, relating and leadership styles, strengths and weaknesses, and so forth. This is a good start in pinpointing passions and prevailing sins.

Next, identify and own your story. How did you become a Christian? What forces or voices prompted you to become a teacher or preacher? What are the formative events in your life? Who are the most influential people? When did you succeed? When did you fail? Where were you wounded? When did you hurt others—say, through an act of sexism or political partisanship—whether intentionally or unintentionally? You might find it helpful to utilize a template to guide this process. When I (Paul) was in seminary, I ran across the "Generalized Time Line" posed by J. Robert Clinton, which is composed of sovereign foundations, inner-life growth, ministry maturing, life maturing, convergence, and afterglow.[41] It has proven helpful in ascertaining major movements in my life. I have also benefited from Terry Walling, a protégé of Clinton's who has expanded upon his ideas, adding constructs such as the "Three Strategic Transitions" of "Awakening, Deciding, and Finishing."[42] The "Preacher's Timeline and Journal" exercise offered in *Preaching with Cultural Intelligence* is useful as well.[43] As far as investigating one's racial identity and experiences, Jemar Tisby gives concrete ways to "Write Your Racial Autobiography."[44] A final recommendation is in order: many leaders and communicators have found Janet Hagberg and Robert Guelich's *The Critical Journey* to be a beneficial

---

39. Kidner, *Psalms 1–72*, 209.

40. https://www.mbtionline.com; https://www.discprofile.com; https://ianmorgancron.com/assessment.

41. J. Robert Clinton, *The Making of a Leader: Recognizing the Lessons and Stages of Leadership Development* (Colorado Springs: NavPress, 1988), 39–55.

42. Terry B. Walling, *Stuck: Navigating the Transitions of Life and Leadership*, rev. ed. (Chico, CA: Leader Breakthru, 2015).

43. Kim, *Preaching with Cultural Intelligence*, 51–60. The cited section describes four vital steps, including writing out one's family dysfunctions, ethnic background, cultural attitudes, and pain. For more on how pain influences us, see Matthew D. Kim, *Preaching to People in Pain: How Suffering Can Shape Your Sermons and Connect with Your Congregation* (Grand Rapids: Baker Academic, 2021).

44. Jemar Tisby, *How to Fight Racism: Courageous Christianity and the Journey toward Racial Justice* (Grand Rapids: Zondervan, 2021), 39–62.

reflective tool.[45] These sources and exercises are vital because they furnish rich insights into the preacher's internal world.

A third practice is regular journaling, which helps sort out your emotional, physical, and spiritual responses to ever-shifting relationships and events. If you don't write it, you may hide it. I (Paul) confess I struggle to consistently engage in this habit. One reason is that I am an Enneagram Type 3, an achiever or "Performer," which tends to be the least inward-facing and self-reflective of that model's nine personality types.[46] Yet I do my best to give attention to the state of my soul by confessing sin and brokenness, assessing areas of confusion and disappointment, and always asking for the grace to "keep in step with the Spirit" (Gal. 5:25) in all things. If you struggle with journaling, let me suggest one writing prompt. A few months back, I took the Holmes-Rahe Stress Inventory, which assigns points to various life events so a person can evaluate whether he or she is approaching a dangerous breakdown zone.[47] Working through that inventory stimulated a gush of thoughts I subsequently put on paper.

Finally, enlist the help of counselors, coaches, mentors, or spiritual directors in exploring your inner world. A number of years ago, I (Paul) saw a therapist to explore some anger and anxiety I was encountering pertaining to the history and dynamics of my family of origin. Then in 2019, after a major ministry initiative collapsed spectacularly and I found myself unexpectedly recovering from burnout after completing my PhD thesis (at the same time!), I hired ministry coach Terry Walling to help me recalibrate my life through spiritual renewal and vocational sharpening.

In a nutshell, while introspection often occurs in a narrow space, the circle must expand to include the wider community. That brings us to the third and final section of our model.

Connection

Regarding connection, the direction is outward and the emphasis is on accountable relationships (cf. Ps. 51:16–19). Psalm 51 closes with a resoundingly social note. David asks God "to prosper Zion" and fortify the walls

---

45. Janet O. Hagberg and Robert A. Guelich, *The Critical Journey: Stages in the Life of Faith*, 2nd ed. (Salem, WI: Sheffield, 2005).

46. See Ian Morgan Cron and Suzanne Stabile, *The Road Back to You: An Enneagram Journey to Self-Discovery* (Downers Grove, IL: IVP Books, 2016); and Todd Wilson, *The Enneagram Goes to Church: Wisdom for Leadership, Worship, and Congregational Life* (Downers Grove, IL: IVP Praxis, 2021).

47. "The Holmes-Rahe Stress Inventory," American Institute of Stress, https://www.stress.org/holmes-rahe-stress-inventory.

surrounding the city (v. 18), and he anticipates that God "will delight in the sacrifices of the righteous" (v. 19). The final thrust is "fellowship with God and his people . . . [and David's desire] to make the community secure."[48]

There is a dynamic interplay between homiletical and communal renewal that cannot be overstated. Preacher and congregation—indeed, all human beings—are irrevocably intertwined. As Martin Luther King Jr. penned from his cell in Birmingham, "We are caught in an inescapable network of mutuality, tied in a single garment of destiny. Whatever affects one directly, affects all indirectly."[49] Another legendary preacher and Nobel laureate, Desmond Tutu, insists, "My humanity is caught up, is inextricably bound up, in yours. . . . A person is a person through other persons. . . . I am human because I belong. I participate, I share."[50] In fundamental terms, "One's identity—even one's very being—cannot be understood apart from others. Personhood is, in part, a socially constructed reality."[51] We could say that a preacher is a preacher through her family, colleagues, mentors, and congregants.

What does this piece of the model look like? We pose two priorities for your consideration.

Participate in a Covenant Community

A famous example of a covenant community is the "Modesto Manifesto" established by Billy Graham and his associates regarding their evangelistic ministry. Together, they decided that "integrity would be the hallmark of both our lives and our ministry" and so they agreed to adopt strict standards in four areas: "money . . . the danger of sexual immorality . . . [to not] carry on their work apart from the local church . . . [to demonstrate] integrity in our publicity and our reporting."[52] They encoded these values into the DNA of their organization: "Billy's team structured the ministry to reinforce guidelines and hold themselves accountable. . . . [They] formed

48. Motyer, "The Psalms," 519.
49. Martin Luther King Jr., "Letter from a Birmingham Jail," in *The Autobiography of Martin Luther King Jr.*, ed. Clayborne Carson (New York: Warner, 1998), 189.
50. Desmond Tutu, *No Future without Forgiveness* (New York: Random House, 1999), 31. Tutu is referring to the African concept of *ubuntu*.
51. James Beitler, citing the thoughts of Desmond Tutu, in James E. Beitler III, *Seasoned Speech: Rhetoric in the Life of the Church* (Downers Grove, IL: IVP Academic, 2019), 139.
52. Billy Graham, *Just as I Am: The Autobiography of Billy Graham* (New York: HarperCollins, 1997), 150–51. Explained differently, they committed to avoid "1. Shady handling of money. 2. Sexual immorality. 3. Badmouthing others doing similar work. 4. Exaggerated accomplishments." Harold Myra and Marshall Shelley, *The Leadership Secrets of Billy Graham* (Grand Rapids: Zondervan, 2005), 55–56.

a board of significant leaders, gave that board authority, and accepted its supervision."[53]

If you are not currently part of something similar, why not create your own Modesto Manifesto?[54] Taking into consideration denominational polity and context, perhaps you could form an accountability group with your local elder board or council, with denominational colleagues or direct reports, or even form an ad hoc group with clergy in your region. We insist that this group be diverse, regularly confess sin, and study Scripture or pertinent books together.[55]

Please do not deny or discount the indispensability of accountable relationships. We belong to each other and need each other to flourish (1 Cor. 12:12–26). Healthy community acts like the mold that shapes the liquid metal of our deliberations and desires; it is the flying buttresses that reinforce the domed walls of our character. Without solid support reinforcing us, our ministries may crack and collapse under the unrelenting weight pulling us downward.

Cultivate Diverse Relationships Rooted in Prayer and Mission

I (Paul) have written elsewhere about how to do this.[56] Our witness is most potent when our practice aligns with our proclamation. Personally, I've gleaned profound lessons by listening to, learning from, praying with, and serving alongside other Christians who don't look, think, act, or talk like me.

It is crucial that we hear and harmonize with the melody ringing forth from the heavenly city right now. It would be a shame to pray "your kingdom come, your will be done, on earth as it is in heaven" (Matt. 6:10) but then fail to recognize and model our lives after the new Jerusalem, the ultimate reality and our eternal future: the "great multitude . . . from every nation, tribe, people and language" worshiping the Lamb of God (Rev. 7:9). Heaven is a dynamic mosaic of males and females, rich and poor, educated and uneducated, and black, white, brown, and yellow skin tones, to name a few variables. However, there is one style of dress (white robes), one voice, one song, and one object

---

53. Myra and Shelley, *Leadership Secrets of Billy Graham*, 57.

54. Our friend Heather Joy Zimmerman helpfully points out: "Some women have concerns that the application of the so-called 'Billy Graham rule' in the Manifesto (of never being 'alone' with a woman) can have the effect of sexualizing any activities with a woman. I have personally experienced the effects of being objectified *by* a man's boundaries that were driven by and applied in fear rather than respect and propriety. I have felt as objectified in Christian institutions as I have by our sexualized society." Conversation with Heather Joy Zimmerman, August 2, 2021. In designing covenants, it is important to consider everyone it involves or impacts.

55. For an example of an accountability group covenant, see appendix B.

56. See Hoffman, *Reconciling Places*, 107–30.

of worship. Toward this inexorable end, we pray, preach, and make disciples in common cause with other brothers and sisters in Christ.[57]

Conclusion

This chapter detailed the personal category, the third step in the seven-step paradigm presented in this book. We contend that homiletical renewal (devotion, introspection, and connection) animates homiletical maturity. First, the homiletician gazes upward and worships the mercy, love, and compassion of God. This includes activities such as prayer and studying Scripture, which fashion and purify one's affections. Second, the preacher gazes inward, gauging the condition of her soul, identifying the milestones in her story, and spotting her distinct personality traits, so they help rather than hinder her holy calling. Third, the herald gazes outward, connecting through covenant community and the nurture of reconciling relationships.

Having covered the theological, contextual, and personal steps of our model, it's time to trek on to the fourth step: the positional. The preacher is a herald, not a heart-changer, and thus controls what is said, not what is received. Let's move forward and explore this further.

Questions for Reflection

1. What role has Psalm 51 played in your life, church, or ministry? After reading this chapter, have you gleaned any new insights from David's penitential prayer? If so, what are they?

2. Homiletical renewal comprises three parts: devotion, introspection, and connection. Of the three, which one do you feel the strongest or most competent at? In which one are you weakest or least competent? A tip: it may prove helpful to take out a piece of paper and rate yourself on all three parts: 1–10, 1 being low, and 10 being high. What is your highest and lowest score?

---

57. This vision continues to catalyze the One Church, One Prayer movement I (Paul) help spearhead. For more information, go to https://www.facebook.com/onechurchoneprayer or see appendix D below.

Practical Next Steps

1. Take an inventory of your prayer life. What methods do you use to pray? How often? How long? Adopt one new practice and try it for six weeks, e.g., spending ten minutes each day in silence or singing aloud to worship music.

2. Assess which personality inventories you have taken previously. Now go and take a new one. Or if you already have taken a few tests and know your personality, instead write out your "Generalized Time Line,"[58] "Preacher's Timeline and Journal,"[59] or "Racial Autobiography."[60]

3. If you do not currently belong to a covenant community or accountability group, start one. Invite a few friends or colleagues and use the sample homiletical integrity covenant (appendix B) as a starting point to create your own. You will not regret it!

58. Clinton, *Making of a Leader*, 39–55.
59. Kim, *Preaching with Cultural Intelligence*, 51–60.
60. Tisby, *How to Fight Racism*, 39–62.

4

The Positional Step

We Are Heralds, Not Heart-Changers

The aim of this chapter is to expound the positional dimension of our model. Homileticians cannot succeed without embracing their role as God's proclamatory vessels. It is best to prioritize the proper preaching and application of the text, rather than obsessing over the audience's response. It is the job of the Holy Spirit to bestow unction upon a speaker, and through that speaker, bring conviction and repentance to the congregation. At the same time, it is vital to recognize numerous Christian traditions and denominations have a history of social and political action in the pursuit of righteousness, justice, and unity. Thus, shepherds and their flocks must collectively discern the will of God in how reconciliation is proclaimed and practiced in their milieu.

A plethora of sticky issues surround homiletical identity and spiritual and social renewal in the church. It is not our purpose to solve them here. Rather, our mission in this chapter is more measured: to provide a flowchart we hope offers some clarity and accessibility regarding change dynamics (see fig. 4.1) and to explicate and apply it.

A Necessary Caveat: Confessing Our Fixation with Outcomes

We believe there exists a substantial lacuna within the ministry and mission methods deployed by the American church over the past half-century. That is,

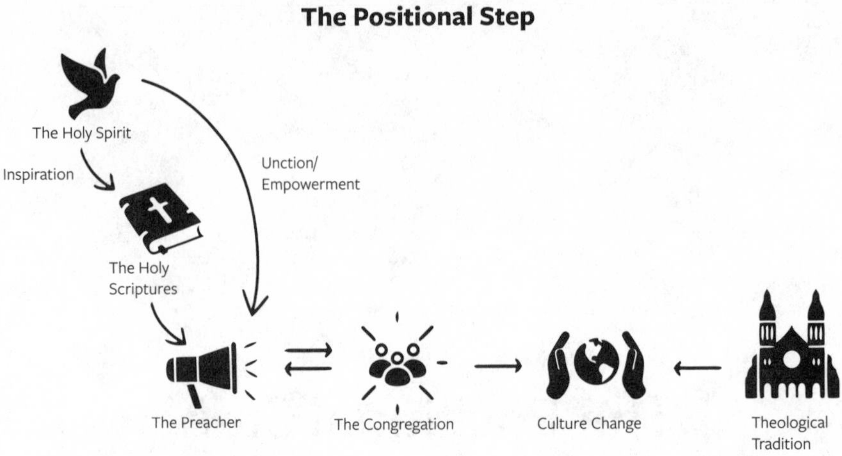

The Positional Step

Figure 4.1

a prominent characteristic of the church is its preoccupation with consumerist, pragmatic approaches to ecclesiology and preaching. Far too many leaders and communicators tend to focus on orchestrating visible, measurable results in areas such as commitments or recommitments to saving faith in Jesus Christ, baptisms, church attendance, membership metrics, and fundraising, to name a few.[1] Growth is not wrong per se: there are numerous instances of the early church increasing exponentially (cf. Acts 2:47; 4:4; 5:14; 6:1; and 6:7). Today, as then, the goal is to depopulate the kingdom of darkness, make and multiply disciples, and promulgate a kingdom-oriented and holistic vision that glorifies the triune God.

In other words, we should declare the Root (the self-emptying Jesus, crucified and risen; cf. Rev. 22:16) rather than worry about fruit ("nickels and noses"—donations and conversions). We ought to announce the only perfect person (the Lord of all) rather than establish a platform (the preacher's personality and social media followers). We should promote the radical gospel, a fully orbed, all-encompassing apprenticeship that beckons every Christian and congregation to forsake ethnocentrism, classism, sexism, and partisanism and embody the dazzling and kaleidoscopic "one new humanity" formed through the cross (Eph. 2:14–18).

1. For exemplary sources that offer alternatives to using these metrics, see Will Mancini and Corey Hartman, *Future Church: Seven Laws of Real Church Growth* (Grand Rapids: Baker Books, 2020); and Jared C. Wilson, *The Gospel-Driven Church: Uniting Church Growth Dreams with the Metrics of Grace* (Grand Rapids: Zondervan, 2019).

We contend genuine transformation is possible inasmuch as the preacher clasps onto a proper appreciation of and dependence upon "the Spirit of truth" (John 14:17; 15:26; 16:13) in the homiletical process and event.

The Person and Work of the Holy Spirit

The ways the third member of the Holy Trinity has been understood by evangelicals in the West vary widely—from ignored, to overhyped, to relegated to an individualized and pietistic role.[2] For instance, Timothy Tennent asserts that Christians have often "greatly limited the active role of the Holy Spirit in the life of the church . . . [restricting] it to applying the work of Christ into our lives (e.g., regeneration) and in personal holiness (e.g., sanctification)."[3] Kirsteen Kim traces this trajectory back to the Protestant Reformers, who tended to emphasize "the illuminating role of the Holy Spirit in the interpretation of Scripture and the sanctifying role of the Spirit in the life of the believer."[4]

Our goal is to momentarily stretch beyond homiletics to consider what missiology, ecclesiology, and pneumatology may offer. This leads us to underscore three aspects of the Holy Spirit: the Spirit is the sovereign leader of God's mission through the church; the Spirit is the Trinity's reconciling agent on earth; and the Spirit is a dynamic iconoclast or boundary-breaker and a signpost to the ultimate kingdom, the new Jerusalem (Rev. 21–22).

Lesslie Newbigin labeled the Spirit "the Sovereign Spirit,"[5] arguing convincingly that the Spirit spearheads the entire mission of the church, not just preaching. While this is readily seen in Acts 2–16, the New Testament presents at least four parts to the Spirit's mission: sanctification and unification—which although internally focused are critical to our witness—along with empowering evangelism and preparing the way for the body of Christ externally.[6] Of particular import for our purposes here is the fourth dimension: what some missiologists have called the *prevenient work* of the Holy Spirit.

---

2. For more on this, see Paul A. Hoffman, *Reconciling Places: How to Bridge the Chasms in Our Communities* (Eugene, OR: Cascade Books, 2020), 72–80; and Paul A. Hoffman, "A Critical Assessment of the Practical Theology of 'Urban Missional Engagement' with Particular Reference to the Writings of Timothy Keller" (PhD thesis, University of Manchester, 2017).

3. Timothy Tennent, *Invitation to World Missions: A Trinitarian Missiology for the Twenty-First Century* (Grand Rapids: Kregel, 2010), 94.

4. Kirsteen Kim, *The Holy Spirit in the World: A Global Conversation* (Maryknoll, NY: Orbis Books, 2007), 5.

5. Lesslie Newbigin, *The Open Secret: An Introduction to the Theology of Mission* (Grand Rapids: Eerdmans, 1995), 20, 56, 58.

6. See Hoffman, *Reconciling Places*, 72–76.

That is, the Spirit "always goes before the church in its missionary journey."[7] The Spirit is the advance scout, moving ahead of the homiletician to probe and soften the hearts of the audience, creating fertile soil to receive the gospel seeds, repent, and be regenerated. He also stimulates deep change in the lives of Christians, as he did with Peter in Acts 10–11.

The second trait of the Holy Spirit is that of chief reconciler.[8] God's revelation necessarily calls for and brings about reconciliation (cf. Rom. 5:6–11; Col. 1:15–22; Eph. 2:11–22; 2 Cor. 5:11–21). The Spirit applies what Jesus's blood shed on the cross has now made possible: the restoring of all broken relationships and the liberation and renewal of all creation (cf. Rom. 8:21; Matt. 19:28). As Amos Yong states, "The goal of Christian mission is the reconciliation of the world in all its complexity to God through Jesus Christ by the power of the Holy Spirit."[9] This mission continues unabated until the consummation of time and history, culminating in the new Jerusalem, brimming with the fullness of God's presence and the flourishing of his people (Rev. 21–22).

Third, until this perfect order comes to fruition, the Holy Spirit gives a foretaste of this sumptuous future by establishing and expanding the church, which is a countercultural—even revolutionary—community. This becomes more apparent when one reflects upon the outpouring of the Spirit on Pentecost in Acts 2, including the declaration of the gospel in numerous foreign tongues, the way Peter's sermon explains this supernatural occurrence as the fulfillment of Joel 2, and ensuing results such as the centrifugal explosion of the church from Jerusalem.

The composition of this new community, birthed and constituted through the Spirit, must not be overlooked. At its core, it exists to be a reconciling and united—yet still diverse—family that reflects the glory of the triune God.[10] On the other hand, the church is also a subversive, alternate society because it reveals the reigning values of heaven, and not those of a temporary, fallen world. Indeed, at Pentecost the Holy Spirit launched

new social structures and relations. . . . In effect, the restoration of the kingdom through the power of the Spirit actually overturned the status quo. . . . Those at the bottom of the social ladder—women, youth, and slaves—would be recipients of the Spirit and vehicles of the Spirit's empowerment. People previously

7. Newbigin, *Open Secret*, 56.
8. See Hoffman, *Reconciling Places*, 76–80.
9. Amos Yong, *The Missiological Spirit: Christian Mission Theology in the Third Millennium Global Context* (Eugene, OR: Cascade Books, 2014), 14.
10. This is why some theologians describe the church as "an icon of the Trinity." See Miroslav Volf, *After Our Likeness: The Church as the Image of the Trinity* (Grand Rapids: Eerdmans, 1997).

divided by language, ethnicity, culture, nationality, gender, and class would be reconciled in this new version of the kingdom.[11]

Willie James Jennings's interpretation of Acts 2 agrees. He sees the Spirit enacting a sweeping epochal shift: "This new world order begins with collapse. God shakes foundations, especially ones that claim divine imprint."[12] Keith Warrington, in exploring the implications of Pentecost, describes how the Spirit births something new:

> The Spirit is interested in inclusion, providing an opportunity for unique cooperation and harmony. Thus, he initiates a community that includes women, men and children, young and old, multi-racial, culturally varied and nationally diverse. The church . . . is a medley of people who are privileged to stand with each other, to relate to each other, to minister together on behalf of the Spirit and thus to reflect God and his purposes.[13]

Maybe it's high time for a refreshed appraisal of the sovereign, subversive, and reconciling Spirit. Our congregants would be well served if the third member of the Holy Trinity is given his due from our pulpits. This is an indispensable way of forging cohesion in the body of Christ by calling it to conform to its identity in the Spirit. We must preach in a way that challenges God's people to embody the Spirit's reality amid a decaying and divided planet.

The Holy Spirit Inspires Scripture

We now shift our attention back to the Spirit's place in homiletics. Preachers proclaim the Holy Scriptures, words and ideas inspired (*theopneustos*, "God-breathed," 2 Tim. 3:16) by God.[14] It is no coincidence the Holy Spirit is sometimes described using "the Hebrew word *ruach* and the Greek word *pneuma* . . . [which] point to the movement of the air . . . [and] can often be translated as 'wind,' 'storm,' 'breeze,' etc."[15] This Spirit "carried along" the human authors who "spoke from God" when inscribing the Scriptures (2 Pet. 1:21). Let's

---

11. Amos Yong, *Who Is the Holy Spirit? A Walk with the Apostles* (Brewster, MA: Paraclete, 2011), 14–15.

12. Willie James Jennings, *Acts: A Theological Commentary on the Bible* (Louisville: Westminster John Knox, 2017), 34–35.

13. Keith Warrington, *The Message of the Holy Spirit* (Downers Grove, IL: InterVarsity, 2009), 141.

14. Thus "Scripture is God's word written." John Stott, *Between Two Worlds: The Art of Preaching in the Twentieth Century* (Grand Rapids: Eerdmans, 1982), 96.

15. Hendrikus Berkhof, *The Doctrine of the Holy Spirit* (Atlanta: John Knox, 1982), 13.

recognize this lovely symmetry: the same Spirit who participated in the forma-tion of the first creation, and thus general revelation (cf. Gen. 1:2), helped create special revelation, which points to Jesus, the ultimate "Word" (*logos*; cf. John 1:1)—God's final revelation (Heb. 1:1–3). Furthermore, the Spirit bookends[16] the story of Scripture itself: we find him in the first chapter depicting the first creation (Gen. 1) and in the final chapter, which portrays the consummation of the final creation: "The Spirit and the bride say, 'Come!'" (Rev. 22:17).

Potent preaching grasps two central truths: the Spirit's role in (1) the forma-tion and superintending of the Scriptures and (2) honoring and maintaining his delicate chain of custody. James Forbes frames it this way:

> [Preaching] is a living, breathing, flesh-and-blood expression of the theology of the Holy Spirit. Consider how the Holy Spirit has been at work to make possible the traditional preaching situation: It is the Spirit who has inspired the scripture lessons of the day. It is the Spirit who has shepherded the word through compilation, translation, canonization, and transmission to the present time. It is the Spirit who convenes a congregation to hear the word of God. And it is the Spirit who opens our hearts and minds to receive anew God's self-disclosure as the living word.[17]

In other words, the Holy Spirit, who inspired and guarded the Scriptures, empowers the preacher and brings conviction to the people. The Holy Spirit is the cord connecting Word–Preacher–People, and it must not be severed.

However, a disclaimer is appropriate. Preachers must never forget the inher-ent power of language apart from the Spirit. The Bible contains no shortage of warnings, such as "The tongue has the power of life and death" (Prov. 18:21) and the assertions in James 3 that the tongue "corrupts the whole body" (v. 6) and "is a restless evil, full of deadly poison" (v. 8). It is not hyperbolic to say that "words create worlds."[18]

This phenomenon has long been studied in rhetorical theory: "The identi-ties of both rhetor [speaker] and audience are fashioned in and through the language we use. The language we use not only *references* but also *shapes* reality. . . . All language functions constitutively."[19] To illustrate, scholars have examined Adolf Hitler's rhetorical techniques, which he masterfully deployed

---

16. In biblical studies this is a literary device called an *inclusio*. It represents perfection or completion of thought.

17. James Forbes, *The Holy Spirit and Preaching* (Nashville: Abingdon, 1989), 19.

18. Abraham Joshua Heschel, *Moral Grandeur and Spiritual Audacity: Essays* (New York: Farrar, Straus and Giroux, 1997), ix.

19. James E. Beitler III, *Seasoned Speech: Rhetoric in the Life of the Church* (Downers Grove, IL: IVP Academic, 2019), 136. In this passage Beitler draws from the thoughts of philosopher Kenneth Burke.

to reap massive destruction.[20] This means responsible speakers must steward their words carefully in every domain, not just in the pulpit.

Nevertheless, the Holy Scriptures remain a sui generis form of communication and thus indispensable to preaching. John Stott notes the efficacy of the Holy Scriptures lies not only in the fact that God's Word is "authoritative" but also in the fact that "God still speaks through what he has spoken." The Bible remains a dynamic force catalyzing change: "When God speaks he acts. His Word does more than explain his action; it is active in itself."[21] Hence, shallow sermons—those that lack a robust engagement with the Good Book—tease, tantalize, and titillate but do not transform. They disrupt the chain of custody by offering scant material for the Spirit to harness. But when Holy Writ is fully proclaimed, the Spirit can move supernaturally through the homiletician. This is sometimes called *unction*.

The Holy Spirit Gives Unction to the Preacher

D. Martyn Lloyd-Jones defines unction as

> the Holy Spirit falling upon the preacher in a special manner. It is an access of power. It is God giving power, and enabling, through the Spirit, to the preacher in order that he may do this work in a manner that lifts it up beyond the efforts and endeavors of man to a position in which the preacher is being used by the Spirit and becomes the channel through whom the Spirit works. This is seen plainly and clearly in the Scriptures.[22]

Unction prompts humility: the communicator must totally rely on the Holy Spirit in the preaching event because only he can arouse repentance for the sins of ethnocentrism, classism, sexism, and partisan polarization. Only he can stimulate godly motivation for reconciliation and unity.

Unction derives from the New Testament concept of *conviction*, which is a key work of the Holy Spirit. Jesus taught, "It is for your good that I am going away. Unless I go away, the Advocate will not come to you; but if I go, I will send him to you" (John 16:7). God the Father and God the Son sent the Holy Spirit to continue, and even to further, Jesus's gospel ministry. What

---

20. Bruce Loebs, "Hitler's Rhetorical Theory," *Relevant Rhetoric* 1 (Spring 2010), available at http://relevantrhetoric.com/Hitler%27s%20Rhetorical%20Theory.pdf.

21. Stott, *Between Two Worlds*, 98, 100, 103. Stott writes that the Bible is "the only authoritative witness there is, namely God's own witness to Christ through the first-century apostolic eye-witnesses" (103).

22. D. Martyn Lloyd-Jones, *Preaching and Preachers*, 40th anniv. ed. (Grand Rapids: Zondervan, 2011), 322.

does that look like? Jesus continued: "When he comes, he will prove the world to be in the *wrong* about sin and righteousness and judgment" (John 16:8). The phrase "prove the world to be in the wrong" can be translated as "convict the world concerning sin." The verb "convict" (*elenchō*) carries the idea of "bring to light, expose, convict or convince, reprove, correct."[23] The Spirit is the prosecutor who presents the world with the evidence of its sin and impending judgment if it does not throw itself upon the mercy of the only righteous Judge.

While this role is reserved first for the Holy Spirit in his missionary or outward-facing capacity, in the context of the local church it is mediated through the gospel herald to God's people. On multiple occasions, the apostle Paul states that *elenchō* is a vital function of the preacher's ministry. He instructs Timothy to publicly "reprove" "elders who are sinning" (1 Tim. 5:20) and "correct" believers with the Scriptures (2 Tim. 4:2); he orders Titus to "refute" Christians who contradict "sound doctrine" (Titus 1:9), and "rebuke," even "silence," "those of the circumcision group" who are divisive and evasive (Titus 1:13).

Furthermore, the convicting work of the Holy Spirit is demonstrated in the evangelistic and apologetic preaching of the nascent church. The book of Acts offers three prime examples of unction, which illustrate positive and negative fruit and thus are instructive for modern preachers. In Acts 2:36, Peter concludes his sermon with the big idea that "God has made this Jesus, whom you crucified, both Lord and Messiah."[24] In the following verse the audience's response is immediate, tangible, and significant: "They were cut to the heart and said to Peter and the other apostles, 'Brothers, what shall we do?'" The phrase "cut to the heart" is a form of the Greek verb *katanyssomai* and is used only here. It conveys the idea of "to *pierce thoroughly* . . . to *agitate* violently."[25] Peter responds that they must "repent and be baptized" and "receive the gift of the Holy Spirit," which leads to three thousand new disciples entering the kingdom of God (Acts 2:38, 41). The convicting work of the Spirit supercharges Peter's sermon and catalyzes the formation of the church. Oh, that we all would proclaim the gospel in a way that summons that level of unction and effectiveness!

23. William F. Arndt and F. Wilbur Gingrich, *A Greek-English Lexicon of the New Testament and Other Early Christian Literature*, 2nd ed. (Chicago: University of Chicago Press, 1979), 249.

24. This is the sermon par excellence that inspired Haddon Robinson's Big Idea philosophy of preaching.

25. James Strong, *The New Strong's Complete Dictionary of Bible Words* (Nashville: Nelson, 1996), 642.

Later in Acts, the Holy Spirit flows through the apostles and Stephen to a degree that elicits a conviction marked by fury. In Acts 5, the apostles "are made to appear before the Sanhedrin to be questioned by the high priest" (v. 27). They have disobeyed their orders to cease teaching in Jesus's name (v. 28). The apostles and Peter assert that their allegiance is to God rather than their oppressors, and they describe God's salvific work through Jesus Christ. They conclude their defense by declaring: "We are witnesses of these things, and so is the Holy Spirit, whom God has given to those who obey him" (v. 32). The response? "They [the Sanhedrin] were furious and wanted to put them to death" (v. 33). The phrase "were furious" is the verb *diapriō*, which also can be translated "they were cut [to the heart]." Its literal meaning is "to *saw asunder* . . . to *exasperate*."[26] The apostles speak truth to power, and rather than bringing conversion, it brings persecution—flogging (v. 40). Only Gamaliel's persuasive speech quells the Sanhedrin's ferocity, dulling their desire to inflict maximum harm.

We run across *diapriō* a second and final time when Stephen declares salvation history to the Sanhedrin in Acts 7. His magisterial discourse accuses the religious leaders of "always resist[ing] the Holy Spirit!" (v. 51). In contrast, Stephen was "full of the Holy Spirit" as he spoke (v. 55). Not surprisingly, "they were furious [*dieprionto*] and gnashed their teeth at him" (v. 54) and then stoned Stephen to death (vv. 57–58). As a result, a "great persecution broke out against the church in Jerusalem," which scattered not only Christians but the gospel as well (Acts 8:1–8).

Here's the bottom line: preaching marked by unction will function as a double-edged sword. On one hand, it often reaps transformation; on the other hand, confronting abusive authorities and unjust powers may arouse hostility, as any provocation is received as a threat that must be extinguished. Sensitive heralds never forget that their message conveys the story of the "Righteous One" who was "betrayed and murdered" (Acts 7:52). As Jesus presciently cautioned, "'A servant is not greater than his master.' If they persecuted me, they will persecute you also" (John 15:20). When confronting sin in general and the -*isms* in particular, we ought to expect reactionary resistance from the fleshly nature and even "the devil's schemes" and "spiritual forces of evil" (Eph. 6:11–12). For instance, I (Paul) have observed that whenever I preach on a vital issue pertaining to repentance, reconciliation, and unity, seemingly out of the blue I experience acute anxiety or find myself ambushed by a familial or leadership conflict, which threatens to siphon my spiritual and mental

---

26. Strong, *New Strong's Complete Dictionary of Bible Words*, 602.

reserves away from the declarative mission at hand. This must never surprise us—such is the hostile territory in which God's heralds operate.

The Preacher as Conduit Dispensing God's Truth

Having explored the person and work of the Holy Spirit, including inspiration and unction, we now move to the next part of the positional step diagram: the role of the gospeler as God's conduit or megaphone. That is, we want to investigate the homiletician's role as a mediating tool (or weapon)[27] used by the Spirit to convey God's story of redemption to an audience of current or emerging disciples. When addressing a group of ministers, Lloyd-Jones asserts, "You are just the instrument, the channel, the vehicle: and the Spirit is using you."[28] We also agree with Warren Wiersbe that "God fills clean, available vessels that humbly want to be used for his glory."[29]

What is the conduit dispensing or distributing? John Koessler spells out one element: "During the act of preaching, the preacher serves as the living voice of the biblical text. . . . [He or she] makes God's written word incarnate by speaking the biblical author's words into the contemporary context. . . . [The objective] is to animate the text without altering it."[30] This is a critical point. To preach with force, the communicator must not compromise, dilute, or intentionally or unintentionally alter the structural integrity of the key ingredient being delivered: God's inspired and inerrant Scriptures. This brings to bear multiple elements, including a thorough historical-grammatical exegesis of the text and discernment of "the *telos* (or purpose) . . . [that is] the Holy Spirit's intention in the passage."[31]

What's more, the faithful messenger comprehends that the sermon "presents four faces": "the face of God, who speaks through His Word," "the face of the biblical text," "the face of the listener, who must see himself both as he is and as he might be by God's grace," and "the face of the preacher."[32] In

27. Cf. Rom. 6:13: "Offer every part of yourself to him as an instrument of righteousness." In the Greek, the word the NIV translates as "instrument" is *hopla*, which can also be translated as "weapon," as in "weapon of righteousness."

28. Lloyd-Jones, *Preaching and Preachers*, 340.

29. Warren W. Wiersbe, *The Dynamics of Preaching* (Grand Rapids: Baker, 1999), 107.

30. John Koessler, *Folly, Grace and Power: The Mysterious Act of Preaching* (Grand Rapids: Zondervan, 2011), 48–49.

31. Jay E. Adams, *Preaching with Purpose: The Urgent Task of Homiletics* (Grand Rapids: Zondervan, 1982), 27. Chapter 6, "Determining the *Telos*," proffers insights regarding broadening application by discovering "telic cues."

32. Koessler, *Folly, Grace and Power*, 51.

this insightful illustration, the herald is just one-fourth of the equation, while the remaining three-fourths is God speaking to people.

Here's the nub. It is astonishing that the preacher—God's chosen vessel—serves as the nexus where the Spirit catalyzes a supernatural synergy between the written Word, God's active voice, and unction. Said differently, the Spirit fuses inspiration, divine presence, human utterance, the herald's personality, and *dunamis* (power). We find a case in point in Acts 4:8–12, when Peter addresses the Sanhedrin. Because he is "filled with the Holy Spirit" he declares the soteriological exclusivity of Jesus Christ. When he concludes, the religious leaders are "astonished" by his unusual "courage" (Acts 4:13). Shortly thereafter, following a dynamic prayer meeting, "all" the Christians present are "filled with the Holy Spirit and [speak] the word of God boldly" (v. 31).

This pattern continues in the ministry of the apostle Paul. On Cyprus, Paul confronts the sorcerer Elymas and, "filled with the Holy Spirit," pronounces God's judgment—blindness (Acts 13:9–11). Consequently, the proconsul becomes a Christian (v. 12). In 1 Corinthians, the apostle attributes the effectiveness of his preaching not to "wise and persuasive words" but to the fact that it was accompanied by "a demonstration of the Spirit's power" (1 Cor. 2:4–5). He anchors this instance to a larger principle: "The kingdom of God is not a matter of talk but of power" (1 Cor. 4:20). And one of my (Paul) personal favorites, which I place at the top of every sermon manuscript, is 1 Thessalonians 1:5: "Our gospel came to you not simply with words but also with power, with the Holy Spirit and deep conviction." This is the impartation trifecta every homiletician, evangelist, and teacher longs for.

So, then, what does this feel like experientially? Various words or phrases can only approximate such a tremendous and transcendent encounter. For some it's like a leaf floating down a river, coaxed along gently by a strong current. The speaker is carried by a force that is simultaneously inexorable, enveloping, energizing, and calming. For others it's akin to what athletes call "the zone," which is "a state of supreme focus. . . . Attention is absorbed into the present. . . . Your mind only processes the thoughts and images that help you execute your task successfully."[33] Perhaps Lloyd-Jones articulates it best: unction provides "clarity of thought, clarity of speech, ease of utterance, a great sense of authority and confidence as you are preaching, an awareness of a power not your own thrilling through the whole of your being, and an

33. "Understand the Zone in Sports," *Sport Psychology Today*, June 19, 2012, http://www .sportpsychologytoday.com/youth-sports-psychology/understanding-the-zone-in-sports.

indescribable sense of joy."[34] Oh that our proclamation would be regularly marked by this special anointing!

The Preacher as Member of the Congregation

It should be noted the herald is more than God's vessel; she or he is a member of the congregation as well.[35] In that sense the homiletician wears multiple hats: shepherd, speaker, and parishioner.

I (Paul) know this well. When Evangelical Friends Church of Newport, Rhode Island, called me to be their pastor in December 2006, my wife Autumn and I became official members of the church. This entailed signing a membership covenant and then being formally approved by a vote of the present in-person members of the congregation. This is unique and tricky. On one hand, I have a strategic role (along with our elder board) in influencing what matters the church body votes on. On the other hand, when the congregation convenes to deliberate and decide on a significant issue, I only get one vote, the same as every other member. This reality keeps me grounded. I must lead and preach never by fiat or force but rather by love and persuasion.

That raises a weighty question: What are the implications of the preacher's various hats when it comes to cultivating repentance, reconciliation, and unity? The answer brings to bear the relational and dialogical aspects of homiletics. Sheer Spirit-empowered proclamation is not enough; for deep change to occur, the gospeler must remain connected to and in continuous conversation with the flock. What does that look like?

The incarnation of Jesus Christ remains the best inspiration and model for imitation. Although we lack adequate space here to broach the beauty and complexity of the condescension of the Son of God, I (Paul) have written about it elsewhere.[36] Suffice it to say that Jesus's emptying of divine glory to sacrificially love and serve sinful and broken humans occupies the core of the Christian faith and life. It also challenges ministers to exemplify Christ-honoring postures such as humility, social inclusion, identification, and mutuality, and to exhort their faith families to do the same.[37] Put differently, every parishioner contributes to the spiritual ecology of the church. The pastor acts as the chief environmental engineer, seeking to cultivate an ecosystem—a

---

34. Lloyd-Jones, *Preaching and Preachers*, 339.

35. We are speaking in general terms. There are itinerant ministries, but even then, that person, to be healthy and mature in Christ, ought to belong to and participate in a local congregation.

36. See Hoffman, *Reconciling Places*, 61–66.

37. Hoffman, *Reconciling Places*, 89–91.

gospel-centered biodome, if you will—that fosters comprehensive and systemic flourishing. Our comprehension of preaching must encompass this field of vision to be effective.

In practical terms, this means the preacher will lead by dispensing the leaven of love among the faith community (cf. Luke 13:20–21). This includes being in relationship with them, listening to them, and praying for them and with them.[38] When this type of caring culture is established, the preacher relationally *knows* his congregation and is also able to exegete the hurts, hopes, sins, strengths, and stories of the people. This is essential to promoting the bonds of reconciliation and unity.

More could be said, but it's time to broach the sticky wicket: the dynamics surrounding spiritual, social, and cultural transformation.

Cultural Change: How Does Deep Change Occur?

This is a complicated question that opens up into a vast domain. As practical theologians, we are convinced that much of ministry is highly local and contextual. The best way forward, then, is to survey some select categories: the driver of change, biblical metaphors of change, and the modalities of change.

The driver of change. Again, we reiterate the person and work of the Holy Spirit. Timothy Tennent reminds us that the Holy Spirit is "the agent of the New Creation."[39] This means the Spirit injects hints of the new Jerusalem into our present world, which is a signpost to the ultimate reality (cf. Rev. 21–22). A key consequence is "the Holy Spirit confronts cultural sin, empowers cultures for change, and draws cultures toward the triune God."[40] This was illustrated earlier in the chapter when we delved into stories from Acts.

Biblical metaphors of change. How does the Bible depict a holistic and social Christlikeness that cultivates reconciliation, righteousness, and unity? Wiersbe spotlights three metaphors that express a metamorphosis is occurring:

From childhood to maturity (1 Cor. 3:1–4)

---

38. See Scott M. Gibson, *Preaching with a Plan: Sermon Strategies for Growing Mature Believers* (Grand Rapids: Baker Books, 2012), 59–60.
39. Tennent, *Invitation to World Missions*, 175–84.
40. Scott W. Sunquist, *Understanding Christian Mission: Participation in Suffering and Glory* (Grand Rapids: Baker Academic, 2013), 252.

From barrenness to fruitfulness (1 Cor. 3:5–9a)

From the world's wisdom to God's wisdom (1 Cor. 3:9b–23)[41]

Notice that these images are organic and process oriented, which is how organisms (bodies) and ecosystems (communities) develop. And yet these images are also challenging because they invite us into a sanctifying liminality, the threshold between the familiar and broken, and God's kingdom bursting forth, stimulating and spreading "righteousness, peace and joy in the Holy Spirit" (Rom. 14:17). The Spirit's activation in proclamation, however, remains unmistakable: "When the Scriptures are preached in divine power, people will have the Word lovingly written on their hearts, they will take off their masks and radiate God's glory, and they will gaze on Christ in his Word and be transformed to become like him."[42] The telos is the Revelation 7:9 vision writ small, an embodied microcosm of the final creation.

The modalities or units of change. Preachers must understand that change is complex and multilayered. It is interpersonal: see the apostle Paul's appeal to Philemon regarding Onesimus.[43] Jesus taught and mobilized units of 12 (cf. Matt. 10), 72 (Luke 10), and 120 (Acts 1). John Wesley spread the gospel (and Methodism) through societies, class meetings, and bands.[44] Missional leaders such as J. R. Woodward highlight the importance of the Four Spaces of Belonging.[45] Last but not least, I (Paul) advocate for the formation of reconciling communities and coalitions.[46]

41. Wiersbe, *Dynamics of Preaching*, 71–73.

42. Wiersbe, *Dynamics of Preaching*, 75–76.

43. Paul A. Hoffman, "Philemon," in *The Big Idea Companion for Preaching and Teaching: A Guide from Genesis to Revelation*, ed. Matthew D. Kim and Scott M. Gibson (Grand Rapids: Baker Academic, 2021), 553–55.

44. See Howard A. Snyder, *The Radical Wesley: The Patterns and Practices of a Movement Maker* (Franklin, TN: Seedbed, 2014); and D. Michael Henderson, *John Wesley's Class Meeting: A Model for Making Disciples* (Wilmore, KY: Rafiki, 2016).

45. Intimate space (group of three to four people to whom you can bare your soul), personal space (group of five to twelve people with whom you practice, learn, and grow), social space (participatory missional experience with a group of twenty to fifty people), public space (gathering of seventy or more people that helps to build momentum for movement). The Four Spaces of Belonging were developed by Joseph Myers, *The Search to Belong: Rethinking Intimacy, Community, and Small Groups* (Grand Rapids: Zondervan, 2003). Cited in J. R. Woodward and Dan White Jr., *The Church as Movement: Starting and Sustaining Missional-Incarnational Communities* (Downers Grove, IL: IVP Books, 2016), 155–60.

46. Hoffman, *Reconciling Places*, 124–30.

Change Is Influenced by Training and Tradition

Preachers are practical theologians and thus *contextual* theologians. This means they are acutely aware that change cannot remain theoretical but must be concretely applied to a particular place, among real people. This surfaces two corollaries.

First, there is normally a gap between the pastor's training and expertise and the congregation's varied education and experience. Some have called this the *curse of knowledge*. The herald can be tempted to mistakenly assume most parishioners study and contemplate the intersection of preaching and change as much as she does. Rest assured, they do not! (This is not a judgment upon the genuineness of their faith, just an honest assessment of reality.) The astute homiletician grasps this, calibrates her expectations accordingly, and realizes it is her responsibility to bridge this chasm and bring the majority of the people (e.g., the center of the bell curve) along at a prudent rate of transition.

Second, discerning communicators understand that congregational change is informed by the church's theological tradition and denominational polity. Each ecclesial entity has a perspective regarding civic and political engagement. For instance, Amy Black has identified five general categories: the "Anabaptist (Separationist) View, the Lutheran (Paradoxical) View, the Black Church (Prophetic) View, the Reformed (Transformationist View), and the Catholic (Synthetic) View."[47] To summarize, she outlines a spectrum of perspectives and behaviors, ranging from detached to involved. On one side is the Anabaptist position, which articulates "the most limited possible Christian involvement in politics."[48] The Black church sits near the "middle": "this tradition speaks truth to power with a prophetic voice. The goal . . . is the relentless pursuit of liberation, justice, and reconciliation. The tradition has a mixed view of the role of government."[49] The other side is occupied by Catholic social teaching and political thought, which "recognizes the essentially political nature of human life, while highlighting the responsibility of the state to cultivate the common good."[50]

Given the challenges of the present era (including partisan polarization, the prominence of social media, and attempts to confront and rectify our ongoing *-isms*), now is a great time for churches to reevaluate their engagement with public life. Unfortunately, "politics" as a concept has all too

47. Amy E. Black, ed., *Five Views on the Church and Politics* (Grand Rapids: Zondervan, 2015).
48. Black, *Five Views on the Church and Politics*, 11.
49. Black, *Five Views on the Church and Politics*, 13.
50. Black, *Five Views on the Church and Politics*, 16.

often been reduced to party (e.g., Democrat or Republican) or policy (e.g., creation and implementation of laws). No doubt both are crucial and hold real-life consequences. But is it possible our preaching could contribute to the formation of a constructive vision of activism? We define *Christian activism* broadly as "forms of public engagement that seek to connect, inspire, and mobilize congregations (and Christians) to proclaim and embody the gospel and reflect the values of the triune God's new creation."[51] This might include acknowledging pain and fear, endorsing and modeling healthy lament, encouraging reconciling actions and lifestyles, and peaceful protest, to name a few.[52]

To recap, the effective preacher is in tune with the complexities of change, the lived experiences of his people, and the ecclesiological traditions and denominational realities surrounding the congregation as the gospel rings forth and the Spirit brings renewal.

Conclusion

This chapter explored the positional step of our paradigm. The herald is best served—and the congregation best helped—when she embraces her role as a vessel that facilitates a crucial chain of custody. It originates with the sovereign Holy Spirit, continues through the creation of the Holy Scriptures, and results in holy saints. Unction brings conviction, which leads to supernatural change. Yet the communicator must remain keen to her many roles: as member of the body, spiritual ecologist, and contextual theologian.

We now move on to the methodological step, to apply and concretize the ideas presented thus far. This fifth step is where bones are covered with flesh, come alive, breathe, and walk.

---

51. Paul A. Hoffman, "Activism 101: How Churches Can Respond to the Death of George Floyd," *ChurchLeaders*, June 15, 2020, https://churchleaders.com/outreach-missions/outreach-missions-articles/377212-activism-101-how-churches-can-respond-tothe-death-of-george-floyd.html.

52. Paul A. Hoffman and Matthew D. Kim, "Four Ways Church Leaders Can Bring Racial Healing," *Influence*, June 10, 2020, https://influencemagazine.com/Practice/Four-Ways-Church-Leaders-Can-Inspire-Racial-Healing.

Questions for Reflection

1. What five words would you use to describe the person and work of the Holy Spirit—theologically or in your personal experience?
2. Have you ever experienced unction while preaching? What do you recall?
3. What is your congregation's or denomination's view of political/social action? Do you agree or disagree?

Practical Next Steps

1. Describe in writing (1) a time you felt convicted by the preaching of another person, and (2) one or two incidents when your audience experienced change or conviction as a result of your preaching. Are there any common factors?
2. Reach out to a clergy friend from a different theological tradition and ask that person to detail his or her understanding and experience of the Holy Spirit or views on social engagement.
3. Write down three ways you would like to see your church grow or change in the coming year (e.g., become more diverse, more socially engaged).

5

The Methodological Step

A Homiletic for Reconciliation and Unity

The previous four chapters poured the foundation for this one, which attempts to create a pathway for promoting reconciliation and unity through our sermons. Earlier, readers have considered our reconciling meta-narrative of Scripture (chapter 1), developed cultural, emotional, and historical intelligences (chapter 2), embraced homiletical renewal (chapter 3), and acknowledged their positional responsibilities (chapter 4). This chapter articulates a workable framework for preaching effectively in our polarizing times. Our homiletical method for advancing reconciliation and unity involves three key steps: acknowledge our centered sets, acknowledge our bounded sets, and include virtue formation.

Centered Sets

We will begin with centered sets, which are our core, shared foundations of the faith (see figs. 5.1–5.4). These centered sets involve four areas of commonality: (1) shared doctrines or essential theological commitments, (2) a shared identity as God's people, (3) shared mission—the Great Commandments and the Great Commission, and (4) shared experiences.[1] In any sermon addressing

1. See Mark D. Baker, *Centered-Set Church: Discipleship and Community without Judgmentalism* (Downers Grove, IL: IVP Academic, 2021).

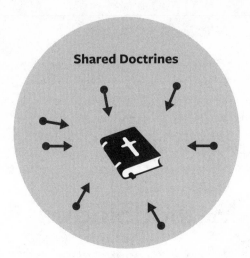

Figure 5.1

a divisive topic, we strongly encourage preachers to begin with at least one of these four centered-set topics (the one most naturally emerging from one's Scripture text or sermon topic).

Shared Doctrines

First, we begin with what unites us: shared doctrines, which we might call essentials of the faith (see fig. 5.1). It's virtually impossible for Christians in one nuclear family, let alone one congregation, to have exactly the same point of view about every belief and practice. However, that doesn't mean we have zero shared doctrinal tenets. So, consider with us three universal areas of doctrinal harmony, low-hanging fruit where we might find common ground with fellow believers: the gospel, the Apostles' Creed, and the kingdom of God.[2] We will briefly explain how we understand each of these unifying factors among Jesus's disciples. What unites us are these shared doctrines or shared essentials of the faith.[3]

First, we are united in the gospel. The gospel has been a contentious concept in recent years. Numerous books have attempted to define what the gospel is.[4]

2. See David W. Bebbington, *Evangelicalism in Modern Britain: A History from the 1730s to the 1980s* (London: Unwin Hyman, 1989), 2–17.

3. Alistair McGrath reinforces our approach. He poses a "hierarchy of doctrines," which differentiates between "fundamental doctrines" such as "the divinity of Jesus Christ" and "the Trinity" and "secondary doctrines" such as "the sacraments" and "baptism." See Alistair E. McGrath, *Studies in Doctrine* (Grand Rapids: Zondervan, 1997), 273–76.

4. See Alisa Childers, *Another Gospel? A Lifelong Christian Seeks Truth in Response to Progressive Christianity* (Carol Stream, IL: Tyndale, 2020); Matthew W. Bates, *Gospel Allegiance:*

The primary division has centered on the person and work of Jesus versus the implications and applications of the gospel (for example, the issue of social justice). In short form, the gospel is the good news of God, who reconciled a sinful world through the person and work of his Son, Jesus Christ: Jesus's virgin birth; his perfect, sacrificial life; his death on the cross; his bodily resurrection from the grave; his ascension to heaven; and his impending return or second coming.

Second, the Apostles' Creed is an important confessional statement that can rally and unite believers. It gives us a balanced perspective on the nature and work of the triune God as well as what God has accomplished for the sake and mission of the church.[5]

Third, we may find common ground in the biblical concept of the kingdom of God (see Matt. 12:28; 19:24) and the kingdom of heaven (see Matt. 3:2; 4:17; 5:3, 10, 19, 20; 7:21; 8:11; 10:7; 11:11–12; 13:11, 24, 31; and 19:23). Christians with a kingdom of heaven mindset prioritize God's kingdom over and above the systems and values of this earthly kingdom. While not negating the importance of earthly matters, unity in Christ enables us to put our ministry energies toward building the kingdom of God, not toward leveraging our earthly entourage or clan for power, prestige, and promotion.

Living into the kingdom means channeling our efforts on eternal matters rather than merely temporal ones. As Jonathan Leeman asks regarding political disagreement between Christians, "Is this an issue which I can disagree [on] and still come to the Lord's table with them? . . . Disagreements between Christians become divisive when we don't make a distinction between ultimate things and important things. Satan loves to tell us that the political things that divide us are the most important things in the world."[6]

Having briefly explored three shared doctrines among professing Christians, we will now provide an example of how safeguarding our centered sets will help us to "keep the main thing the main thing."

An Example of Centered Sets: Four Principles for Establishing Commonness

In an attempt to preserve unity at all costs, Gordon Hugenberger, pastor emeritus of the historic Park Street Church in Boston, wrote a paper

What Faith in Jesus Misses for Salvation in Christ (Grand Rapids: Brazos, 2019); and Lisa Sharon Harper, _The Very Good Gospel: How Everything Wrong Can Be Made Right_ (Colorado Springs: WaterBrook, 2016).

5. See J. I. Packer, _Affirming the Apostles' Creed_ (Wheaton: Crossway, 2008).

6. Jonathan Leeman, quoted in Kate Shellnutt, "In Essentials, Unity. In Conspiracy Theories, Truth," _Christianity Today_, February 2021, https://www.christianitytoday.com/pastors /2021/february-web-exclusives/pastor-politics-capitol-trump-conspiracies-preach-divided.html.

addressing the divisive topic of women in leadership (for our purposes, the category of sexism).[7] He draws our attention to four principles that center on our commonness—in other words, around our centered sets:

1. priority to safeguard each other's conscience
2. substantial common ground between complementarians and egalitarians
3. deeper unity in our common loyalty to the Word of God
4. no warrant for division in Christ's church over such secondary issues[8]

In sum, Hugenberger notes: "It is my conviction that there is no excuse for Christians to disfellowship one another, to become embittered against each other, or to separate over the issue of gender roles."[9] We would also add ethnocentrism, classism, and political partisanism. But, sadly, we do break fellowship over nonessential matters without differentiating among the categories of orthodoxy, heterodoxy, and heresy as helpfully laid out by Michael Svigel.[10]

Jesus's high priestly prayer in John 17 is a charge to pursue Christian unity in perpetuity so long as it doesn't violate orthodox biblical teaching (or doctrinal essentials). In promoting unity, we are not seeking to minimize or merely gloss over theological and ministry philosophy divides. They do matter. And yet, they should not matter to the point of breaking fellowship with other Christians, or cause us to shame other Christians—publicly or privately—who hold a different understanding (again, as long as they are committed to doctrinal essentials). (See appendix C.)

Shared Identity[11]

Identity is a foundational theme in the Bible. God's constant reminders to Israel—who they were as God's chosen and beloved people—are of paramount importance. Why? Their identity shaped who they were, who they would become, what they would do, how they would navigate their collective

7. See Gordon P. Hugenberger, "Women in Leadership," April 14, 2008, unpublished paper, 1–3, available at https://www.csmedia1.com/cpcnewhaven.org/women_in_leadership_hugen berger.pdf.

8. Hugenberger, "Women in Leadership," 1–4.

9. Hugenberger, "Women in Leadership," 3.

10. See Michael Svigel, "A Case for Retro Christianity," Credo House blog, May 9, 2009, https://credohouse.org/blog/a-case-for-retro-christianity.

11. Some of this section on shared identities is adapted from Paul A. Hoffman, "The Identity Imperative: Three Keys to Preaching on Identity in an Era Marked by Identity Confusion and Construction," *Preaching* 36, no. 3 (Spring 2021): 10–13. Used with permission.

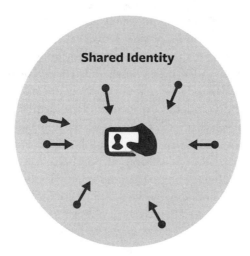

Figure 5.2

suffering, and how they treated others. Similarly, it is helpful for us to draw from the language Scripture employs for our common identities in Christ (see fig. 5.2).

First, and foremost, we as human beings are God's image-bearers.[12] Second, we have a shared spiritual DNA in that we are all born into this world as sinners. Romans 3:22–24 spells out the human predicament of our depravity: "There is no difference between Jew and Gentile, for all have sinned and fall short of the glory of God, and all are justified freely by his grace through the redemption that came by Christ Jesus." Third, the apostle Paul is crystal clear in Galatians 3:26, saying, "In Christ you are all children of God."[13] The apostle Paul reveals the primary identity of every Christian, those who have been redeemed, regenerated, justified, and adopted through the blood of Jesus Christ (vv. 26–28). Being children of God is our ultimate identity and the crux of our faith. Timothy Keller asserts that our identity as God's children is "the climax of the gospel" and "the heart of the Christian life."[14]

But being the children of God is not all. Delve a little deeper into Galatians 3:26–28. Notice the apostle Paul does not say that ethnicity ("Jew nor Gentile"), class or socioeconomic status ("slave nor free"), or biological sex ("male and female") have been obliterated or abolished in Christ. They still

12. See Matthew D. Kim, "Preaching on Race in View of the Image of God," in *Ministers of Reconciliation: Preaching on Race and the Gospel*, ed. Daniel Darling (Bellingham, WA: Lexham, 2021), 1–11.

13. The verb *este* is in the second person plural: "you are all."

14. Timothy Keller, *Galatians for You* (Epsom, UK: Good Book, 2017), 89.

exist and offer credible meaning. Indeed, it appears these categories will continue to exist in some form in the new Jerusalem.

It is critical, therefore, that preachers underscore the difference between primary and secondary identities. Our shared primary identity is the foundation for enduring unity and robust connectivity in our fractured, tribal world. Sadly, in the ancient world and today, secondary identities have been overly accentuated (read: weaponized) by the world, the flesh, and the devil to cause division. This is why elsewhere, I (Paul) have labeled ethnicity, class, and sex the "Galatians 3:28 triad."[15] When abused, they become a terrible triumvirate: deep fault lines rending the shared ground upon which we stand.

To be clear, we do not deny the existence of ethnocentrism, classism, and sexism within the church. They are real and pervasive. We must lament the sins afflicting the body of Christ and seek to remedy them. That is precisely why our approach to preaching is more crucial now than ever. Our hope is not in highlighting our differences only; rather, it is found in the person and work of Jesus Christ, who conquers all our foes, including the powers of death, sin, Satan, and the evil systems of our dark and fallen world.

In our hyper-individualistic culture, shared identities may not mean as much as they would in a collectivistic culture. Drawing from our Western, individualistic experience in American evangelical culture, we tend to focus on *me* over *we*: for example, "I am a child of God" rather than "We are God's children." However, one vital implication of Christians' new identity is that it is a profoundly social or communal identity. By definition, we are children in our heavenly Father's new family. Unfortunately, this can easily be overlooked in our individualistic, autonomous, and self-expressive society.

One way to highlight our shared identity in Christ is by planning a preaching series around it. At the beginning of 2017, I (Paul) devoted eight weeks to preaching on the Christian's identity in Christ to mobilize the church around Easter outreach. I based the sermon series on John Driver's book *Images of the Church in Mission*. Helpfully, Driver outlines fifteen communal images of the church from the New Testament, organized in four major categories: "pilgrimage images: the way, sojourners, the poor; new-order images: the kingdom of God, new creation, new humanity; peoplehood images: the people of God, the family of God, the shepherd and the flock; and images of transformation: salt, light, and a city, a spiritual house, a witnessing community."[16]

15. See Paul A. Hoffman, *Reconciling Places, How to Bridge the Chasms in Our Communities* (Eugene, OR: Cascade Books, 2020), 29–34.

16. John Driver, *Images of the Church in Mission* (Scottdale, PA: Herald, 1997), 9. Driver states, "The Bible employs nearly one hundred different images for the church, thus developing a composite picture that, like a great painting, is filled with inexhaustible meaning."

The congregation heartily received these messages. Numerous parishioners expressed a newfound understanding that God's people exist as one entity, sent together to share the gospel with the world. This is one possible outcome when preachers emphasize our shared corporate identity in Christ.

With that in mind, we must remember that our shared identities—which sometimes lead to misplaced identities—have a bearing on how we treat others. In the prayer of the Pharisee and the tax collector, in Luke 18, we witness a prime example of a shared identity gone wrong or a shared identity that becomes an idol. Read through Luke 18:9–14. The Pharisee takes ultimate pride in his own identity as a Pharisee, a religious person, and looks down on the tax collector, whom he determines to be a sinner or a person of lower status than himself. His self-righteousness alienates another person, causing him to pray as he does—in a posture of superiority. Jesus explains that the posture of the Christian is one of utter submission and humility before a holy and righteous God. The tax collector, recognizing his sinfulness, prays and requests mercy rather than seeking praise. In our fractured culture, our shared identity—whether it's ethnicity, gender, class, or politics—can become a collective or individual source of pride and self-righteousness. Jesus's example in Luke 18 is a microcosm of our divided culture today and a reminder that brothers and sisters should not aspire to be like this self-righteous Pharisee, lest they fall into Pharisaism, which is "an overreliance on superficial indicators of righteousness that in practice bely their opposite."[17] Our shared identities in Christ must lead to greater reconciliation, unity, and purpose for advancing the mission of God in our world.

Shared Mission

Third, what unites us is our common or shared mission: actively pursuing and fulfilling the Great Commandments and the Great Commission (see fig. 5.3). First, Jesus imparted two Great Commandments in Matthew 22:36–40. Loving God and loving neighbor are not seen as mutually exclusive but rather are simultaneous and overlapping goals in the Christian life. We cannot claim to love God without loving people: "Whoever claims to love God yet hates a brother or sister is a liar. For whoever does not love their brother and sister, whom they have seen, cannot love God, whom they have not seen" (1 John 4:20). While we could spend a lot of time here, suffice it to say that it's critical for us as Christians to prioritize loving others above loving division. Our

17. David Zahl, *Seculosity: How Career, Parenting, Technology, Food, Politics, and Romance Became Our New Religion and What to Do about It* (Minneapolis: Fortress, 2019), xvii.

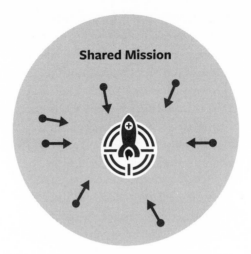

Figure 5.3

mission in life is twofold: to intentionally embody and live out as best we can the Great Commandments and the Great Commission.

Matthew 28:18–20 articulates Jesus's Great Commission. As disciples of Jesus, we are commanded to go and make and multiply disciples of all people and nations. The words used to flesh out making disciples are *go, teaching,* and *baptizing.* This entails leaving our places of comfort, winsomely declaring the gospel of reconciliation, and enfolding former outsiders into our family. Unfortunately, instead of living out our shared mission, all too often Christians have allowed infighting over nonessential matters to distract and stall our directive from the Son of God. We've forgotten that people who don't hear and embrace the gospel will go to a literal hell for eternity. Brothers and sisters, our shared mission must occupy the forefront of our minds daily—not obsessing over and making a spectacle of our differences.

Shared Experiences

The fourth part of our centered sets relates to shared experiences (see fig. 5.4). The Scripture is scattered with examples and stories of God's people moving and worshiping together as one connected community. We might be drawn to biblical accounts such as the wanderings of the Israelites in the wilderness in the book of Exodus, the discipleship experience of Jesus and the twelve disciples, the Spirit-infused encounters of Pentecost, and the life-giving witness of the early Christians and the early church in Acts 2:41–47. Shared experiences often created collective knowledge, values, and purpose.

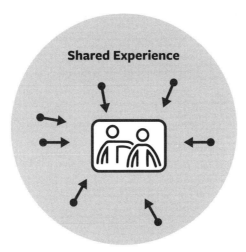

Figure 5.4

Part of the process of moving toward unity and reconciliation is to listen to and lament with those with whom we disagree and those who have different experiences than we do (see fig. 5.4).

How Do We Get There? Shared Listening Informs Shared Experiences

The first step toward cultivating a homiletic that fosters reconciliation and unity is to listen to the perspectives and stories of others. In his letter to the Jewish diaspora, the apostle James admonishes: "My dear brothers and sisters, take note of this: Everyone should be quick to listen, slow to speak and slow to become angry" (James 1:19). When there are divisions among us, we often do the opposite: we are quick to tune others out, quick to speak, and quick to become angry. What would it look like for Christians to understand their shared experiences? In *The Politics of Ministry*, Bob Burns, Tasha Chapman, and Donald Guthrie point out four functions of human interests:

1. People have different interests.
2. Those interests reflect the way people think life should be.
3. People gather together around similar interests.
4. People promote and defend their interests.[18]

18. Bob Burns, Tasha D. Chapman, and Donald C. Guthrie, *The Politics of Ministry: Navigating Power Dynamics and Negotiating Interests* (Downers Grove, IL: InterVarsity, 2019), 57.

To comprehend a person or group's experiences, we would benefit from active listening. In active listening, one is not thinking about one's position, response, or rebuttal. Rather, the active listener is fully invested in what the other person is sharing, and following up with questions for the purpose of greater understanding. It involves six listening skills: (1) paying attention, (2) withholding judgment, (3) reflecting, (4) clarifying, (5) summarizing, and (6) sharing.[19] From experience, we know that people (including pastors and preachers) have varying degrees of listening skills. Preaching to a divided nation will require development of the skill set for listening to and understanding others.

Shared Listening Leads to Shared Empathy

Why are we so quick, as Christians, to dismiss people who think and believe differently than us without even a modicum of striving to figure out how they arrived at their particular conclusions? Until we can move collectively from apathy to empathy and lament, there is little "heart space" for reconciliation and unity. How can we reconcile and unite when we care not to feel the pain of others?

In January 2020, one of my (Matt's) sons became very ill after going to a friend's sleepover birthday party. We believe most of the kids at that party were stricken with COVID-19 (although they were not diagnosed, since COVID-19 had not yet become common knowledge). In any event, we ended up needing to take him to the emergency room after witnessing high fevers and uncharacteristic behavior. After six hours or so of monitoring, the doctors decided to send my wife and son in an ambulance to Boston Children's Hospital. (He was eventually diagnosed with the flu and encephalitis.) But during those hours in our local hospital's emergency room, nurses and doctors who had no knowledge of our son's prior medical history kept trying to give him the flu vaccine and other medicines that we didn't want being put into his body. The history they did not know is that throughout his life, his body has reacted negatively to almost all forms of prescription medicine and vaccines. As an emergency medical technician (EMT) rode with my wife in the close confines of an ambulance for fifty minutes en route to Boston, she listened to my wife's story. After hearing our son's medical history, the

---

19. See "Use Listening Skills to Coach," August 24, 2021, Center for Creative Leadership (website), https://www.ccl.org/articles/leading-effectively-articles/coaching-others-use-active-listening-skills. We also recommend Glenn E. Singleton, "Four Agreements of Courageous Conversations," in *Courageous Conversations about Race: A Field Guide for Achieving Equity in Schools*, 2nd ed. (Thousand Oaks, CA: Corwin, 2015), 70–78.

EMT told my wife that without any knowledge of our son's life and health challenges, the healthcare professionals at the hospital were labeling us "anti-vaxxers" behind our backs and saying negative things about us. When my wife shared with her that all three of our sons suffer from seizures and that our children have numerous health issues and food allergies, the EMT said she understood our pain; she tried to empathize with our reasoning. All it took for some understanding was her ability and willingness to listen to our story.

People quickly assume that if your problem doesn't affect them directly, or is not true of their experience, then your problem is not real—it's untrue. That's the erroneous attitude that Christians need to examine to build a greater level of understanding and empathy. When we listen well, we will have an opportunity to be transformed from apathy to empathy. To be apathetic toward another's hardship reveals a calloused heart toward humanity. Apathy literally means no (*a-*) feeling (*-pathy*). For unity to become a congregational priority entails movement from apathy ("no feeling") to empathy to l ament.

Shared Empathy Leads to Shared Truth-Telling and Lament

Last, talking about our shared experiences invites opportunities for truth-telling and lament. Mark Charles and Soong-Chan Rah, in *Unsettling Truths*, observe, "The spiritual practice of lament could counteract the human tendency towards self-elevation. . . . Without lament, human effort and human success emerge as the driving force in the activity of the church. The message of a messiah who suffered and died for humanity is lost in the avalanche of triumphalism. The practice of lament is a necessary truth telling."[20] As we tell the truth, we embark on a new journey toward a mutual life based on common grace and a desire to understand and affirm others.

Some time ago, I (Matt) was asked by a pastor friend to preach at his church on the topic of racism. After sharing from Scripture and from my personal testimony of the hardships my family and I have faced living on the North Shore of Boston as Asian Americans, a well-meaning older Caucasian woman approached me after the worship service. In her attempt to empathize with me, she uttered, "I know what it's like to be Asian American." ("Oh, really?" I thought to myself). She continued, "I had terrible acne growing up, and it was a very painful experience for me." Your mind is probably racing just like mine did at that moment. How did you feel when you read

---

20. Mark Charles and Soong-Chan Rah, *Unsettling Truths: The Ongoing, Dehumanizing Legacy of the Doctrine of Discovery* (Downers Grove, IL: InterVarsity, 2019), 9.

those words? (Take a few minutes to ponder that. Now, were you appalled, disgusted, horrified, or confused? Did you laugh or get angry?) By God's grace, I kept my composure—even though this woman's well-intentioned words were insensitive in comparing my God-designed ethnicity to unsightly blemishes. In hindsight, I may have winced. However, the credit belongs to my godly wife, who upon hearing this woman's comments concluded that this was her attempt to show empathy. This sister in Christ genuinely felt that these were the empathetic words I needed to hear. This was her way of connecting with me. This was her honest, vulnerable response to identify with my pain. It's the best she could do as a white person who hasn't experienced racial/ethnic trauma.[21] Can we fault her for something she has never experienced? There's no way she could fully comprehend what it means to be discriminated against based on skin color, so she drew from the pain of her own life experience of being rejected for her physical appearance (a centered set—shared experience of prejudice due to appearance, such as acne). Have you ever compared your pain with others in an attempt to sympathize or empathize with them? While it may not have been an apples-to-apples comparison, she tried.

As painful as those words were to hear in that sanctuary, listening led to empathy and empathy led to lament. Lament enables us to concretize our centered sets (shared doctrines, shared identity, shared mission, and shared experience). Tish Harrison Warren exhorts: "If we don't want a culture of outrage, we can't only be a reasoned culture or distracted culture or a numbed or busy culture. We must learn to be a lamenting culture. As a church, we must learn to slow down and let emptiness remain unfulfilled."[22] Choose lament. Choose lament over quick solutions. Allow the discomfort of our sin and shame to linger. Provide the Holy Spirit space to prod us toward confession and repentance for sins committed against God and against one another. Most of us never lament long enough to experience and empathize with the pain of another human being. When we have lamented long enough (days, weeks, months), we will know when it's time to run to the Savior's arms for warmth and healing.

After we have properly lamented and engaged in shared experiences, we can then move our sermon from centered sets to bounded sets. Toward the beginning of the sermon, name the centered set(s) that we can unite around. In most cases, we would not recommend that you start with what divides us.

---

21. See Sheila Wise Rowe, *Healing Racial Trauma: The Road to Resilience* (Downers Grove, IL: InterVarsity, 2020).

22. Tish Harrison Warren, *Prayer in the Night: For Those Who Work or Watch or Weep* (Downers Grove, IL: InterVarsity, 2021), 45.

Figure 5.5

Once the congregation understands our centered sets, we can journey into the bounded sets and identify our divisions.

Bounded Sets

In contrast to centered sets, bounded sets are used for fence-keeping and determining insiders and outsiders. As Jennifer Durham explains, "By definition, a bounded set view is one in which belief and behavior determines who is in the club, and who is excluded. It draws boundary markers by which one is considered 'in-group' or 'out-group.'"[23] Here, the bounded sets address the four primary -*isms* that we have spoken about throughout this book that exacerbate our divisions within the body of Christ: ethnocentrism/racism, classism, sexism, and political partisanism (see fig. 5.5). While we may disagree about aspects of bounded sets, preaching on divisive issues will require the preacher to first establish our unity through centered sets and then move toward bounded sets—that is, our various -*isms*. We can name our divisions and then present a gospel-centered approach to overcoming our chasms. The -*isms* are bounded sets that pertain to tribalism, self-righteous attitudes, and idolatry regarding class, ethnicity, politics, and

23. Jennifer M. Durham, "Bounded Set Trends and Conformity to Group Norms at a Non-Denominational Church" (DMin thesis, Ashland Theological Seminary, 2005), 3.

sex. Where in the sermon could you point out one or both of the following bounded-set principles?

We Are Divided by Self-Righteousness and Tribal Preservation

First, whenever appropriate, we might remind our listeners that bounded sets perpetuate our divisions on account of our self-righteousness and tribal preservation. A major stumbling block impeding our unity as a church is the spiritual malady of narcissism—a ubiquitous disease infecting many Christians, including pastors.[24] Scrolling through social media these days, it's quite easy for us to quickly dismiss others and their viewpoints. The sins of self-righteousness and pride loom large in short sound bites and jabbing tweets, especially among self-professing Christians. To demonize others instantly without knowing anything about them and their lives is the skill set of the day. Since when does affiliation with one nonessential issue determine one's value? How does it turn someone into less than a human being who is made in God's image? How easily we fall prey to judgment and criticism of others without listening first. What about #Cancelled and Farewell _____ (enter the name of a supposed fallen Christian/Christian leader/pastor)? Who are we to judge other human beings? How quickly have well-known evangelical pastors condemned others to the fires of hell? Who put us in the position of God alone? Is there no possibility for these individuals to come back to the Lord before they die?

Thinking about self-righteousness brings to mind Jesus's teaching in Matthew 7:1–5 in his Sermon on the Mount: "Do not judge, or you too will be judged. For in the same way you judge others, you will be judged, and with the measure you use, it will be measured to you. Why do you look at the speck of sawdust in your brother's eye and pay no attention to the plank in your own eye? How can you say to your brother, 'Let me take the speck out of your eye,' when all the time there is a plank in your own eye? You hypocrite, first take the plank out of your own eye, and then you will see clearly to remove the speck from your brother's eye." The absurdity of Jesus's analogy causes us to pause and reflect on this disturbing, even grotesque, image. The difference between the size of a "speck of sawdust" and a "plank" is laughable. Another translation for "plank" is "log." Jesus explains that when we judge others we simultaneously fail to see the log of hypocrisy in our own life. And yet, in our fractured day, it's become second nature for us to immediately judge others because of one comment made or one social media post. What

24. Chuck DeGroat, *When Narcissism Comes to Church: Healing Your Community from Emotional and Spiritual Abuse* (Downers Grove, IL: InterVarsity, 2020).

we are encouraging through this book is for preachers to help listeners grow in sanctification via how they treat others, especially those with whom they disagree. As Jonathan Leeman and Andy Naselli note, "Christian maturity . . . knows how to both disagree with someone and yet still show compassion."[25] Bounded sets are exclusionary by nature. When we engage in divisive forms through tribalism, whether the tribe is biblical, doctrinal, theological, philosophical, or political, we are in fact sinning against God by perpetuating disunity. Preaching to a divided nation and a divided church involves regular opportunities for individual and congregational repentance for the sin of judgment against another Christian. Let us make it clear again: we do not write a blank check for theological heresies. Essential doctrines of the faith must remain essential. We do not capitulate to the culture's demonic voices and demands. However, while orthodoxy hinges on particular theological minutiae, we cannot stand for breaking fellowship on account of secondary doctrines and ministry philosophies.

We Are Divided by Prioritizing Idols over God and His People

Ethnicity, sex/gender, class, and politics all can be good things. Yet if any of them cause divisions within the body of Christ, they have become idols. A heavy contributor to the disunity we see in the church today stems from promoting the idolatry of being right on a particular divisive issue—allowing "rightness" to supplant our unity in Christ and in the gospel. Remember, there is a caveat pertaining to unity: division may be necessary when it comes to essential doctrines. Yet, whenever possible, we must go back to the two fundamentals of the Christian faith. That means we revert to the two Great Commandments mentioned by Jesus in Matthew 22:37–40, where he instructs: "'Love the Lord your God with all your heart and with all your soul and with all your mind.' This is the first and greatest commandment. And the second is like it: 'Love your neighbor as yourself.' All the Law and the Prophets hang on these two commandments.'"

Unity is possible when we choose to love God and love our neighbor more than we love the issues (idols) and being right. Some might say it this way: "We value people over positions." Based on Jesus's instruction in Matthew 22, we have no excuse not to love God and love his people. Later in the New Testament, the apostle Paul pens in Ephesians 2:14, "For he [Jesus Christ] himself is our peace, who has made the two groups one and has destroyed the barrier, the dividing wall of hostility." Jesus made a way for the kingdom

---

25. Jonathan Leeman and Andy Naselli, *How Can I Love Church Members with Different Politics?* (Wheaton: Crossway, 2020), 9–10.

to be opened to all who would put their faith in him. The contentious, volatile, myopic moment in which we find ourselves is a reflection of how God's people have promoted and prioritized idols more highly than God and people. There is no doubt that issues currently debated in churches and in the public square are significant matters—but our idolization of particular issues, and our idolization of our own point of view about them, renders reconciliation and unity impossible. For our sermons to promote reconciliation and unity, we must put to death the various idols in our congregations: the idol of patriarchy, the idol of ethnic supremacy, the idols of nationalism, political partisanship, socioeconomic class distinctions, and more. In the final section of this chapter, let's envision a type of preaching that seeks to inform and transform our passions and desires through virtue formation.

Virtue Formation: Humility, Kindness, and Charity

As we maintain our centered sets and seek to acknowledge and overcome our bounded sets, we complete the homiletical paradigm by preaching on virtue formation. Psalm 133:1 is as relevant in our fragile Christian culture as it was when King David wrote it: "How good and pleasant it is when God's people live together in unity!" To become a "people [who] live together in unity," virtue formation is a key ingredient of relational connection and transformation. Due to our aversion to moralistic preaching, we've been shy about naming Christian virtues gone awry. Preaching to a divided nation necessitates preaching regularly on core virtues such as humility, kindness, and charity.

Preach Regularly on Humility

While many virtues are salient to successful relationships, a virtue that is sorely lacking in our turbulent times is humility. The apostle Paul underscores the need for Christian humility in Philippians 2:1–4: "Therefore if you have any encouragement from being united with Christ, if any comfort from his love, if any common sharing in the Spirit, if any tenderness and compassion, then make my joy complete by being like-minded, having the same love, being one in spirit and of one mind. Do nothing out of selfish ambition or vain conceit. Rather, in humility value others above yourselves, not looking to your own interests but each of you to the interests of the others." A primary reason why Christians cannot live in unity is that we are doing the opposite of what Paul instructs: we are doing practically everything out of selfish ambition and vain conceit, and we do not value others above ourselves, and we are looking out only for our own interests. Years ago, John Killinger wrote a book with the startling, abrasive title *If Christians Were Really Christian*. His premise is that as Christians, we have allowed the culture to shape much of who we are, dictate our aspirations, and manipulate what we live for. Here is a sample of the chapter titles: "If Christians Really Prayed for God's Kingdom," "If Christians Really Loved Everybody," "If Christians Really Followed Jesus," "If Christians Really Lived in the Spirit."[26] No Christian wants to be called a hypocrite, an actor, or a phony by fellow Christians or by the unbelieving world. And yet, so many of the divisions in our world could be avoided by exhibiting some humility.

It bears repeating: humility is one of the primary missing ingredients in our self-important world. None of this surprises God. As Paul writes to Timothy, "There will be terrible times in the last days. People will be lovers of themselves, lovers of money, boastful, proud, abusive, disobedient to their parents, ungrateful, unholy, without love, unforgiving, slanderous, without self-control, brutal, not lovers of the good, treacherous, rash, conceited, lovers of pleasure rather than lovers of God" (2 Tim. 3:1–4). Why pursue humility? Scott Sauls elucidates: "Jesus and Christianity do not discriminate between good people and bad people. Instead, Jesus and Christianity discriminate between humble people and proud people. 'God opposes the proud but gives grace to the humble' (James 4:6)."[27] Sauls reminds us: "Because Jesus Christ has loved us at our worst, we can love others at their worst. . . . Our gentle answer will be costly as well. We must die to ourselves, to our self-righteousness, to our indignation, and to our outrage."[28]

A question then begs to be asked. Can we teach ourselves or others how to be humble? Scripture teaches us how: by decreasing our self-interest and increasing in others-interest, as Philippians 2:1–11, James 4:1–6, and other passages educate us. Francis Chan writes in *Until Unity*: "What if we each made it our goal to strive for a level of humility we've never had? We could spend our circle time on our knees crying out to the God of truth, begging Him to expose any pride or deception that has crept into our own lives. We need to stop thinking that our primary duty toward our fellow believers is to critique them. It's not. Our primary duty is to love them."[29] Expression of humility involves daily reminders—confessing our pride, repenting and asking forgiveness for our arrogance, and pursuing friendship with those with whom we disagree.[30] Humility is a virtue indispensable to our discipleship. Therefore, preach and teach on it regularly.

26. John Killinger, *If Christians Were Really Christian* (St. Louis: Chalice, 2009).
27. Scott Sauls, *A Gentle Answer: Our "Secret Weapon" in an Age of Us against Them* (Nashville: Nelson, 2020), 10–11.
28. Sauls, *Gentle Answer*, xxv.
29. Francis Chan, *Until Unity* (Colorado Springs: David C. Cook, 2021), 16–17.
30. Chan, *Until Unity*, 32–33.

Preach Regularly on Kindness

The church will do better if Christians gravitate away from meanness toward kindness. Meanness is not the way of Christ, and yet it's evident everywhere we look.[31] It's an ingrained and socially acceptable character trait. We have come to expect people to be mean toward each other; it no longer shocks us. Meanness is embodied even in the church. Some of the meanest people we know are professing Christians.

The opposite of meanness is kindness. We see this virtue espoused by Paul as a fruit of the Spirit in Galatians 5:22–26: "But the fruit of the Spirit is love, joy, peace, forbearance, kindness, goodness, faithfulness, gentleness, and self-control. . . . Those who belong to Christ Jesus have crucified the flesh with its passions and desires. Since we live by the Spirit, let us keep in step with the Spirit. Let us not become conceited, provoking and envying each other."

In *Love Kindness*, Biola University president Barry Corey relates how the virtue of kindness has slipped away from many Christian communities. He shares: "Kindness has become far too often a forgotten virtue. Christians often bypass kindness to begin a shouting match, or we just talk among ourselves about how awful the other side is. . . . This is our challenge: living from a Christ-centered core that spills out into a life of kindness. It's a life with a firm center and soft edges."[32]

In order for believers to act with Christian kindness, Corey encourages us to hold fast to the essential doctrines of the Christian faith—that is, have a "firm center" (centered sets) and yet demonstrate "soft edges" (concerning bounded sets) when it comes to more divisive issues. It's a cultural paradigm shift in a congregation to react to others with kindness first, rather than meanness. In aggregate, what others see and hear can make a powerful impression. At our best, how we use language, our verbal tones, our body language, our facial expressions, postures of humility, grace, compassion, and acts of kindness will exemplify a congregation that's committed itself to kindness within a nation and church that is deeply divided.

Preach Regularly on Charity

The virtue of charity also is sorely lacking in our world. By charity, we do not mean simply a handout or allowing ourselves to become a biblical or theological doormat. Christian charity can take many different forms. While we often associate it with giving or generosity, charity also involves praise.

31. See Killinger, *If Christians Were Really Christian*.
32. Barry H. Corey, *Love Kindness: Discover the Power of a Forgotten Christian Virtue* (Carol Stream, IL: Tyndale, 2016), xviii, xxii.

Again, Francis Chan helps us in this regard: "Our lack of praise may actually be the biggest cause of our divisions. Once we stop worshiping, all hope for unity is lost. This is what unites us: we can't stop talking about the treasure we have in Jesus. . . . Worship is our path to unity."[33]

While we agree fully that our collective focus on the worship of God facilitates unity, we will add that praising others with whom we disagree may also foster reconciliation and unity. To be charitable with our words and actions with those with whom we have discord may be the very antidote to reverse the curse of Christian ruptures. When I praise another human being, it forces me to remember the person's good qualities (*imago Dei* qualities) rather than myopically seeing only the divisive issue that separates us.

Think about the following lighthearted example: a person you are "friends" with on social media has just posted a picture of himself on the beach relaxing on a long-awaited vacation. What's your first gut-level response to this self-advertisement? Did you immediately judge that person for the extravagant self-congratulatory splurge? Or did you say to yourself with a spirit of charity, "I know he's probably had a very difficult year and I'm so glad that he's able to enjoy a sorely needed time of refreshment and relaxation." A spirit of charity suspends and withholds judgment. It considers the other side of the equation. Charity celebrates with those who need some rest and relaxation or encourages those who are going through the doldrums of life.

Another illustration of our divisions might elicit a more toxic response. How did you feel when you saw that social media post of a person deciding against getting the COVID-19 vaccination? Or, on the opposite side of the spectrum, proudly holding up her COVID-19 vaccination card with the sticker "Just got vaccinated!" Can you love your neighbor in either camp?

Preach in such a manner that your congregants relearn how to love others first. Invite them to form the virtue of charity. Explain and show them what charity looks like in your particular Scripture text. Help them identify the toxicity of a divisive and contentious spirit—a heart that Satan adores. In your sermon, move rapidly in your explanation and application of what virtue formation entails here and now. Preaching to a divided nation will explore opportunities to elevate virtue formation, which is missing in many congregations today.

Conclusion

In this fifth chapter, we have articulated a homiletical method that can gradually encourage a congregation to become reconciled and unified. While not

33. Chan, *Until Unity*, 15–16.

comprehensive, this step encourages us to unite around our centered sets and acknowledge the glaring tensions of our bounded sets. Ultimately, our homiletical goal is to increase virtue formation and Christlikeness in the congregation through expressions of humility, kindness, and charity.

The subject of our next chapter is the practical step. We will share some pre-sermon, mid-sermon, and post-sermon practices that put flesh on centered and bounded sets and virtue formation.

Questions for Reflection

1. How can you promote greater unity through emphasizing centered sets?
2. Which bounded set is most contentious today in your church (ethnicity, class, gender, or politics)? How do you feel about preaching on it? Would it help or hurt your congregation?
3. What other bounded sets (divisive issues) are palpable in your local congregation?
4. Which virtue could you preach about in an upcoming sermon or sermon series?

Practical Next Steps

1. Would you consider inviting a pastor/preacher to speak to your congregation who does not share your view on a particular bounded-set issue? Why or why not?
2. Make a list of your most valued centered sets of shared doctrines, shared identities, and shared experiences.
3. Take each of the four bounded sets and prayerfully prioritize which -*ism* you might preach on in the next six to twelve months. Seek counsel from your church's leadership board.

6

The Practical Step

Pre-Sermon, Mid-Sermon, and Post-Sermon Practices

In this penultimate step, our objective is to offer some best practices for preaching to a divided nation and congregation while considering the centered and bounded sets mentioned in chapter 5. They include pre-sermon, mid-sermon, and post-sermon exercises.

- *Pre-sermon.* We'll consider five preliminary questions: What's your sermon's purpose? Have you done a SWOT analysis (we'll detail that shortly)? Is this the right time? How is your congregation divided? What are your personal biases?
- *Mid-sermon.* We'll explore homiletical activities that we recommend while preaching the sermon.
- *Post-sermon.* We will conclude with some ideas for intentional congregational participation in reconciliation and unity after we preach the sermon.

We acknowledge that these suggestions are not comprehensive nor are they magic wands that will eradicate all of our divisions. Only the Holy Spirit can transform individuals and congregations. Yet they represent a practical place to start the journey.

Pre-Sermon Considerations

Let's start with five salient questions to ask before drafting a sermon.

1. What's Your Sermon's Purpose?

When considering addressing a contentious topic, the shrewd homiletician gives thought to what the objective or aim is for this sermon or sermon series. Haddon Robinson writes, "No matter how brilliant or biblical a sermon is, without a definite purpose it is not worth preaching."[1] Can you clearly state the goal of the sermon or sermon series as you embark upon the potentially hazardous terrain of a divisive issue?

Three traditional purposes in every sermon are to explain (describe), prove (give evidence), and apply.[2] To Robinson's schema, we add a fourth category: *form*, as in form affection or identity. As you carefully determine the purpose of your sermon on a divisive topic, consider these four potential purposes, which are discussed below. In most cases, the applicational aim will center on either one's *being* (change of character or personal identity) or one's *doing* (change of behavior or responding with action). Of course, in certain cases, the sermon's purpose may include two or more of the elements.

Inform Perspectives (Explain)

A primary agenda for your sermon or sermon series on one of the -*isms* presented in this book (ethnocentrism, classism, sexism, and partisanism) may be to educate the congregation on two or three major views on a given topic in a balanced, evenhanded way. Think in the vein of publishers' popular series like *Two Views on Women in Ministry*, *Baptism: Three Views*, or *Homiletics and Hermeneutics: Four Views on Preaching Today*.[3] In these series, editors choose leading voices to represent and defend their views on a given subject with healthy rebuttals. The purpose of these series is not persuasion per se; rather, they are informational in nature, offering major perspectives.

When I (Matt) was a pastor in Colorado, I preached a sermon series titled "What Do I Believe?" We covered twelve or so topics that the church wanted to hear a biblical sermon about. I had asked the congregation by "secret vote"

---

1. Haddon W. Robinson, *Biblical Preaching: The Development and Delivery of Expository Messages*, 3rd ed. (Grand Rapids: Baker Academic, 2014), 71.

2. Robinson, *Biblical Preaching*, 77.

3. James R. Beck, ed., *Two Views on Women in Ministry* (Grand Rapids: Zondervan Academic, 2005); David F. Wright, ed., *Baptism: Three Views* (Downers Grove, IL: IVP Academic, 2009); and Scott M. Gibson and Matthew D. Kim, eds., *Homiletics and Hermeneutics: Four Views on Preaching Today* (Grand Rapids: Baker Academic, 2018).

what topics they wanted me to cover, and I did my best to oblige them. The topics included creation care, women in ministry, Christians and yoga, and Reformed or Arminian views on the nature of election, among others. Instead of polarizing members of the congregation against each other, the preacher's purpose in a series of this sort is to present a balanced sermon that provides a biblical rationale from various perspectives, integrating appropriate Scripture passages. (You may or may not divulge your own position; there's wisdom on either side depending on the topic.) Surprisingly, when as part of this series I preached on the doctrine of election, providing scriptural evidence for and against both Reformed and Arminian views, after the worship service one of my leaders came up to me and said: "Pastor Matt, I used to believe that I was Reformed. But after hearing your sermon, I've changed my mind. I think I'm an Arminian!" Yes, I can sense the glaring eyeballs. This switching of congregants' theological camps would be anathema for some preachers.

Provide Pastoral Care (Apply)

Preaching on divisive issues can serve as a form of pastoral care. It's quite possible that many of your listeners are mourning silently in the pews. They've been hurt by pastors, church leaders, fellow Christians, and nonbelievers in the exploitative areas of ethnocentrism, sexism, classism, and politicism. Perhaps one of the ways we can demonstrate care for the congregation is to preach on one or more of these -isms that have wrought pain and suffering. We might preface the sermon or the series by peeling the bandage off these open wounds. For the pulpit to remain permanently silent on issues of domestic or sexual violence or economic injustices, to pick some examples, fails to show how the gospel permeates every part of our lives.

Promote Peace, Reconciliation, and Unity (Apply)

Preachers are leaders by virtue of their vocation, so we cannot sit idly and watch our congregations remain divided. Leadership requires us to bridge the divides in our churches over theology, politics, tension between social classes, gender-related issues, and other controversial matters. We agree with William H. Willimon that "preaching and leadership are inseparable."[4] It's not good enough for members of the family of God to make it through a worship service without engaging in physical or verbal warfare with a neighbor in the pew. There is a greater purpose for the church. As Jim Samra notes, God, in

---

4. William H. Willimon, *Leading with the Sermon: Preaching as Leadership* (Minneapolis: Fortress, 2020), 10.

his sovereign wisdom, "designed and created the church for our benefit and for his glory. . . . We love the church because it is a gift from God. We participate in the church because God does. We do not give up on the church, because God refuses to."[5] Part of this benefit is the opportunity to model for the world that Christians can live peaceably, live in unity, and even reconcile with one another.

Concerning God's desire for harmony among Christians, the apostle Paul penned these magisterial words:

> For he himself [Christ] is our peace, who has made the two groups one and has destroyed the barrier, the dividing wall of hostility. . . . His purpose was to create in himself one new humanity out of the two, thus making peace, and in one body to reconcile both of them to God through the cross, by which he put to death their hostility. He came and preached peace to you who were far away and peace to those who were near. (Eph. 2:14–17)

Agreeing to disagree may suffice for some. Yet ultimately God's plan for the "one new humanity" is that we will intentionally live out our ontological identity in Christ. This means intentionally choosing to love our neighbors and intentionally choosing reconciliation, unity, and peace, especially with those with whom we disagree. Later in this chapter we will provide some preaching principles to guide us on how to "put to death [our] hostility."

Preach to Persuade (Prove)

In some cases, a preacher may feel persuasion is the most desirable outcome of a particular sermon or sermon series. R. Larry Overstreet shares that there are several different outcomes of persuasive preaching, including persuasion as winning over, persuasion as obedience, persuasion as confidence, persuasion as being convinced, persuasion as faith or trust, and persuasion as empathic declaration.[6] Perhaps the preacher believes that the congregation is misinformed about biblical positions, or misguided—or even that certain congregants are misaligned with Scripture. In such cases, the preacher deems it necessary to persuade, convict, or move the congregation toward a proper biblical/theological understanding.

Take, for instance, the hot-button matter of same-sex marriage. As evangelical pastors, we the authors maintain that Scripture conveys a clear

---

5. Jim Samra, *The Gift of Church: How God Designed the Local Church to Meet Our Needs as Christians* (Grand Rapids: Zondervan, 2010), 16–17.

6. R. Larry Overstreet, *Persuasive Preaching: A Biblical and Practical Guide to the Effective Use of Persuasion* (Wooster, OH: Weaver, 2014), 41–49.

stance on the issue: that same-sex marriage goes against God's design for heterosexual marriage between a man and a woman for life. Although the wider culture, and even the Supreme Court, have been swayed to pronounce same-sex marriage not just permissible but also a union to be celebrated, the preacher's responsibility in this example may be to accomplish all of the above: winning over, obedience, confidence, being convinced, faith or trust, and empathic declaration. We seek to persuade or prove to our listeners that a biblical stance is warranted on this topic—even though listeners may disagree.

Preach to Form Affections (Form)

The fourth dimension we are adding to Robinson's triad (explain, prove, and apply) is form, or formation, which pertains to shaping one's desires and, consequently, one's identity.[7] James K. A. Smith observes in *You Are What You Love*, "Discipleship doesn't touch just our head or even just our heart: it reaches into our gut, our *splagchna*, our affections."[8] When something is rooted in our affections, we respond with guttural reactions that reflect our deepest longings and reveal our sense of self (personhood) and priorities. Essentially, affections are passions. We can become so passionate about a particular issue that we are willing to abandon our most basic form of discipleship, which is love of God and love of neighbor. That's what is foundational to the life of a disciple—not one's view of politics, economic policies, gender issues, or the like. In pursuing our affections, if we lose sight of the ultimate object of worship (the triune God), eventually our misshapen affections demonize and mentally discard anyone who disagrees with us or gets in the way of our deepest desires. Francis Chan contends: "Too many people call themselves Christian who have never experienced a deep connection with God. Because so few people have experienced His love, even fewer are able to share it. If our relationship with God is robotic or nonexistent, our bond of love with others will be equally weak. When love is shallow, all it takes is something as trivial as a disagreement to divide

---

7. Affections and identity interact in a mutual feedback loop: desires drive worship, which forms identity. For example, Psalm 135:15–18 states those who worship idols become like them: mute, blind, and deaf. Conversely, 2 Cor. 3:18 indicates when we "contemplate" or behold Christ, we are "transformed into his image." I (Paul) have observed this at my church regarding the conflicts over whether to wear masks during the COVID-19 pandemic. Many Christians have made either wearing a mask or not wearing a mask into an idol and have used Scripture out of context to support their claims. More than anything, we want to encourage Christians to demonstrate love for neighbor regardless of one's position on mask wearing.

8. James K. A. Smith, *You Are What You Love: The Spiritual Power of Habit* (Grand Rapids: Brazos, 2016), 9.

us."[9] In order to love people, we desire to continually form a relationship with God and experience his love.

Another purpose of the "affection formation-type" sermon, then, might be to diagnose these affections and explain why a normally good desire (the pursuit of a worthy cause) can become detrimental and hurtful to the body of Christ (when that worthy cause becomes an idol, leading to relational strife or hatred). Scott M. Gibson offers this insight: "If the gospel informs our character, then the contours of the gospel are to shape how we live our lives. The prioritizing of a political position over one's faith (even though one might think that his or her faith is equal to the political position), dare I say, is a demonstration of spiritual immaturity."[10] The preacher's purpose might be to reframe the hierarchy of affections in a way that leads listeners toward greater spiritual maturity and greater discipleship, so that they will not allow disagreement to disrupt peace and unity among Christians.

2. Have You Done a (Prayerful) SWOT Analysis?

It might be beneficial to do a prayer-infused analysis before preaching on a controversial topic within the local church context. SWOT analysis (strengths, weaknesses, opportunities, threats) is frequently used in business and the military. In the church it is a useful way to gauge whether or not one should pursue a homiletical moment to speak into congregational divides. We've added a spiritual element: prayer. Prayer is foundational in the preaching process to discern whether the Spirit is leading us to preach on a given topic.

Let's explore an example: preaching on gender roles, or more specifically, a church's position on women in ministry. Whether one is an egalitarian or a complementarian or a comple-galitarian (yes, we just made that up!), there will be some aspect of SWOT to analyze.

- *Strength*. If I am a male preacher, preaching on gender issues and the treatment of females can be a strength in my desire to encourage and empower women in the church to exercise their gifts (according to my position of complementarianism or egalitarianism).
- *Weakness*. However, as a male preacher, I also have a glaring weakness: I am a man preaching from a limited male perspective.
- *Opportunity*. Women in the congregation will feel heard and empowered to serve.

9. Francis Chan, *Until Unity* (Colorado Springs: David C. Cook, 2021), 31.
10. Scott M. Gibson, "Preaching to a Politically Divided Congregation," *Preaching Today*, https://www.preachingtoday.com/skills/2021/preaching-to-politically-divided-congregation.html.

- *Threat.* Men or women in the church may hold a different view and get upset. Depending on which topic we preach on, we must face the fact that we may lose some church members for any number of reasons.[11]

3. Is This the Right Time?

In *Prophetic Preaching*, Leonora Tubbs Tisdale asks, "Why do we avoid speaking truth in love regarding some of the burning issues of our day? And why are we often fearful of what becoming prophetic witnesses will mean for our lives?"[12] She observes seven common fears about preaching on justice issues:

1. An inherited model of biblical interpretation that marginalizes the prophetic dimensions of Scripture
2. Pastoral concern for parishioners
3. Fear of conflict
4. Fear of dividing a congregation
5. Fear of being disliked, rejected, or made to pay a price for prophetic witness
6. Feelings of inadequacy in addressing prophetic concerns
7. Discouragement that our own prophetic witness is not making a difference[13]

We may be passionate about a divisive issue, but is this the proper time to preach on it, if ever? Put differently, is this a *kairos* moment or a *chronos* moment? A *kairos* moment is when the Holy Spirit leads us to seize an opportunity and address an important matter in the life of the congregation and in our world today. It's a time or season we don't want to miss.[14] We might think of a *chronos* moment as just another Sunday, another sequence in time. Take a second to jog your memory. In retrospect, do you wish you had postponed any planned sermons and instead preached on a major event

---

11. For instance, Scott Sauls shares in a National Association of Evangelicals podcast that people left his church after he preached on politics and offered a "third-way" approach for his congregation. Sauls, "Post-Election Guidance for Christians," National Association of Evangelicals podcast, November 15, 2020, https://www.nae.org/saulspodcast.

12. Leonora Tubbs Tisdale, *Prophetic Preaching: A Pastoral Approach* (Louisville: Westminster John Knox, 2010), 3.

13. Tisdale, *Prophetic Preaching*, 11–20.

14. See David Schnasa Jacobsen, *Kairos Preaching: Speaking Gospel to the Situation* (Minneapolis: Fortress, 2009).

in your community or the nation?[15] What about devoting a Sunday to celebrate something positive happening in the world? That's a *kairos* homiletical moment that we cannot retrieve. If an issue seems urgent, discerning prayer and reaching out to survey your church leaders or fellow pastors can help you decide whether to preach on that topic. As preachers, part of our homiletical wisdom is in knowing the difference between a *kairos* and *chronos* moment.

Before preaching on controversial topics, it would be prudent to inform the elder board, pastoral staff, or denominational contacts beforehand. Provide a communal space where the congregation can engage in discussion after the worship service. Don't drop a bomb, flee the blast zone, and leave your parishioners to face the shockwaves. Prepare for possible repercussions by discussing the topic in advance with small group leaders who can shepherd the people through ongoing conversations and prayer gatherings. Consider: as the preacher, how can you help the congregation process the sermon and the information shared? What about feedback from online and podcast listeners not immediately in the congregation's reach? How will they respond? How might a sermon be perceived outside of the immediate church context? In other words, we must plan ahead and pray before we preach on divisive topics. Not everything we say will be well received even if our motives are well intended. Prepare your staff or leadership for the aftermath.

4. How Is Your Congregation Divided?

Not every congregation will be struggling with the same *-isms* at the same time. Thus, as a congregational exegete, you will need to ascertain the specific divides that confound your specific local church. It would be ill-advised to preach on all of the *-isms* just to stir up the pot. Some congregations are deeply divided, for instance, on political issues. A. J. Swoboda shares, "I pastor a church made up of (at best guess) 40 percent Democrats, 40 percent Republicans, and 20 percent unaffiliated. In short, that's a rather politically inclined (and charged) church community. It creates, I admit, quite the homiletical headache. . . . Just about everyone is looking for something different; a reality that might just drive just about *any* preacher insane."[16] Yet it's beneficial

---

15. I (Paul) have discerned *kairos* moments and changed my sermon schedule at the last minute around ten times during my fourteen years shepherding our church. To name a few, I did it after the Sandy Hook Elementary School shooting, after COVID-19 was declared a national emergency, after the insurrection at the US Capitol on Jan. 6, 2021, and numerous times after racial tensions in the US reached a crescendo.

16. A. J. Swoboda, "God's Huckster: Preaching Jesus in a Politically Charged Climate," *Preaching Today*, https://www.preachingtoday.com/skills/2016/june/gods-huckster.html.

to know beforehand the potential problems the sermon may create among listeners who are blindsided by the sermonic blast.

In *A Gentle Answer*, Scott Sauls puts his finger on the pulse of the cultural moment we find ourselves in. He writes: "Outrage has become something we can't get away from, partly because we don't seem to want to get away from it. Instead of getting rid of all bitterness, rage, and anger as scripture urges us to do (Eph. 4:31), we form entire communities around our irritations and our hatreds."[17] When we allow personal perspectives to govern how we interact with our congregants, this leads to a divided congregation. We must know the hot-button issues that permeate and splinter the church in different ways. People in the pews are hurting over these *-isms*, and we should respond pastorally.[18]

5. What Are Your Biases?

"To be human is to have bias. If you were to say, 'I don't have bias,' you'd be saying your brain isn't functioning properly! . . . As logical and fair as we try to be, we are nearly always operating with a degree of bias, without ever being aware of it," express the authors of *The Leader's Guide to Unconscious Bias*.[19] What is unconscious bias? We concur with this definition: "Unconscious biases, also known as implicit biases, are the underlying attitudes and stereotypes that people unconsciously attribute to another person or group of people that affect how they understand and engage with a person or group."[20] Assuming this is correct, how can you name your personal biases if you don't even know what they are? Tough question. Perhaps you can ask yourself a follow-up question: What are my conscious biases?

Rather than hopelessly trying to name every single type of bias imaginable, let's focus on our four-part diagnostic of ethnocentrism, classism, sexism, and political partisanism. What might bias look like in ministry, and in particular, a preaching ministry?

Bailey Reiners articulates twelve unconscious biases in the workplace that we might appropriate here for preaching: affinity bias, confirmation bias,

---

17. Scott Sauls, *A Gentle Answer: Our "Secret Weapon" in an Age of Us against Them* (Nashville: Nelson, 2020), xxii.

18. See Matthew D. Kim, *Preaching to People in Pain: How Suffering Can Shape Your Sermons and Connect with Your Congregation* (Grand Rapids: Baker Academic, 2021).

19. Pamela Fuller, Mark Murphy, and Anne Chow, *The Leader's Guide to Unconscious Bias: How to Reframe Bias, Cultivate Connection, and Create High-Performing Teams* (New York: Simon & Schuster, 2020), 1.

20. Bailey Reiners, "16 Unconscious Bias Examples and How to Avoid Them in the Workplace," Builtin.com, updated September 30, 2021, https://builtin.com/diversity-inclusion/unconscious-bias-examples.

attribution bias, conformity bias, the halo effect, the horns effect, contrast effect, gender bias, ageism, name bias, beauty bias, and height bias.[21] Since we don't have time to go into each of them, allow us to focus on one that impacts preaching most directly. According to Reiners, "Affinity bias, also known as similarity bias, is the tendency people have to connect with others who share similar interests, experiences and backgrounds."[22]

Subconsciously, we gravitate toward those who are like us. For preachers, that means we naturally have an affinity for others who may share our denomination, doctrine, ministry philosophy, views on secondary theologies such as women in ministry and baptism, and who generally think—and even preach—like we do. This can extend to race, ethnicity, gender, class, and political leanings.

Here's a litmus test for affinity bias for pastors and communicators. Do we read books from only a particular theological view or publisher, that is, only those who think and believe as we do? Do we demonize, ignore, vilify, or become self-righteous around those who think and believe differently? Do we surround ourselves with only like-minded pastors and friends? If we answered yes to these and similar questions, we struggle with affinity bias.

We all struggle with affinity bias in different ways. The bottom line is this: How will we treat parishioners who think and believe differently, and how will we preach with them in our hermeneutical and homiletical views?

Pre-Sermon Prayer

In addition to asking yourself these preliminary questions, we cannot emphasize enough the importance of pre-sermon prayer. Hearts can be transformed only by a move of the Holy Spirit through individual and corporate prayer. As Ezekiel 36:26 reminds us, "I [God] will give you a new heart and put a new spirit in you; I will remove from you your heart of stone and give you a heart of flesh." We urge you to invite your entire congregation to pray leading up to your sermon on any divisive issue. Congregational unity in prayer will loosen the soil of hardened hearts. There may be unspoken tension or even open hostility in the sanctuary. Encourage all members of the church family to pray with you and pray for the unity of the church body. Pray that they can rightly hear the proclamation of God's Word. Pray that they can listen to each other. Pray that the Spirit would invite open hearts and minds to bring healing and restoration to broken relationships. Pastors, we are foolish if we

---

21. Reiners, "16 Unconscious Bias Examples."
22. Reiners, "16 Unconscious Bias Examples."

believe we possess the potency to change the hearts of our church members merely through preaching a sermon. Heart work requires prayer work.

In Edward M. Bounds's *The Weapon of Prayer*, he avers: "In all God's plans for human redemption, He proposes that [we] *pray*. . . . The progress to consummation of God's work in this world has two basic principles—God's ability to give and [our] ability to ask. Failure in either one is fatal to the success of God's work on earth."[23] Therefore, will we join in committing to pray for unity? We don't want to just write or read a book on reconciliation and unity. We want to embody it in our own families, churches, and communities. We pray for a move of the Spirit to unify Christians both nationally and globally. Everything begins and ends with fervent prayer. Nothing can happen without it.

As you bravely embrace the pastoral responsibility of bridging congregants' divides, the opportunity presents itself to rally your congregation to pray individually and collectively. Perhaps you might covenant together for a fourteen-day, twenty-one-day, or thirty-day commitment to pray and fast for unity in the body.

Start with Unity and Move toward Diversity

As explained in chapter 5, the general principle for preaching on divisive issues is to begin the sermon with what unites us rather than what divides us. Start with the centered set(s) of doctrines, identities, mission, and experiences and then open the listeners' hearts to acknowledge the differences and preferences that can be stumbling blocks to unity. As you prayerfully select a topic and a text, determine the unifying theme you will preach at the outset of your sermon. A topical paper by Gordon Hugenberger provides a blueprint for finding common ground on contentious issues.[24] Launch your sermon with unity!

The gospel is always a solid place to start. When broaching heated and contested topics, remind your listeners of the gospel. The gospel, in simple terms, is the plan of God to redeem and reconcile a fallen world through the person and work of Jesus Christ, who lived a sinless and sacrificial life, died on the cross, was buried in the tomb, was resurrected on the third day, ascended to heaven, and shall return one day as king and judge. This story binds Christians together.

23. Edward M. Bounds, *The Weapon of Prayer: A Study in Christian Warfare* (New York: Revell, 1931), 51, 57.

24. See Gordon P. Hugenberger, "Women in Leadership," April 14, 2008, unpublished paper, available at https://www.csmedia1.com/cpcnewhaven.org/women_in_leadership_hugenberger.pdf.

Next, find commonality in your sermon text. In what areas can you confidently affirm your listeners' unity in beliefs and practices? State them clearly. Smile as you invite listeners to pursue reconciliation and unity. Remind your listeners they are gospel-centered, Christ-centered, God-exalting, Spirit-led, forgiven sinners—disciples of Jesus who have been redeemed by the blood of the Lamb. Where can we find mutual agreement in the midst of diverse views on ethnicity, class, sex, and politics? Once we establish unity and encourage peace, then we can proceed to the various *-isms* that divide us.

We have touched on some of the preparatory work for preaching on divisive topics. But what can we do more intentionally while *in* the pulpit to help our listeners more effectively hear difficult sermons? We humbly pose some mid-sermon and post-sermon practices that may assist in this cumbersome process.

Mid-Sermon Considerations

Handle with Care

When one purchases fragile items, the seller often labels the box with four important words: "Fragile: Handle with Care." Your congregation is fragile when it comes to the four *-isms*. Some members of the congregation might have experienced trauma and pain from these divisive issues. Some might be struggling with one or more of these *-isms* on any given Sunday. Proper sermonic delivery involves using nuanced vocabulary, tone, and body language that are palatable for all who hear. Giving attention to one's verbal and nonverbal communication can set a warm and winsome mood when addressing tense topics. While some preachers may argue that writing a sermon manuscript (word for word) is not for them, we strongly encourage you—if you are emboldened to preach on a divisive issue—to write out your entire sermon (every word of it). Once you've written your manuscript, practice reading it aloud and record your sermon. Observe your language and tone. You might even want to practice in front of a video camera (or smartphone) and press record. Watch your body language, review your facial expressions, and consider your use of gestures. This is rarely a fun exercise for any preacher, but the discipline of self-review will be worth it. Perhaps even get another pair of ears and eyes to evaluate your sermon and provide input.

The language you use deserves careful thought. We can avoid hostility by choosing our words carefully. Refrain from various forms of adversarial speech, such as these categories of political language: "Negative Campaigning: language that is entirely focused on an opposing candidate; Uncivil Language: language that does not follow social conversation norms concerning respect and politeness; Polarizing Language: rhetoric that expresses points of views that are far from the middle of the ideological spectrum; and Divisive Rhetoric: language that has the distinct intention of pitting groups against each other."[25] Avoid sweeping political labels, such as calling people in your congregation *liberals, conservatives, right wing, left wing, Alt-Right, Alt-Left,* or *extremists.*

With regard to racial and ethnic cultures, studiously avoid boundary-set terms like *you people, your people, those people,* or *us versus them,* which distance others rather than drawing them closer. Whenever possible, use words that describe specific ethnicities, rather than broad racial categories.[26] Be careful not to incite and perpetuate racial hatred and violence with epithets and ethnic/racial slurs such as referring to whites as *crackers, white supremacists,* or *lynchers,* calling Asian Americans *chinks, gooks, Japs, bananas,* or *model minorities,* or calling COVID-19 the *China Virus* or the *Kung Flu.* Don't call Latinos/Hispanics *the illegals, the help, beaners,* or *spics.* Don't refer to Black people as *negroes* or use the N-word. Don't refer to Arab Americans as *terrorists* or *jihadists.* This may sound absurdly horrific, but we never know what might come out of our mouths—since our hearts all have a propensity toward prejudice.

Moreover, in our subconscious we may perpetuate harmful ethnic and cultural stereotypes by using fetishizing language such as Asian American women being *exotic* or *petite,* or Latino men being *macho* or *swooning lovers,* or African American women being *strong* or *feminists.* A recent example was Rickshaw Rally, a children's Vacation Bible School curriculum, which cast Asian Americans as foreigners from the "Far East" who practice peculiar non-American customs.[27] We may think it's innocent, or even humorous, but promoting such damaging cultural stereotypes further separates people.

With regard to sexism, be slow to label groups as *feminists, misogynists, wife beaters, patriarchists,* or other sexist slurs. With regard to classism, avoid *rednecks, white trash, ghettos, ghettoization, pimps,* and more. If you must use similar language regarding any of our *-ism* categories, quickly define your words so that you will not be easily misunderstood or summarily dismissed

25. See Trevor Winans, "Divisive Rhetoric and Adverse Language in American Political Discourse" (master's thesis, Boston University, 2019), accessed September 3, 2021, https://www.bu.edu/polisci/files/2019/06/Winans.pdf. The full text of the thesis is available at https://open.bu.edu/ds2/stream/?#/documents/388947/page/1.

26. See Sarah Shin, *Beyond Colorblind: Redeeming Our Ethnic Journey* (Downers Grove, IL: InterVarsity, 2017), 12–16.

27. See John Rutledge, "LifeWay Apologizes to Asian-Americans for Rickshaw Rally," *Baptist Standard,* November 8, 2013, https://www.baptiststandard.com/news/baptists/lifeway-apologizes-to-asian-americans-for-rickshaw-rally.

when you use terms such as *white privilege, white supremacy, critical race theory (CRT),* or *Black Lives Matter (BLM).* These loaded terms can trigger all different types of responses from our listeners. If you use them during a sermon, you will want to spend adequate time explaining their meaning and why it's necessary to bring up in the message.

How we speak our carefully chosen words is crucial, so we'll reiterate: we encourage you to practice your sermon out loud and record yourself. Play it back as a form of self-review to see if your body language and facial expressions match what you're communicating. While we never get our sermons quite right, it will not hurt us to practice the sermon before we preach it. However, don't be overly paranoid or scripted. Remember to smile when it's appropriate to smile and frown when you need to frown. Display body language and use gestures that promote dialogue, warmth, encouragement, unity, and hope by opening wide your arms, when appropriate.

Lead with Questions, Not Answers

Throughout the sermon, ask provocative questions and leave sermonic space for listeners to reflect. Allow your listeners to wrestle with contrarian ideas and perspectives they haven't thought much about previously or may avoid thinking about. Sporadic, intentional moments of silence can feel awkward at times, but these spaces for constructive thinking may be the only time in a person's chaotic week to ponder significant ideas, philosophies, and practices. Whether they choose to engage in the mental exercise or not, provide them with this gift of quieted grace.

Ask listeners to consider what their questions are, and have them write those questions down in a bulletin or on their phone. Invite them to send their questions to you or your office assistant throughout the week. Compile them. Pray over them. Consider a follow-up sermon or sermon series based on those questions. Perhaps they would be a good foundation for a Bible study series or small group discussion. Don't ignore them. When preaching on divisive issues, we want to enable our listeners to think for themselves, so prompting questions rather than dictating answers is often a best practice. That doesn't mean we don't provide scriptural evidence throughout—that's a given.

Encourage Deference over Difference

Our final suggestion about mid-sermon considerations is that we encourage you to elevate deference over difference. I (Matt) heard a memorable sermon on 1 Corinthians 11:17–34 on the Lord's Supper. The preacher focused the sermon on the apostle Paul admonishing the Corinthian Christians to defer to one another rather than concentrate on how they differed. What does that mean?

Class was a significant issue in the Corinthian congregation. Paul challenged the human tendency to flaunt or show off our resources before others. In verse 22, he asks: "Don't you have homes to eat and drink in? Or do you despise the church of God by humiliating those who have nothing?" Rather than focusing on our differences—in this case, the difference of class—Paul instructs the believers to defer to the other in verses 33–34: "So then, my brothers and sisters, when you gather to eat, you should all eat together. Anyone who is hungry should eat something at home, so that when you meet together it may not result in judgment."

How is deference manifested here? Paul is telling the rich to eat at home so that those who have less can sit at the table and get their proper share of the meal, and in some cases get even more than those whose bellies are already full. When we defer to the other, we are celebrating the *imago Dei* in that person. Deference demonstrates the other person is more important than our own immediate pursuit of gratification, in whatever form. Clearly, we see that difference separates people while deference includes people (in this situation, it includes them in table fellowship). As you preach and teach God's Word, provide practical, concrete examples of how as a church community you can elevate deference over difference. Explain deference in everyday terms. Help your congregation to see that the way of Christ is to defer to others rather than expose differences, which only separates, segregates, and isolates.

Post-Sermon Work

Sometimes, Let a Church "Hash It Out" in Love

Sometimes it's best to let people speak the truth of how they really feel. Bottling up our opinions, hurts, and frustrations can quickly lead to unexpected or unintended explosions (even for pastors). There may be fallout either way. We cannot shield our congregations from disagreements and even some heated arguments. As in a nuclear family, the best approach may be to allow a spiritual family to "hash it out." The point is not to encourage physical brawling or harm. The dilemma is that if we refuse to acknowledge the elephant in the room, we don't say what we need to say and don't confess the things that are actually in our hearts. In short, we're not being honest or "speaking the truth in love" (Eph. 4:15).

Just as families sometimes need to vent and clear the air, spiritual families need time to be real with each other. Too frequently we perpetuate a Christian culture of niceness. We think being nice is being Christian. Being nice means not saying or doing anything to offend another person. Being nice means saying the politically correct thing or keeping quiet so as to not poke the sleeping bear. Derek Vreeland writes: "Some white Christians are afraid to speak out and avoid the deep soul-searching required to acknowledge our own complicity in a culture of white dominance." What we actually need, according to Vreeland, is to confess our ignorance, apathy, denial, playing nice over truth-telling, colorblind rhetoric, politics, tribalism, theological insufficiency, fear, and uncertainty.[28] We should be able to tell a brother or sister in Christ that they've hurt us, or to admit that we didn't appreciate their comments—or that we felt slighted when someone gave us a dirty look or when everyone but us was asked for their opinions. "Christian nice" has only led to Christian community "death." Sometimes, we simply must be transparent with our feelings.

A small group meeting, leadership meeting, or church town hall gathering can be a good setting. Set the ground rules for the session at the beginning: speaking the truth in love is not permission to openly slander another person. Speak truth with kindness and gentleness. Practice charity in your speech. Let us reemphasize: there is no place for hateful rhetoric or defamation of character. And yet, let's admit we can be so afraid of offending others that we fail to do the hard work and "heart" work of being truly vulnerable and exposing our hidden sins. Speaking the truth in love may involve calling out, confessing, and repenting of the sins of racism, ethnocentrism, xenophobia, sexism, classism, pride, arrogance, superiority, ageism, political posturing, and more. When it is called for, do your very best to make the situation whole by enacting righteousness and justice.[29] In the final analysis, providing the opportunity for church members to "hash it out" in love will require much prayer and careful planning. Know who will attend and how to safeguard a safe space.

Actively Pursue Reconciliation and Unity

So, you've courageously preached a sermon on one of the *-isms*. Now what? To preach on a divisive topic, and not follow up afterward with concrete

---

28. Derek Vreeland, "Why Do White Christians Remain Silent?," *Missio Alliance*, March 25, 2021, https://www.missioalliance.org/why-do-white-christians-remain-silent.

29. This may involve restitution, and not just reconciliation. See Duke L. Kwon and Gregory Thompson, *Reparations: A Christian Call for Repentance and Repair* (Grand Rapids: Brazos Press, 2021).

conversations and application, would be a disservice to your congregation. To commit to proclaiming reconciliation and unity requires the preached Word and the lived Word—a congregational commitment to pursue peace and harmony together in concrete and embodied ways.

In our opinion, Jemar Tisby provides a constructive and valuable framework. Although his focus is on combating racism, his principles should prove useful in addressing all the *-isms*. To engage the battle against racism (and all *-isms*) he offers the ARC of Racial Justice (awareness, relationships, and commitment):

> Awareness: First, we need to learn about who they are. Instead of being scared of differences, we can celebrate them.
>
> Relationships: We should also be excited about being friends with all kinds of people. People who have different hair, clothes, food, and languages than we do. We might discover something new to like about the world, and people with lots of different friends do the best job of getting along with others.
>
> Commitment: But just like you have rules in school, you'll have rules as a grown up too. Have you ever thought a rule was unfair? . . . The question is what are you going to do about it? If you see something wrong, you absolutely have the ability to raise your voice, take action, and try to change the rule. You won't always be able to make the changes you want, but it's trying that counts.[30]

Your congregation will be at varied levels in terms of practicing this simple rubric of awareness, relationships, and commitment. We encourage you to pursue ARC throughout the year. You might preach a short sermon series inviting listeners to grow in each of these three areas. You might covenant as a congregation to make them part of your church's mission, vision, and values. You might provide monthly or quarterly opportunities to develop intellectual awareness, interpersonal relationships, and ecclesial commitment by bringing in experts on ethnicity, class, gender, and politics to give workshops and training, and to encourage active engagement with local organizations. These types of activities will enhance the impact of your preaching and teaching.

Our actions, or lack thereof, have real consequences. An Asian American woman was beaten brutally in broad daylight on the streets of New York City. A video captured this hate crime, and also showed three men witnessing this horrific beating who did nothing to stop it and nothing to help her in the

---

30. Jemar Tisby, *How to Fight Racism: Courageous Christianity and the Journey toward Racial Justice* (Grand Rapids: Zondervan, 2021), 57–58.

aftermath. They saw the crime in real time, and yet one of them cowardly pressed a button to close the door, as if closing the door nullified the crime.[31]

Please hear this prophetic call: Are we so numb to hatred, division, and violence that we would close the door (literally and figuratively)? May these sobering words from priest and author Tish Harrison Warren nudge us to remember that today is the day for reconciliation: "For all of us, recalling the inevitability of death reminds us that the day to seek God, the day to repair relationships, the day to help others and bless the world around us is *today*—because it may be our last. Facing mortality leads us to ask necessary questions: Who are we, and what is life for?"[32] It is our prayer that all Christians—ministers and congregants—will wake up. Wake up, dear Christian brothers and sisters. Wake up and exercise the gospel that reconciles and unites in your midst!

Conclusion

This chapter presented some best practices when preaching on divisive topics. We encourage you to review these pre-sermon, mid-sermon, and post-sermon practices as you prepare and preach your sermon or sermon series. There may be other welcome practices that you could share with fellow pastors in your town, networks, and denominations. We hope that all preachers will continue to develop in winsomely communicating the gospel and scriptural truths in our turbulent times. In chapter 7, we will finish the loop with step seven, the categorical step exploring biblical themes and texts.

Questions for Reflection

1. How is your congregation's collective prayer life?
2. In what ways does your church lack reconciliation and unity?
3. Which of the *-isms* is most pressing for your congregation? If you had to choose one *-ism* to prayerfully consider preaching about, which one would it be?

31. Nicole Hong, Juliana Kim, Ali Watkins, and Ashley Southall, "Brutal Attack on Filipino Woman Sparks Outrage: 'Everybody Is on Edge,'" *New York Times*, updated April 6, 2021, https://www.nytimes.com/2021/03/30/nyregion/asian-attack-nyc.html.

32. Tish Harrison Warren, "In a Year of Death, Ash Wednesday Offers Unexpected Hope," *Christianity Today*, Feb. 16, 2021, https://www.christianitytoday.com/ct/2021/february-web -only/covid-19-coronavirus-ash-wednesday-lent-hope.html.

Practical Next Steps

1. What pre-sermon, mid-sermon, and post-sermon practices might help you immediately as you consider preaching on a divisive topic?

2. Identify some current struggles in your church that may stymie the pursuit of reconciliation and unity today.

3. Pray with your church's leadership on when and how to begin pursuing Tisby's ARC (awareness, relationships, and commitment).

7

The Categorical Step

Biblical Themes and Texts

We now arrive at the seventh and final step in our homiletical model. To recap, thus far we have explored pride, prejudice, reconciliation, and unity through a reconciling hermeneutic (the theological step), developed three intelligences (the contextual step), addressed how a preacher can grow in maturity through homiletical renewal (the personal step), examined the role of the Holy Spirit working in and through the herald to stimulate godly change (the positional step), explored how to promote reconciliation and unity through a centered-set approach and virtue formation (the methodological step), and posed some sermonic pre-, mid-, and post-sermon exercises that are constructive (the practical step).

This final chapter endeavors to equip communicators with salient themes and texts that are concrete and applicational. That is, we aim to present the topics and passages that will pack the greatest homiletical punch. While we maintain that "all Scripture is . . . useful for teaching, rebuking, correcting and training in righteousness" (2 Tim. 3:16), some texts are particularly germane when it comes to the task at hand. Although this list is far from exhaustive, it should serve as a robust entry point.

Creator: The Trinity Exemplifies Unity amid Diversity

The apostle Paul instructs Christians to "follow God's example, therefore, as dearly loved children" (Eph. 5:1). What does that mean? There are countless aspects of God's nature and character that could be emulated. However, harmony and distinction, unity and diversity are exemplified in the intra-trinitarian relations, sometimes referred to as the *immanent* Trinity. Ross Hastings contends that "the nature of the Trinity as persons-in-relation is not a subsidiary doctrine or even an attribute of God among others. It is who God is, and it is the very center of Christian theology and therefore of mission."[1] The way God interacts within himself is a model for how God's people are to share *koinonia*, or fellowship. Indeed, the Father, Son, and Holy Spirit "have loved, adored, served, and enjoyed one another from all eternity. . . . [They] are 'other-oriented.'"[2] Theologians call this *perichoresis*, which is defined as "the togetherness, the joy, the self-giving, self-surrendering passion and life shared by the Father, Son and Spirit."[3] For a moment imagine what would happen if God's family cultivated these kinds of relationships and reflected them to the world. It would glorify God, give us deep satisfaction, and fortify and verify our gospel witness before the cosmos.

To preach on the nature of the Trinity we suggest starting with passages such as Matthew 3:16–17, John 14–17, 2 Corinthians 13:14, Ephesians 4:1–13, and 1 Peter 1:1–2.

The First Creation

At the first creation we see the Trinity collaborating together (cf. Gen. 1:2, 26–28; John 1:1–5) and everything was "good." As a reminder, this word carries the idea of "lovely and wholesome, bursting with *shalom*—complete delight and flourishing experienced in God's undiluted presence."[4] There is relational comity, a deep and abiding interconnectedness between Creator and creation. At the same time, we also discover the emergence of a

1. Ross Hastings, *Missional God, Missional Church: Hope for Re-Evangelizing the West* (Downers Grove, IL: IVP Academic, 2012), 84.
2. Timothy Keller, *Center Church: Doing Balanced Gospel-Centered Ministry in Your City* (Grand Rapids: Zondervan, 2012), 33–34.
3. J. R. Woodward and Dan White Jr., *Church as Movement: Starting and Sustaining Missional-Incarnational Communities* (Downers Grove, IL: InterVarsity, 2016), 121.
4. Paul A. Hoffman, *Reconciling Places: How to Bridge the Chasms in Our Communities* (Eugene, OR: Cascade Books, 2020), 52.

God-ordained diversity. God commands the first humans to "be fruitful and increase in number; fill the earth and subdue it" (Gen. 1:28). Brenda Salter McNeil writes, "'The Cultural Mandate' accounts for unity and diversity. That is, migration creates difference, which God commanded in Genesis 1."[5] Unity is not uniformity; God values variety and difference.

This variety and difference are evidenced in the creation of male and female as equally made in the image of God. Here, we discover vital doctrines that inspire concord. One is the *imago Dei*, which has been discussed previously.[6] This belief not only calls for justice (cf. Gen. 9:6) but also imparts dignity and equality. C. S. Lewis famously penned: "There are no *ordinary* people. You have never talked to a mere mortal. . . . It is immortals whom we joke with, work with, marry, snub, and exploit—immortal horrors or everlasting splendors."[7]

So, the next time you preach, consider having parishioners turn to the people next to them and make a statement like "You are precious to God," "You are loved by your heavenly Father," "You are God's masterpiece," "You are fearfully and wonderfully made," "Thank you for being here today," "I love you," or other similar expressions. This action conveys each person's God-given worth and establishes a culture of honor and respect in the congregation.

A second doctrine that merits underscoring is God's common grace. After Jesus instructed his followers, "Love your enemies and pray for those who persecute you" (Matt. 5:44), he noted that God "causes his sun to rise on the evil and the good, and sends rain on the righteous and unrighteous" (v. 45). Common grace "accounts for sinful man's ability to arrive at a modicum of justice. . . . [It] is the grace of preservation by which man's rapacity is restrained. Indeed, if it were not for common grace, the world would fall into anarchy and disorder."[8] God's unmerited goodness and generosity infuse and sustain the created order. God's people are to declare and incarnate the grace of our heavenly Father to a fallen and fractured world. It continually binds us to God and one another.

To teach on the first creation, we recommend beginning with texts such as Genesis 1, Genesis 9:1–17 (which includes the Noahic covenant), Psalm 145:8–9, and Acts 17:16–34.

5. Brenda Salter McNeil, *Roadmap to Reconciliation: Moving Communities into Unity, Wholeness and Justice* (Downers Grove, IL: InterVarsity, 2015), 23–26.

6. Also see the sermon on sexism, "Equal in God's Eyes," in appendix G.

7. C. S. Lewis, *The Weight of Glory* (New York: HarperOne, 2001), 45–46.

8. Donald G. Bloesch, *Essentials of Evangelical Theology*, vol. 1, *God, Authority, and Salvation* (New York: HarperCollins, 1978), 91.

Alienation: Original Sin and Total Depravity

The pervasive nature of sin is another significant basis for reconciliation and unity. Sin does not discriminate regarding ethnicity, class, sex, or political affiliation. King David's observations are universally accurate: "All [humans] have turned away, all have become corrupt; there is no one who does good, not even one" (Ps. 14:3). The apostle Paul crystallizes the truth of human nature and behavior: "Jews and Gentiles alike are all under the power of sin. . . . All have sinned and fall short of the glory of God" (Rom. 3:9, 23; cf. Eccles. 7:20). In other words, human corruption due to sin is universal *and* comprehensive. Robert Reymond asserts that "man in his raw, natural state as he comes from the womb is *morally and spiritually corrupt in disposition and character*. Every part of his being—his mind, his will, his emotions, his affections, his conscience, his body—has been affected by sin."[9]

Worst of all, every person lies to himself or herself, and others, regarding their condition: "The heart is deceitful above all things and beyond cure. Who can understand it?" (Jer. 17:9). We are deceived about our deception, blinded to our blindness, ignorant of our ignorance. A pitiful condition indeed! Moreover, this deceit goes beyond the self or individual sin and flows into a communal, collective, corporate, systemic sin that undergirds the errant treatment of others within the entire family of God. We would do right, as the Israelites did (e.g., 2 Sam. 21 and Ezra 9), to corporately confess our sins, which often precedes genuine reconciliation and unity.

The result? We affront the almighty God's holiness, transgress his commands, and are legally guilty rebels trapped under Satan's domain. God's wrath—his perfect justice—is activated to oppose our filth. We are relationally alienated from our caring Creator, and the trajectory of our fate is toward condemnation and eternal death—forever separated from God's loving presence.

Our corruption, however, may offer one possible upside: a camaraderie rooted in commonality. When I (Paul) was in seminary, my wife worked for the American Cancer Society doing fundraising and development. As a supportive spouse, I volunteered (or was I voluntold?) at this wonderful organization. I helped haul daffodils during Daffodil Days, petted the pretty puppies during Dogswalk, and assisted in the execution of the inspirational Relay for Life— including placing votive candles around the high school track to remember and honor those who died of cancer. Along the way, I discovered a plucky solidarity, an esprit de corps among those battling this awful disease. The members of this club exhibited a palpable sense of belonging, animated by

9. Robert L. Reymond, *A New Systematic Theology of the Christian Faith* (Nashville: Thomas Nelson, 1998), 450.

deep-seated compassion and empathy. I perceived a similar connection among the family, friends, loved ones, and caregivers supporting the patients who sought to overcome the "C-word." The shared struggle forged a beautiful bond that encircled a resilient community.

Is it possible to view our common affliction—sin—through a similar lens? It is prudent for the preacher to remind the congregation that our shared spiritual condition verifies the truism "the ground is level at the foot of the cross." The diagnosis of depravity caused by original sin means we are all equally lost, destitute, and desperate. Our condition of complete corruption "denotes the total inability of sinful man to please God or come to him unless moved by grace."[10] Outside intervention by the Great Physician is our only hope for healing (cf. Luke 5:31–32).

To expound on original sin and total depravity, we suggest you start with passages such as Genesis 3, Psalm 14:1–3, Psalm 51, and Romans 1–3.

Reconciliation: The Vast, Superabounding, Atoning Love of Jesus Christ

Although the disease is ubiquitous, the antidote is as well. Every person—whatever their ethnicity, socioeconomic status, or partisan identity—is saved from their sins using the same means: by grace through faith (cf. Eph. 2:8–9). Each human must be born again (cf. John 3:3) and regenerated (cf. Titus 2:14; 3:1–6). This revolution culminating in our total renovation can occur only through the completely efficacious blood of Jesus Christ, the sinless Lamb of God (cf. John 1:29; Heb. 9:1–10:18). Jesus's blood is powerful: "With your blood you purchased for God persons from every tribe and language and people and nation" (Rev. 5:9).

What prompted such an astonishing and undeserved sacrifice? The superabounding grace and love of God (Rom. 5). God's grace "reigns" (Rom. 5:21), turning "enemies" (Rom. 5:10) into "dearly loved children" (Eph. 5:1). The prolific composer Charles Hutchinson Gabriel eloquently and evocatively exulted in God's love this way: "I stand amazed in the presence of Jesus the Nazarene, and wonder how he could love me, a sinner, condemned unclean. How marvelous! How wonderful! and my song shall ever be; How marvelous! How wonderful! is my Savior's love for me!"[11] Recently, a guest worship

---

10. Bloesch, *Essentials of Evangelical Theology*, 1:90.

11. C. Michael Hawn, "History of Hymns: 'I Stand Amazed in the Presence,'" Discipleship Ministries of the United Methodist Church, July 2, 2013, https://www.umcdiscipleship.org /resources/history-of-hymns-i-stand-amazed-in-the-presence.

leader played this hymn as the closing anthem during our worship services. I (Paul) felt a surge of emotion completely engulf me, leaving me dumbstruck— unable to sing. My sentiments were revealed in the form of salty tears, which expressed my gratitude: "This is *how much* Jesus loves *me!*"

The richest, most vibrant forms of unity emerge from God's love. Through his Son, Jesus Christ, and in the power of the Spirit, God the Father showers his children with affection, attention, joy, and delight (Zeph. 3:17). This love purifies and liberates us from insecurity, fear, selfishness, prejudice, and exclusion. God's holy ardor captivates us, and when we bask in its magnificence, it dispels all resentments and antipathies.

Proclaim this love so passionately it gushes from your soul, spilling into and saturating the hearts of your listeners.

To declare the incomparable love of our Redeemer, commence with Scripture texts such as Psalm 136, Isaiah 53–55, John 3:1–21, Romans 8:31–39, and 1 John 4:7–21.

The Final Creation: Justice and the Revelation 7 Vision

A final theme meriting attention is that of God's righteous judgment and establishment of the new creation. The Apostles' Creed avows that Jesus Christ "will come to judge the living and the dead."[12] Because "God does not show favoritism" (Rom. 2:11), every single person will "stand before God's judgment seat" and "give an account" of their lives before God (Rom. 14:10–12). And the just Judge does not grade on a curve: everyone will be weighed according to the same identical standards. All the shallow, external variables humans presently deploy to categorize, marginalize, and reject one another will vanish when God perfectly punishes sin and evil, once and for all. This inescapable destiny ought to keep us humble and sober-minded. It hedges against discrimination and retribution as the Lord guarantees he will deal with all forms of unrighteousness.

Yet on the other side of judgment sits the gloriously remade Eden. Hallelujah—there are no hierarchies in heaven: rewards, yes; bigotry and injustice, no. The crown, the zenith of the Trinity's reconciling and restoring mission is the inestimable community of disciples worshiping the Lamb (Rev. 7:9). In heaven, there's a breathtaking diversity:

God's redeemed children are not white washed like eggs in a carton. Instead, each retains some vestige of their ethnicity, sex, and national status. There are

12. Apostles' Creed, available at https://www.crcna.org/welcome/beliefs/creeds/apostles-creed.

people of every ethnic composition, male and female,[13] and, presumably, Christians from the global north and west (generally wealthy while on earth) and the global south and east (generally less affluent).[14]

Interestingly enough, a major class distinction—fashion—appears to have vanished. In fact, there's a void of designer clothing, save one item: everyone is "wearing white robes" (Rev. 7:9). In the new Jerusalem two common denominators are preeminent: the imputed righteousness of Jesus Christ and the unceasing worship of the only worthy King, who sits regally on his throne— and they are intertwined because the former makes the latter possible. Pause and just process that portrait: at the core of the ultimate reality there exists a harmonious balance between unity and diversity. How can a herald *not* spend the bulk of his or her life and breath announcing this vision? What is more satisfying or desirable than this?

To preach on the final judgment and creation we propose the following sampling of texts: Isaiah 61–65, Daniel 12, Revelation 7:9–19, and Revelation 20–22.

Biblical Texts

Now that we have identified the primary biblical themes, we will devote the rest of this chapter to enumerating some recommended Scripture passages for preaching on six topics: classism, ethnocentrism, political divisions, reconciliation, sexism, and unity. Due to space limitations, we will not offer a comprehensive list. However, we will provide brief annotations for less commonly preached Old Testament verses and passages, and then we suggest some New Testament passages directly or indirectly linked to these topics. Depending on whether you endorse preaching through a book (verse-by-verse exposition) or topical sermons, you'll want to make appropriate decisions about how best to incorporate these biblical texts. Any of these texts could be preached as a positive or negative example on these biblical themes. That is, you could take a negative case study/passage and expound on how your listeners might incorporate positive applications and implications in their lives.

13. According to Matthew 22:30, in heaven "people will neither marry nor be given in marriage; they will be like the angels in heaven." So human sexuality will look different in heaven, but that does not mean maleness or femaleness is erased. Christ's own resurrected body appeared male to his followers (see, e.g., Matt. 28:5; Luke 24:28).

14. Paul A. Hoffman, "The Identity Imperative: Three Keys to Preaching on Identity," *Preaching* 36, no. 3 (Spring 2021): 10–13.

Classism

1 Samuel 16:7

"People look at the outward appearance, but the LORD looks at the heart." God's instructions to Samuel present an invitation for us to mimic the value God places on the heart, rather than physical appearance (or, we might add, rather than whether a person is wealthy or impoverished).

Nehemiah 5

Nehemiah's treatment of the poor is to be emulated and celebrated. There's much to teach a congregation about sacrificial love toward the least of these in this text.

Psalm 12:5

God's heart for the poor and vulnerable is clearly expressed in this psalm. God protects those in need, and so should we as his people.

Proverbs 28:27

God encourages Christians to have a generous heart toward the economically disadvantaged.

Ecclesiastes 5:8-20

The teaching here on how to properly view wealth and money is a helpful sermon topic in addressing classism.

New Testament

The topics of socioeconomic class and classism can also be preached from these passages: Matthew 6:1–4; 18:21–35; 19:16–30; 22:1–14; 25:44–46; Mark 10:23; Romans 12:16; 1 Corinthians 11:17–34; 16:2; Ephesians 4:32; James 1:27; 2:1–10; 2 Thessalonians 3; 1 Timothy 6:10–19; Philemon (an important text for discussion of slavery in the Bible); James 2:1–17; 4:13–17; and 1 John 3:17.

Ethnocentrism

Genesis 10

The Table of Nations represents God's plan and heart for diverse people groups.

Exodus 1 and Exodus 5

We see how the Israelites are mistreated by the Egyptians under Pharoah's leadership. Threatened by Israel's numbers in their favor, Pharoah sets in place structures to oppress them (making their brick-making task harder by not providing straw, in Exodus 5).

Deuteronomy 10:18-19

This passage elevates the foreigner and sojourner in our midst.

Ruth

The narrative of Ruth is impactful in drawing attention to her ethnicity as a Moabitess. She is an unlikely heroine as a Moabite woman—a young immigrant from a group of people who were enemies of Israel—who would eventually become the great-grandmother of King David.

Daniel

The book of Daniel tells his story and that of his friends while in Babylonian captivity. A preacher might be able to draw some parallels with cultural assimilation and appropriation and how not to force them on minority groups.

Jonah

The book of Jonah is a key Old Testament book on the topic of ethnocentrism. Jonah's hatred and fear of the Assyrians is worth explaining, and the preacher can link Jonah's narrative to modern-day xenophobia and racial injustice.

Jesus's Healing of Gentiles

Throughout the Gospels, Jesus heals non-Jewish people such as the Syrophoenician woman in Mark 7:24–30, which opens an opportunity to teach one's congregation why the Gospel authors mention gentile people groups and what this tells us about God's heart for the nations.

Luke 10:25-37

The parable of the good Samaritan is a chief example of Jesus flipping the script on how gentiles now become God's exemplars of Christian love as Jesus says: "Go and do likewise."

Book of Acts

Acts highlights God's missionary heart for the world. A preacher could draw from any number of texts to emphasize unity amid diversity: Acts 6:1–4 (Hebraic and Grecian Jews), Acts 8 (Philip and the Ethiopian eunuch), Acts 10 (Peter's vision), Acts 15 (Council of Jerusalem), or Acts 13–20 (Paul's missionary travels).

Romans 11:11-32

God's expansion of salvation to gentiles is a pivotal text for preaching on expressing the message of salvation of God to all people and all people groups.

1 Corinthians 9:22

In saying, "I have become all things to all people," Paul prioritizes the gospel over ethnic divisions and his Jewish identity. It also reveals a willingness to encounter and engage other cultures in a fresh way.

Revelation 7:9

John's vision of heaven is a prime illustration of deconstructing ethnocentrism. God plays no favorites in terms of who can enter paradise. All those who place their faith in Jesus may dwell with him forever.

Political Divisions

1 Samuel 8-11

Saul's appointment as Israel's first king has many connotations for assessing political allegiance to God or to national leaders.

1 Samuel 16-24, 26; 2 Samuel 2

David's rise to power sets up division between himself and King Saul. Saul's jealousy of David's rise to fame creates tension, rivalry, and hostility between households. What can we teach our congregants about the important characteristics of leaders?

Gospels

Regular teaching on the kingdom of God/kingdom of heaven (e.g., Matthew 18:1–9) may be an effective way to preach on political divisions. While politics matters, we need to remind our listeners that Christians are citizens of a different kingdom (cf. John 18:33–37).

Matthew 22:15-22; Mark 12:13-17; Luke 20:20-26

Jesus's rebuke of the Pharisees on paying taxes to Caesar has political and governmental implications.

Romans 13

Paul's teaching on how Christians honor government officials lays important groundwork for reflection on how Christians view, interpret, and obey human laws.

Reconciliation

Genesis 16

The story of Hagar, and of Sarai's mistreatment of her slave, reveals Sarai's hostility and inner pain expressed toward Hagar. What can we learn from Hagar and Sarai's story with respect to the dos and don'ts of reconciliation?

Genesis 33

This famous story of Jacob and Esau is a prime testimony of sibling reconciliation.

Ezra 10

Preaching on corporate, public confession is a proper biblical value to spread within Western congregations that often view confession as private. We can apply corporate confession to the sin of division among God's people today.

New Testament

New Testament passages teaching on reconciliation include Matthew 5:23–26; 18:15–17; 25; Luke 17:3; Romans 14:19; 1 Corinthians 12:14–21; 2 Corinthians 5:18–21; 13:11; Ephesians 4:32; and Hebrews 12:14.

Sexism

Consider preaching back-to-back sermon series on men of the Bible and women of the Bible. Exegesis of biblical characters will take some extra effort, but it may well be worth it to educate your congregation on less known Bible characters. In the past, I (Matt) have done so, and the sermon series were well received.

Genesis 1:27-28

The sample sermon on sexism in appendix G points out the importance of preaching on the image of God in both males and females, and celebrates both sexes.

Genesis 19

Lot offering his daughters to be raped by the men of Sodom is a volatile passage that seems to exacerbate the denigration of women and proliferation of sexual violence.

Numbers 27:1-11 and Numbers 36

Moses's accounts regarding Zelophehad's daughters seeking their inheritance and property underscores the patriarchal culture of the ancient Near East. A preacher who spends time exegeting the ancient Near Eastern culture will have much to discuss with today's listeners.

Judges 4 and 5

Deborah's story as a female judge offers a positive case study in female leadership.

John 4

Jesus treats the woman at the well with dignity in spite of cultural and gender differences that normally separated Jews and Samaritans.

John 7:53-8:11

Jesus's treatment of the woman caught in the act of adultery is a critical passage for preachers to expound on men, women, and sexual sin. In particular, it's important to raise the issue of double standards in discussing and handling sexual sin.

1 Peter 3:7

Peter's instructions on how men and women treat each other in the marital relationship is helpful here.

Unity

Genesis 13:11-12

This passage regarding Abram and Lot is ripe with conversation about unity and disunity. When is it helpful to separate oneself from a loved one?

Genesis 37:12-36

The story of Joseph's brothers selling him into slavery reveals a spirit of disunity among siblings. Preachers could spend some time unpacking the emotions and logic of each of the brothers mentioned in this narrative.

Leviticus 11

This text regarding clean and unclean foods may not immediately pop into our consciousness, but it might be a worthy sermon passage on unity and disunity (in relation to Acts 10:9–23, Peter's vision). With whom we associate and share table fellowship is a necessary consideration for Christian unity.

Deuteronomy 13

Moses's instructions regarding the worship of other gods may offer preaching points on the nature of Christian unity and disunity. Are there any false gods we are worshiping today in our congregation instead of the one, true, living God?

Ruth

The entire story of Ruth and Naomi is a profound expression of familial loyalty and unity.

Ezra 3-4

The rebuilding of the altar and the temple during the time of Ezra is a vision for unity as the people of God united around common goals to reinstate worship to the Lord.

Psalm 133:1

"How good and pleasant it is when God's people live together in unity!" David's psalm provides rich imagery for what it looks like when Christians pursue unity in relational harmony.

New Testament

Here are New Testament passages that may guide one's preaching on the topic of unity: John 17:23; Acts 4:32; 15:36–41; Romans 6:1–5; 1 Corinthians 1:10; 12:12–13; Galatians 3:26–28; Ephesians 1:3–10; 4:1–6; 4:11–13; Philippians 1:27; 2:1–4; 4:3; Colossians 3:13–14; 1 Peter 3:8; and 1 John 3.

Questions for Reflection

1. What are some biblical themes that you've preached on to frame our various divisions in the church?
2. In the last year, have you preached from any biblical passages that address our -isms but shied away from addressing the key divisive themes mentioned in the Scripture text? What passages and themes were they?

Practical Next Step

1. Prayerfully plan a sermon series for the coming year on one of the -isms. Which biblical themes and passages will help you most effectively preach on these topics?

CONCLUSION

We conclude where we began. The challenges lying before preachers, teachers, and ministry leaders are legion. The weight of this burden—Christian disunity—has led some heralds and laborers to a place of acute pessimism. For instance, pastor Michael Graham asserts:

> The tectonic plates are shifting underfoot. This fracturing will likely be irrevocable not because our Gospel essentials are not unifying enough but because the divergence of ethical priorities, cultural engagement, racial attitudes, political visions/illusions, and their implications for philosophy of ministry mean that unity is fundamentally no longer tenable.[1]

While we may not totally agree with his sentiments, this perspective is justified given the real chaos presently afflicting the United States.

However, the convictions expressed in this book continue to undergird our tenacious hope. To review, the theological step tells us the triune Creator is one, the world he formed (the first creation) was unified before the fall, Jesus prayed for and died for our union (reconciliation), and the dysfunctions and divisions besetting us do not have the final word *because they are not* the final word. The harmony displayed in Revelation 7 is occurring right now, and one day, when we reach the fullness of time at the final creation, it will be the *singular* experience of God's restored people. To riff off Dr. King's renowned declaration, we will prevail because the arc of God's story bends toward reconciliation and unity.[2]

---

1. Michael Graham, "The Six Way Fracturing of Evangelicalism," *Mere Orthodoxy*, June 7, 2021, https://mereorthodoxy.com/six-way-fracturing-evangelicalism.
2. The original quotation is, "We shall overcome because the arc of the moral universe is long, but it bends toward justice." Martin Luther King Jr., "Remaining Awake through a

Next, the contextual step is demonstrated by the incarnation of Immanuel. The Son of God is the example par excellence of historical intelligence: he entered history, lived in a specific, time-bound milieu, faced it head on, and redeemed it by enacting God's new narrative—the renewal of all things through the cross, resurrection, and ascension.

The third step—the personal—is modeled by the greatest preacher-rabbi of all time. If anyone exemplified homiletical renewal, it is the one and only Messiah. His life revealed a seamless intertwining of devotion, introspection, and connection. No one before or since Jesus has operated in such a state of pure homiletical wholeness.

Regarding the positional step, Jesus, the Logos, allowed the Holy Spirit to use him as a holy conduit through which he poured his precious and powerful unction. Indeed, this book has been written and is being read because the Spirit-inspired *kerygma* has surged like a continuous electrical current from Jesus's lips to ours, to yours, to your congregants', and will move forward for years to come.

Steps five through seven—the methodological, practical, and categorical—are also embodied in the second member of the Holy Trinity. Jesus personified a centered-set orientation as he proclaimed the kingdom of God and concretized it through his virtuous character. As the ultimate pastor, Jesus fostered peace, unity, and reconciliation. As the ultimate preacher, he reinforced these values, communicating the truth in a way that explained, proved, and applied it, with the aim of stimulating affectional formation in his listeners. And last, Jesus's teaching demonstrated a commitment to core themes and categories that highlighted the gospel. He never wasted time bandying about trendy, arcane, or kitschy topics to attract more clicks or followers. He was always on mission because he understood the stakes and thus had no time to waste.

May the same be said of our generation.

Reconciliation and Unity Are Possible: A Contemporary Story

It would be all too easy to finish this book, close it, put it on a shelf, and continue to be demoralized—even paralyzed—by the despair permeating the culture and church. But we believe a modern-day story will sufficiently show that God is still blessing the diligent efforts of preachers, teachers, and ministry leaders who come together to promote unity and reconciliation in their communities.

Great Revolution" (speech, Oberlin College, Oberlin, OH, June 1965), https://www2.oberlin.edu/external/EOG/BlackHistoryMonth/MLK/CommAddress.html.

During the process of writing this book, I (Paul) visited Austin, Texas, for the first time. Thomas Cogdell gave me a tour of the city and shared a tale that reenergized my passion for reconciliation and unity.[3]

Austin has a reputation as a progressive city. This is encapsulated in its slogan, which lays bare its ethos and raison d'être: *Keep Austin Weird*.[4] Unfortunately, this metropolis is not all that weird in that for many years it was deeply divided along racial lines. As is often the case, this chasm was blatantly expressed by the city's highways. Interstate 35 not only runs north–south through the heart of the city; it also demarcates the place of power from the place of poverty. The west side of I-35 is occupied by the Texas state capitol, the University of Texas, corporate skyscrapers dominating the skyline, and the uber-cool bars and music venues of Sixth Street—the epicenter of the famed South by Southwest music and film festivals. The east side of I-35 is occupied by racial and ethnic minorities forced to settle there through zoning decrees dating back to the 1920s.[5]

In 1975, a major attempt was made to cross this divide. Dr. J. J. Seabrook, a Black pastor and the first permanent president of Huston-Tillotson University, a historically Black university in east Austin, helped spearhead a community-wide initiative to rename 19th Street (which connects east and west Austin) Martin Luther King Jr. Boulevard. Not surprisingly, this effort was opposed by many business owners on the west side, who argued the proposed name change should apply only to the portion of 19th Street east of I-35. At a critical juncture, when the resistance was heaviest, Dr. Seabrook addressed the city council at an explosive meeting. Shockingly, in the middle of his impassioned speech, he collapsed at the podium and died of a heart attack. J. J. Seabrook literally sacrificed his life for the cause of righteousness, reconciliation, and unity.

When the city council reconvened a week later, they voted unanimously to rename the entire street—the west and east sides—after Dr. King.

3. Thomas is an Austin native and one of the founders of Christ the Reconciler in central Texas, a diverse community of lay followers of Jesus committed to living out John 17. I am sharing a truncated version of what Thomas shared with me. For a fuller account, see http://www.christthereconciler.org/the-jj-seabrook-story; https://www.bobodellauthor.com/east-and-west-austin; and "A View Too Small: First Steps," in Bob O'Dell and Gideon Ariel, *Five Years with Orthodox Jews: How Connecting with God's People Unlocks Understanding of God's Word* (Hebron, Israel: Root Source, 2020), 289–302.

4. See Joshua Long, *Weird City: Sense of Place and Creative Resistance in Austin, Texas* (Austin: University of Texas Press, 2010).

5. "How East Austin Became a Negro District," East End Cultural Heritage District (website), accessed October 15, 2021, http://www.eastendculturaldistrict.org/cms/gentrification-redevelopment/how-east-austin-became-negro-district.

Fast forward to the 1990s, when concerted efforts were made by local faith leaders to unite Austin's pastors across denominational, racial, class, and economic barriers. Thomas recounted how one meeting became a major inflection point: "The white pastors were meeting with some black pastors to invite them to a pro-life gathering. One African American pastor fired a shot of truth across the bow of this gathering: 'The only time we see you is when you come invite us to cross I-35 for your events.' A young white pastor who was new to the city stood up, and responded, 'I'll take that challenge!' The two pastors started the reconciling journey: they met regularly, developed a friendship, and began to share each other's pulpits."

But there's more. This relationship helped birth a March for Jesus in Austin. The success of that event spurred further collaboration among diverse groups: Blacks, Latinos, and whites, men and women, young and old, lower-, middle-, and upper-class residents, churches, businesses, and civic organizations, to name a few. They became a loose coalition, working together to bring shalom to *all* of Austin's inhabitants (cf. Jer. 29:4–7). The Spirit of God was blowing a fresh wind through the atmosphere of the state capitol.

Then, in 2010, God orchestrated a defining moment, a marker indicating change was occurring. Thomas, his friend Bob O'Dell, and the Rev. Joseph Parker of David Chapel, a prominent east Austin church, felt compelled to coordinate a "Remember J. J. Seabrook Day" on the 35th anniversary of his death (May 1). On that day, hundreds of people representing dozens of diverse congregations from the area gathered to honor "a hero for the entire city." Numerous speakers drew upon their historical intelligence to explain the significance of that moment, stressing how far the city had come, as well as how far there still was yet to go.

Finally, the coup de grâce. Cheryl Cole, Austin's first Black female city councilwoman, stepped to the microphone. She announced that by order of the city council, every May 1 would be recognized as "J. J. Seabrook Day" in Austin. Using a strong voice saturated with elation, she continued: "In the next city council meeting, I will bring before my colleagues a motion to name the bridge across I-35, that bridges east and west on MLK Jr. Blvd.—the J. J. Seabrook Bridge!"

That's right, the bridge that once epitomized the city's divisions now symbolizes reconciliation and unity. Perhaps God's plan is to *Keep Austin Weird* in a different way than the slogan imagines.

Is it possible the triune God wants to make your church, city, state, and nation "weird" for his glory and your satisfaction? Dream with us for a moment: your congregation and community could become a gleaming oasis emitting the fragrant aroma of the countercultural kingdom of God, a place of flourishing, a living icon of the Revelation 7 reality—right here and right now.

What are you willing to sacrifice to make it happen? Jesus gave it all. Can we give any less?

Now, go forth and preach the gospel of reconciliation and unity: theologically, contextually, personally, positionally, methodologically, practically, and categorically.

Your King is *with* you and *for* you. May *his* heart and *his* story shine through all you proclaim and teach, today and forevermore. Amen.

Appendix A

Reflections on Critical Race Theory

In the American evangelical domain, the use of critical race theory (CRT) is controversial, as many consider it incompatible with the historic, orthodox Christian faith.[1] Numerous pastors and theologians appear to critique CRT without offering a clear definition. We support Nathan Cartagena's description of CRT as

> a *movement* aimed at providing an antiracist understanding of the relationships between "race" and law. This movement contains competing and complementary traditions. . . . Each tradition houses multiple methods and claims. CRT therefore is not a single theory, method, or analytic tool. It's a diverse, contested, multi-layered movement.[2]

1. For example, on one hand, see Kate Shellnutt, "Southern Baptists Keep Quarreling over Critical Race Theory," *Christianity Today*, December 3, 2020, https://www.christianitytoday.com/news/2020/december/southern-baptist-critical-race-theory-debate-crt-seminary-s.html. On the other hand, see Jemar Tisby, "Southern Baptist Seminary Presidents Reaffirm Their Commitment to Whiteness," *The Witness*, December 1, 2020, https://thewitnessbcc.com/southern-baptist-seminary-presidents-reaffirm-their-commitment-to-whiteness. We acknowledge Tisby's concern (stated in the abovementioned article) that many white evangelicals have reactively used CRT as a straw man or "epithet" to summarily dismiss potentially legitimate critiques.
2. Nathan Cartagena, "What Christians Get Wrong about Critical Race Theory—Part I," *Faithfully Magazine*, February 2020, https://faithfullymagazine.com/critical-race-theory

With that in mind, we offer five short responses to CRT:

1. We hold the Scriptures as our highest authority and standard. Like all other disciplines that interact with the Holy Scriptures, CRT should be engaged with discernment and skill, not haphazardly or uncritically. We recognize valid criticisms of CRT have been posed by a wide variety of credible thinkers, including Timothy Keller[3] and Thaddeus J. Williams,[4] to name a few. However, we underscore that this does not preclude exploring and dialoguing with CRT in a genuine and robust fashion. Nathan Cartagena, Rasool Berry, David French,[5] Jeff Liou,[6] and Ed Uszynski[7] offer laudable examples.

2. It is wise to keep the doctrine of common grace at the forefront of theological reflection. God speaks through sources and people who may not recognize his reign. Yet inasmuch as a person's insights comport with Scripture and illuminate issues in God's world, they are to be received. Rasool Berry writes,

> The gospel reveals not only a personal pietistic plan of salvation, but a plan of restoration that redeems and restores. Jesus critiques unjust political, economic and social systems as well as personal sins. CRT is on the lookout for systemic, institutionalized racism and injustice. Because of its philosophical assumptions, CRT will not accurately analyze all it seeks to critique. But because of common grace, it will see things we should see; and because of our sin, we know we don't always read the Bible rightly and so we need to listen to other voices. The critiques of [Max] Horkheimer, Derrick Bell, Kimberlé Crenshaw

-christians. Cartagena goes on to write that "CRT scholars share two interests and five conclusions," which he helpfully summarizes.

3. Timothy Keller, "A Biblical Critique of Secular Justice and Critical Theory," Gospel in Life, October 2020, https://quarterly.gospelinlife.com/a-biblical-critique-of-secular-justice-and-critical-theory.

4. Thaddeus J. Williams, *Confronting Injustice without Compromising Truth: 12 Questions Christians Should Ask about Social Justice* (Grand Rapids: Zondervan Academic, 2020), 4–5, 107–8, 136–37.

5. David French, "On the Use and Abuse of Critical Race Theory in American Christianity," The French Press, *The Dispatch*, September 13, 2020, https://frenchpress.thedispatch.com/p/on-the-use-and-abuse-of-critical.

6. Raymond Chang and Michelle Reyes, "Jeff Liou on Justice and Critical Race Theory," *The Reclaim Podcast*, December 16, 2020, https://aaccreclaimpodcast.libsyn.com/episode-9-jeff-liou-on-justice-and-critical-race-theory.

7. Ed Uszynski, interview by Preston Sprinkle, "Critical Theory and Race Relations in America," *Theology in the Raw Podcast*, September 21, 2020, https://www.prestonsprinkle.com/theology-in-the-raw/720-ed-uszynski.

are surpassed by Jesus. The gospel gives us insight to respond and subversively fulfill CRT with something greater.[8]

3. As stated earlier, it is oftentimes more constructive for Christians to first identify and build around commonalities (e.g., tackling injustice and poverty). Then, after a basis of mutual concern has been established, we can tackle disagreements (e.g., underlying ideologies and applications).

4. We find it curious that pastors and preachers who espouse the doctrines of total depravity and original sin would completely shun a discipline that could potentially act as a tool that excavates theological and hamartiological (the doctrine of sin) gems and thus might refract new light upon the full panoply of the redemptive work of Christ.

5. Texts such as Jeremiah 17:9–10 and Proverbs 16:2 teach that humans are masters at self-deception and hence blind to their own blind spots. The social sciences are to be welcomed whenever they help heralds discover new insights into their souls, communities, and culture that they have been heretofore oblivious to.

---

8. Rasool Berry, "Critical [G]race Theory: The Promise and Perils of CRT," *P2C Students* (blog), February 16, 2021, https://p2c.com/students/articles/critical-grace-theory-the-promise -and-perils-of-crt.

Appendix B

Sample Homiletical Integrity Covenant

To honor the triune God through my preaching ministry, I _____ (name) commit to participate in this homiletical integrity covenant.

This means I will prioritize connecting with a diverse group of brothers and sisters to do the following:

1. On a regular basis, I will make myself accountable to them and available to them whenever they need help or encouragement.
2. On a regular basis, I will pray for my covenant members by name, and specifically, for God's power to transform them and mature them into the image of Christ.
3. When we gather _____ (frequency, e.g., monthly or quarterly) I will confess any ethnocentrism, classism, sexism, or partisan polarization in my thoughts, speech, or actions, including on social media. I grant them the authority to lovingly confront me (Eph. 4:15) and gently restore me as led by the Holy Spirit (Gal. 6:1).
4. When we gather, I will join them in studying the Holy Scriptures and resources that edify us as preachers and leaders committed to fostering unity and reconciliation within our congregations, communities, and the wider body of Christ.

5. I will "consider how we may spur one another on toward love and good deeds" (Heb. 10:24) by maintaining a community that shares testimonies and stories, explores best practices, and celebrates successes and achievements.

Appendix C

Essential and Nonessential Doctrines, and Gospel Implications

What can be categorized as essential versus nonessential doctrines of the Christian faith? It depends on who you ask, of course. Yet here are some guiding doctrines for evangelical Christians across history. Not to be overly simplistic, but essential doctrines are core teachings of Scripture that we must uphold for biblical orthodoxy and doctrinal fidelity.

If we had to choose only one essential statement that binds all Christians, it would be the Apostles' Creed.

Examples of Essential Protestant Doctrines
- God is Creator of the heavens and the earth.
- The Trinity: God is three persons in one.
- Human depravity: we are born into sin and have a sinful nature.
- The virgin birth of Christ.
- The full divinity and humanity of Christ.
- The life and work of Christ: his perfection, his sacrificial life, his bodily death, burial, and resurrection.
- Confession and repentance: a sinner must confess their sins and need for Christ.
- Salvation comes through Christ alone and is not based on human works.

- The two Great Commandments and the Great Commission.
- The second coming of Christ: Jesus will return.
- The five *solas* of the Reformation: *sola Scriptura*, *sola fide*, *sola gratia*, *sola Christus*, and *soli Deo gloria*.

Nonessential doctrines are those that should not divide Christians, since they can be debated from more than one biblical argument. Yet they often do create factions.

Examples of Nonessential Doctrines or Differences in Ministry Philosophy
- Baptism (paedo vs. believer)
- Denominationalism and nondenominationalism
- Millennialism (views of Christ's return: amillennial, premillennial, and postmillennial)
- Spiritual gifts (continuationism vs. cessationism)
- Women's and men's roles in ministry and in the family
- Ordination of women
- Worship music style

Some contentious gospel topics have implications for social and political issues in the culture at large. They are important matters for all Christians to act upon, as applications and implications of the gospel, but they are not critical for salvation. However, that does not excuse Christian apathy. Christians ought to be concerned and live out social issues as the Spirit leads them.

Examples of Topics with Gospel Implications
- Creation care
- Healthcare
- Human sexuality
- Immigration reform
- Politics and party affiliation
- Poverty
- Racism and ethnocentrism
- Refugees
- Science and Christianity
- Social justice

Sample Multichurch Prayer and Unity Service

The service order below is the template the One Church, One Prayer Coalition uses during its monthly prayer meetings—both in person and on Zoom. For more info, see https://www.facebook.com/onechurchoneprayer.

1. Attendees greet one another.

2. A designated pastor gives the statement of purpose, including reading Revelation 7:9 and Matthew 6:10, and explains the service format. Essentially, we are praying the Revelation 7 vision "will be done" in our community "as it is in heaven."

3. Opening prayer led by a pastor

4. Opening worship songs

5. Pastor/prayer leader explains prayer point #1, "A request for grace to confess our sins and to humble ourselves,"[1] prays, and opens floor for others to pray.

6. Worship songs

---

1. Prayer points #1, #2, and #3 above come from C. John Miller's "three basic traits of frontline prayer." Cited in Timothy Keller, *Center Church: Doing Balanced, Gospel-Centered Ministry in Your City* (Grand Rapids: Zondervan, 2012), 73.

7. A different pastor/prayer leader explains prayer point #2, "A compassion and zeal for the flourishing of the church and the reaching of the lost," prays, and opens the floor for others to pray.

8. Worship songs

9. A new prayer leader or pastor explains point #3, "A yearning to know God, to see his face, to glimpse his glory," prays, and opens the floor for others to pray.

10. Closing song

11. Benediction

Appendix E

Ministries Pursuing Reconciliation and Unity

This list is not exhaustive, and our inclusion here of an organization does not mean we endorse every aspect of the group's beliefs or ministry practices.

- Alleluia Community (https://www.alleluiacommunity.org)
- Antioch Network (https://antioch-network.org)
- Austin Prays / Unceasing Prayer Movement (http://austinprays.org)
- Be the Bridge (https://bethebridge.com)
- Campus Renewal Ministries (https://www.campusrenewal.org)
- Christ the Reconciler (http://www.christthereconciler.org/home)
- Civil Righteousness (https://civilrighteousness.org)
- Concerts of Prayer Greater New York (https://lead.nyc/concerts-of -prayer)
- Coracle (https://inthecoracle.org)
- The Initiative (http://theinitiative.org)
- International Reconciliation Coalition (https://reconciled1.com/inter national-reconciliation-coalition-overview)
- Jerusalem House of Prayer for All Nations (https://jhopfan.org)
- John 17 Movement (https://john17movement.com)
- Kingdom Mission Society (https://kingdommissionsociety.org)

- Quellen (https://quellen.org)
- Together Advance the Gospel (https://www.togetheradvancethegospel.com)
- Toward Jerusalem Council II (http://www.tjcii.org)
- UniteBoston (https://www.uniteboston.com)
- Voice of Calvary Ministries (http://vocm.org)

Appendix F

Further Reading

Classism

Barnes, Kenneth. *Redeeming Capitalism*. Grand Rapids: Eerdmans, 2018.

Fikkert, Brian, and Kelly M. Kapic. *Becoming Whole: Why the Opposite of Poverty Isn't the American Dream*. Chicago: Moody, 2019.

Lester, Terence. *I See You: How Love Opens Our Eyes to Invisible People*. Downers Grove, IL: InterVarsity, 2019.

Nelson, Tom. *The Economics of Neighborly Love: Investing in Your Community's Compassion and Capacity*. Downers Grove, IL: InterVarsity, 2017.

Sider, Ronald J. *Rich Christians in an Age of Hunger: Moving from Affluence to Generosity*. 6th ed. Nashville: W Publishing, 2015.

Ethnocentrism

Bell, Derrick. *Gospel Choirs: Psalms of Survival in an Alien Land Called Home*. New York: Basic Books, 2006.

Gray, Derwin L. *Building a Multiethnic Church: A Gospel Vision of Love, Grace, and Reconciliation in a Divided World*. Nashville: Nelson, 2021.

Harvey, Jennifer. *Dear White Christians: For Those Still Longing for Racial Reconciliation*. Grand Rapids: Eerdmans, 2020.

Loritts, Bryan. *Insider Outsider: My Journey as a Stranger in White Evangelicalism and My Hope for Us All*. Grand Rapids: Zondervan, 2018.

Williams, Jarvis J. *Redemptive Kingdom Diversity: A Biblical Theology of the People of God*. Grand Rapids: Baker Academic, 2021.

Political Division

Cho, Eugene. *Thou Shalt Not Be a Jerk: A Christian's Guide to Engaging Politics*. Colorado Springs: David C. Cook, 2020.

Giboney, Justin, Michael Wear, and Chris Butler. *Compassion (&) Conviction: The AND Campaign's Guide to Faithful Civic Engagement*. Downers Grove, IL: InterVarsity, 2020.

Leeman, Jonathan. *How the Nations Rage: Rethinking Faith and Politics in a Divided Age*. Nashville: Nelson, 2018.

Padgett, Timothy D. *Dual Citizens: Politics and American Evangelicalism*. Bellingham, WA: Lexham, 2020.

Schiess, Kaitlyn. *The Liturgy of Politics: Spiritual Formation for the Sake of Our Neighbor*. Downers Grove, IL: InterVarsity, 2020.

Political Divisions–Nationalism

Goldberg, Michelle. *Kingdom Coming: The Rise of Christian Nationalism*. New York: Norton, 2007.

Stewart, Katherine. *The Power Worshippers: Inside the Dangerous Rise of Religious Nationalism*. New York: Bloomsbury, 2020.

Whitehead, Andrew L., and Samuel L. Perry. *Taking America Back for God: Christian Nationalism in the United States*. New York: Oxford University Press, 2020.

Reconciliation

Darling, Daniel, ed. *Ministers of Reconciliation: Preaching on Race and the Gospel*. Bellingham, WA: Lexham, 2021.

Leong, David P. *Race and Place: How Urban Geography Shapes the Journey to Reconciliation*. Downers Grove, IL: InterVarsity, 2017.

McNeil, Brenda Salter. *Roadmap to Reconciliation 2.0: Moving Communities into Unity, Wholeness and Justice*. Revised and expanded edition. Downers Grove, IL: InterVarsity, 2020.

Perkins, John, and Karen Waddles. *One Blood: Parting Words to the Church on Race and Love*. Chicago: Moody, 2020.

Villodas, Rich. "Racial Reconciliation Requires a Painful Level of Self-Awareness." *Christianity Today*, March 12, 2021. https://www.christianitytoday.com/pastors /2021/spring/racial-reconciliation-painful-level-self-awareness-villodas.html.

Sexism

DeYoung, Kevin. *Men and Women in the Church: A Short, Biblical, Practical Introduction*. Wheaton: Crossway, 2021.

Everhart, Ruth. *The #MeToo Reckoning: Facing the Church's Complicity in Sexual Abuse and Misconduct*. Downers Grove, IL: InterVarsity, 2020.

Gupta, Nijay K. "Why I Believe in Women in Ministry." *Crux Sola* (blog). *Patheos*, June 4, 2019. https://www.patheos.com/blogs/cruxsola/2019/06/why-i-believe-in -women-in-ministry-gupta.

Langberg, Diane. *Redeeming Power: Understanding Authority and Abuse in the Church*. Grand Rapids: Brazos, 2020.

Lee-Barnewall, Michelle. *Neither Complementarian nor Egalitarian: A Kingdom Corrective to the Evangelical Gender Debate*. Grand Rapids: Baker Academic, 2016.

Unity

Baker, Mark D. *Centered-Set Church: Discipleship and Community without Judgmentalism*. Downers Grove, IL: IVP Academic, 2021.

Chan, Francis. *Until Unity*. Colorado Springs: David C. Cook, 2021.

Ince, Irwyn L., Jr. *The Beautiful Community: Unity, Diversity, and the Church at Its Best*. Downers Grove, IL: InterVarsity, 2020.

Muehlhoff, Tim, and Richard Langer. *Winsome Conviction: Disagreeing without Dividing the Church*. Downers Grove, IL: InterVarsity, 2020.

Van Opstal, Sandra María. *The Next Worship: Glorifying God in a Diverse World*. Downers Grove, IL: InterVarsity, 2015.

Appendix G

Sample Sermons

Sermon on Classism
Text: James 2:1–7
Title: No Dishonor Allowed
Preacher: Paul A. Hoffman

Introduction

It's sad but true: most Americans tend to judge others based on their appearance. Studies consistently indicate that on average, taller people are paid more than shorter people, skinnier people are paid more than heavier people, and—no surprise to anyone—blondes are paid more than people with other hair colors. If your spouse is sitting next to you, and he or she has brown, black, or red hair, do not move or say a word! I am trying to keep you out of trouble!

A while back, model Tyra Banks tested this phenomenon on her talk show. She donned a suit that made her appear to weigh 350 pounds. You can google the photo: Tyra Banks is unrecognizable. Then, a cameraman discreetly followed her as she rode the bus and went shopping around Los Angeles. Tyra was stunned at how people treated her. She confessed, "The people that were staring and laughing in my face—that shocked me the most . . . As soon as I entered the store when I went shopping, I immediately heard snickers. Immediately! I was appalled and hurt!"

The apostle James labels this sad reality "favoritism." And in James 2, he asserts it is sinful and something Christians should never engage in. Before we jump into that text, it would be wise to give you some background info on this letter. Many of the early church fathers and modern scholars believe that James, the half brother of Jesus, authored it. James was a prominent leader in the early church in Jerusalem, and likely led the momentous Jerusalem Council described in Acts 15. It appears James wrote this first-century letter to a group of Jewish Christians who were enduring persecution for their faith in Jesus Christ. Scholar Gordon Fee asserts that this letter contains two thrusts, the communal and the practical. That is, James is concerned with how God's people share life together concretely. In fact, James 1:2–4 states that God's ultimate goal is for his family to become mature and complete. Let's see how this plays out in today's text, James 2:1–7. Please turn there in your Bibles. [Read James 2:1–7.]

The first point I am highlighting is found in verses 1–4 and it's this:

1. Christians reject classism (2:1-4)

Right about now, some of you might be wondering, "Hey, wait! I thought you said this passage was about favoritism. Why are you bringing 'classism' into the mix?" Well, I am proposing that classism is a type of "discrimination," which is the word James uses in verse 4. Put simply, classism is a particular form of discrimination. And I believe this text is referring to classism because in verses 5–7, James makes multiple references to a conflict in their community centered around two groups of people: the poor and the rich.

Before I continue, for the sake of clarity, let me give you my definition of classism, so we can share a common understanding. Classism is a form of sin in which one person or group holds an attitude of superiority or resentment against another person or group, specifically due to their real or perceived socioeconomic status or identity. In America we tend to have three categories: the lower, middle, and upper classes. Class is influenced by race, "privilege, immigration or citizenship status, wealth, poverty, geography, education, socialization, and cultural factors."[1] Educator Ruby Payne points out that class is also shaped by "hidden rules, language or discourse patterns, and social networks."[2] Classism is a posture that commonly leads to expressions of exclusion, derision, scapegoating, and systemic marginalization. I hope to flesh out this definition a bit more as we go along.

1. Paul A. Hoffman, *Reconciling Places: How to Bridge the Chasms in Our Communities* (Eugene, OR: Cascade Books, 2020), 31.
2. Ruby K. Payne, *A Framework for Understanding Poverty*, 4th ed. (Highlands, TX: Aha! Process, 2005), 2–3.

All right, let's swing our attention back onto James 2. This passage is a little tricky because the exact setting is unclear. The scholarly consensus centers on two options: (1) the public worship services, or (2) some kind of church court where the community has gathered to arbitrate a judicial case. The second option is similar to 1 Corinthians 6, where the apostle Paul rebukes the Corinthian Christians for suing one another in the secular courts rather than having the church body adjudicate matters internally. Many scholars lean toward the latter interpretation, as James employs a lot of legal terminology in this passage.

Assuming this text refers to a church court, here's the crux: those judging the case are giving "special attention," or the best seat, to the rich man. We know he belongs to the upper class because in those days, gold rings were a sign of wealth and prosperity. On the other hand, "the poor man in filthy old clothes," as verse 2 describes him, is forced to sit on the floor. Thus, the community is giving preferential treatment based on external criteria—that is, signs indicating one's status in society. This kind of discriminatory treatment, dividing the two parties according to their perceived class identity or socioeconomic position, will almost inevitably lead to a miscarriage of justice. Let's be realistic: what are the odds the poor man will win this case, whether he's the plaintiff or the defendant?

Now before you and I shake our heads in disgust toward these Christians, let's stand in front of the mirror for a minute and be honest. Has this ever happened to you: you were walking on the sidewalk and encountered a person who appeared disheveled, or appeared to be struggling with mental illness or food or housing insecurity, and you walked down a side alley or crossed the street to avoid contact with him or her? Why? Because it felt uncomfortable and you assumed he or she would ask you for money? Or conversely, back in the pre-COVID days when churches had a greeting time during the worship service, perhaps you made a point of introducing yourself first, or even exclusively, to someone who was well-groomed and attractive rather than someone who lacked fashionable clothes, white teeth, and perfectly coiffed hair? That's classism: discriminating based on one's external, class-based appearance. By the way, this is a sin any person, whatever his or her class status, can commit.

Or how about this: have you ever laughed at, lingered over, retweeted, or liked a social media post or meme that mocked a whole group of people? Maybe something along the lines of, "All hillbillies are ____" or "Those trust fund babies are so ____."

Anyone here feeling just a little convicted, a tiny bit of, "ouch, that hurts!"? The mood in the room has become a tad more awkward—but that's a good thing!

Classism is insidious. It can easily become the default setting of our hearts unless we intentionally identify it and ask the Holy Spirit to convict us and reveal to us his heart for people.

You get it, right? James 2:1–4 commands Christians to reject classism. But something's missing. It's the question, *Why* reject classism? That brings us to the second point, which is the big idea:

2. Christians reject classism because it blasphemes the noble name of Jesus (2:5-7)

In verse 1, James calls Christians "believers in our glorious Lord Jesus Christ." Then in verses 6–7, he asks two rhetorical questions: "Is it not the rich who are exploiting you?" and "Are they [the rich] not the ones who are blaspheming the noble name of him to whom you belong?"

Wow! That's some strong language. James states that Jesus, the founder and leader of the church, is both glorious and noble. And to discriminate or commit classism is to blaspheme Jesus's name and character. In the original language, "to blaspheme" means to "slander God or speak evil against God."

Why is classism akin to blasphemy? In verse 5 James asks, "Has not God chosen those who are poor in the eyes of the world to be rich in faith and to inherit the kingdom he promised those who love him?" What James is getting at is that our heavenly Father identifies with materially poor Christians, and to a certain extent, with all poor people. Now to be clear, James 2 is not an outlier. God's preference for the poor is stated repeatedly throughout Scripture. For example, in Luke 6:20 Jesus says, "Blessed are you who are poor, for yours is the kingdom of God," and Proverbs 14:31 says, "Whoever oppresses the poor shows contempt for their Maker, but whoever is kind to the needy honors God." To attack the poor is to attack those whom God loves and identifies with. Hence, to engage in classism or discrimination of any sort is a reprehensible sin.

But did you notice that James is more specific than that? He argues that *Christians are to reject classism because it blasphemes the noble name of Jesus.* Classism not only blasphemes our heavenly Father, but it also blasphemes his glorious and noble son. Why? Jesus identifies with the poor. In Matthew 25:40, Jesus says, "Whatever you did for the least of these brothers and sisters of mine, you did for me." Regarding Jesus identifying with the poor, Timothy Keller gives this insight:

> In the incarnation and death of Jesus we see God identifying with the poor and marginal. . . . Jesus was born in a feed trough. When his parents had him circumcised the offering they made—two pigeons—was that prescribed for the

poorest class of people in the society. He lived among the poor and marginalized, who were drawn to him even as the respectable were repulsed by him. . . . At the end of his life he rode into Jerusalem on a borrowed donkey, spent his last evening in a borrowed room, and when he died he was laid in a borrowed tomb. They cast lots for his only possession, his robe, for there on the cross he was stripped of everything. He died naked and penniless.[3]

Furthermore, classism not only blasphemes the noble name of Jesus, but it also undercuts the core of the gospel. Second Corinthians 8:9 says, "For you know the grace of our Lord Jesus Christ, that though he was rich, yet for your sake he became poor, so that you through his poverty might become rich." Make no mistake: classism contradicts the essence of the gospel of grace.

You get it—the bottom line of James 2 is *Christians must reject classism because it blasphemes the noble name of Jesus.*

Conclusion

Now what? How are we to live in light of this convicting and challenging passage? To keep things simple, let me give you three "R" verbs to follow. First, *repent* of any classist or discriminatory attitudes or actions. Ask the Holy Spirit to reveal them to you and help you lament this sin through prayer. You could go one step further and confess it to a safe friend and ask for accountability. Ask that person to set a reminder on his or her smart phone and check in with you weekly or monthly.

Next, after repenting, *research* classism so you can better understand it and identify it. I suggest three books to start with: John Perkins's *With Justice for All,* Timothy Keller's *Generous Justice,* and Ruby Payne's *A Framework for Understanding Poverty.*

Finally, after you repent and do research, *resource* non-profit agencies that serve impoverished or underresourced communities. Pray. Donate money if you can. Volunteer some time. I recommend you begin with the highly regarded Christian Community Development Association. Go to www.ccda .org for more information.

Repent. Research. Resource. These are three ways you can reject classism, which blasphemes the noble name of Jesus Christ. Let's close in prayer.

3. Timothy Keller, *Generous Justice: How God's Grace Makes Us Just* (New York: Penguin, 2010), 185.

Sermon on Ethnocentrism
Text: Ephesians 2:11–18
Title: One New People
Preacher: Ralph Douglas West

Introduction

In 323 BC, Alexander the Great died in Babylon after a wine-drinking binge. He had conquered the largest empire in history up to that moment. Yet he could not conquer himself. It was his plan that all humans would form a unified empire through sharing "one great loving-cup."[1]

Yet Alexander died at the same age as Jesus did on the cross. Alexander died from a wine cup, not a loving cup. Jesus died from a loving cup. Alexander's plot was only one scheme out of many to unite humans in an ideal community.

The nineteenth century witnessed multiple attempts to unify humanity around a human scheme. The Shakers lived in celibate communities practicing simple living and shared tasks. Being celibate, of course, they have died out. Jim Jones horrified the world with the deadly end of his unified community, unified around a demonic cult leader. The fiery end of David Koresh and his unified cult demonstrated the same failure.

The Qumran community of the Jews, the monastic movement of the Catholics, and the hippy communities of the '60s all hoped for the same thing: unified community, oneness, *koinonia*. Qumran is now a ruin near the Dead Sea, monks fight one another in the very basilica where Jesus was buried and rose, and hippies have vanished into grandparents driving RVs. There is still no unity. God has a plan to create unity: Christ is our peace.

You may take an example from geometry. If two points draw closer to a central point, they must by the laws of geometry draw closer to one another. So also, if two persons draw closer to Christ they must by the same spiritual law draw closer to one another. Using a series of images, Paul shows us how

---

Ralph Douglas West serves as founder and senior pastor of The Church Without Walls in Houston. He completed degrees from Southwestern Baptist Theological Seminary and Beeson Divinity School, where he received the Doctor of Ministry degree. He serves as W. Winfred and Elizabeth Moore Visiting Professor of Ministry Guidance at the George W. Truett Theological Seminary, Baylor University. Sermon adapted from https://ralphdouglaswest.com/about.

1. Plutarch, *De Alexandri magni fortuna aut virtute* 1.6, in *Moralia*, trans. Frank Cole Babbitt (Cambridge, MA: Harvard University Press, 1936), 4, available at http://data.perseus.org/citations/urn:cts:greekLit:tlg0007.tlg087.perseus-eng1:1.6.

this works in the magnificent manifesto of metaphors, this soaring song of similes, this poetic picture of purpose.

One New People Making Peace

Remember "that at [a] time you were separate from Christ" (v. 12). We forget the hopelessness of the pagan world, the futility of the Greco-Roman culture into which God sent his Son. In the National Museum of Greece in Athens you can stand before carved grave markers from that time. They are all carvings of catastrophic chasms of calamity and hopelessness in the face of death. Pagan mothers give up their little ones, husbands and wives shake hands gravely as they depart forever, a dying woman gives her little jewel box to her servant lady. These are poignant and permanent reminders of an ancient world without Christ. The resurrection bursts into that world with hope.

One of the great categorical expressions in Ephesians is "Christ is our peace." In the Greek, it is in the intensive form, calling attention to Christ and Christ alone. Of all the terms by which our Lord is known, none is more endearing than "he himself is our peace" (v. 14).

When we announce the great benediction found in the last chapter of Hebrews, we hear about our God of peace in Hebrews 13:20. He is known as the God of peace. In the patriarchal days, when Jacob called his sons, he came to Judah and blessed his son in Genesis 49:10. "Shiloh" is the Hebrew word recalling peace. Isaiah the poet prophet called Him Prince of Peace (Isa. 9:6). The angels sang of peace on earth and of good will toward men (Luke 2:14). The new humanity will begin only when we decisively understand that He and He alone is our peace.

Sometimes, we preach peace as if it were some separate action of Christ. It seems as if peace is like an isolated monument built by the Lord. It seems as if peace were some external actions, or as if peace can be arranged. No, only by knowing Jesus personally do we know the peace of God. He, Himself, is our peace.

We must be clear: we do not know peace by reciting some creed. I know Baptists who can recite the Baptist Faith and Message, line by line, and yet they are walking civil wars. I know people who recite the Apostles' Creed, others who are flawless in their orthodoxy, and yet they are walking contradictions. Nothing embitters a person more than religious activities without any relationship to the God of peace. It will sap your soul. It will leave you dehydrated and lifeless. It will make you impotent spiritually.

Paul emphasizes that Christ—He, Himself—is our peace: He, alone, is our peace. The incredible tragedy of the modern world is that peace cannot and will not be seen. The resolution of peace is the result of our acknowledgment that we are alienated from God and because of that, we are not reconciled to one another.

The United Nations is the greatest deliberative body in the history of the planet, and yet it has not brought peace. We live in the century of the expertise of the social scientist. The psychologists and the sociologists analyze us individually and collectively. In the Western world, we have known the greatest egalitarian, democratic education available; still, in the coming together of these forces we have no peace. We have no peace between man and man or between man and God. Remember, it was in the last century that in the most educated nation ever produced in Western civilization we saw the crucible for chaos. In Germany were the greatest educational institutions. It was there that the greatest atrocities in history took place.

Why do we not see Christ alone as our peace? Paul gave us the answer. Except the "eyes of your heart . . . be enlightened" you will never see (Eph. 1:18). We keep trying to separate what God has joined together. A lawyer came to Jesus and asked, "Of all the commandments, which is the most important?" And Jesus said, "'Hear, O Israel: The Lord our God, the Lord is one. Love the Lord your God with all your heart and with all your soul and with all your mind and with all your strength.' The second is this: 'Love your neighbor as yourself.' There is no commandment greater than these" (Mark 12:29–31). We have tried to pull apart those two commandments and to bring about reconciliation with our neighbor while not making reconciliation with God.

You may say, "No one will ever hear us with that narrow scope." That is not our responsibility. Our responsibility is not to make men hear that Jesus Christ is the only solution, not only for personal but also for international needs and for a new humanity. Ours is simply to preach it and to preach it again. When we are ignored, to say it louder; when we are scorned, to say it with dignity; when we are patronized, to say it kindly; and when we are confronted, to say it courageously.

We must understand that He, Himself, is our peace. The Greek goddess of peace was named Eirene, the same as our name for a lady, Irene. She was always presented with a cornucopia, a horn of plenty, filled with good things. Peace is not just the absence of conflict. Peace is the presence of abundance. There is peace in a cemetery, but there is no life. The peace of Christ is radiant with life, filled with vitality, a surplus of joy, a positive overflowing presence of peace.

One New People Breaking Walls

Paul also explains that Christ "has made the two groups one and has destroyed the barrier, the dividing wall of hostility" (Eph. 2:14). "Mending Wall," a poem by Robert Frost, offers us a point of reflection on our responsibility to break down walls. A stone wall separates the speaker's property from his neighbor's. In spring, the two meet to walk the wall and jointly make repairs. The speaker sees no reason for the wall to be kept. There are no cows to be contained, just apple and pine trees. He does not believe in the wall. The neighbor resorts to an old adage: "Good fences make good neighbors." The speaker remains unconvinced and mischievously presses the neighbor to look beyond the old-fashioned folly of such reasoning. His neighbor will not be swayed. The speaker envisions his neighbor as a holdover from a justifiably outmoded era, a living example of a dark-age mentality. But the neighbor simply repeats the adage.

This is graphic, emotive language because in Herod's Temple there was a wall that separated the Court of the Gentiles from the rest of the Temple, and on that wall were inscriptions in Latin and in Greek forbidding gentiles to enter. Josephus spoke of these inscriptions, and in excavations made in 1871 and 1934 two of these inscriptions were found and displayed in the Archaeological Museum in Istanbul and the Rockefeller Museum in Jerusalem. They read: "No foreigner may enter within the barricade which surrounds the sanctuary and enclosure. Anyone caught doing so will have himself to blame for his ensuing death."

Paul says Christ tore down this odious barrier by His death. Now Jew and gentile alike have access to God and have spiritual unity. The ultimate answer to vertical and horizontal alienation is not intellectual or political or social, but spiritual. The answer comes when we cross the broken barrier and thus come near to God and then near to each other (1 John 1:3, 4).

The wall that divided Communist East Germany from the western enclave in Berlin stood as the symbol of suppression. On June 12, 1987, President Ronald Reagan with the dramatic backdrop near the Brandenburg Gate challenged Soviet leader Mikhail Gorbachev to "tear down this wall." He added: "Secretary Gorbachev, if you seek peace, if you seek prosperity for the Soviet Union and Eastern Europe, if you seek liberalization, come here to this gate. Mr. Gorbachev, open this gate! Mr. Gorbachev, tear down this wall!"

And the wall came tumbling down. But not only did the government tear down the wall, the people tore down the wall. When Jesus died on Calvary the curtain in the temple was torn in two. The wall of separation in the sight of God came down. No longer did you have to show your ID to access God.

There is no room for ethnic idolatry since the Lord has torn down the walls. We live in an age after the death of George Floyd where many are attacking critical race theory as the greatest threat to the gospel of Jesus Christ we have ever seen. But we must be careful with this kind of revisionist approach to discerning what threatens the people of God. One does not have to be an advocate of critical race theory to recognize that the reason why it exists in the first place is because the true gospel was not preached when Black people were placed on auction blocks and separated from their families. The church in America did not stand up when after slavery the Black Codes were instated, and a new kind of slavery was introduced. When Martin Luther King Jr. wrote his letter from the Birmingham Jail, it was because the preachers were not upholding the truth of the gospel and protesting the evils done to people of color. But the world must recognize, the wall has been torn down. Through the blood of the cross, we are all the people of God, we are all God's children. The wall is no more!

But we must ask, how did Christ's death bring down the wall? Picture the wall leveled, the *thanatos* inscriptions lying under the rubble and the nations joyfully stepping across as Jew and gentile, brothers and sisters. Christ's death brought down the wall!

What did He do? He abolished the law. He created a new humanity. He reconciled the new humanity to God. Christ abolished the ceremonial code, and second, He created a new humanity. His purpose was to create in Himself one new man out of the two, thus making peace.

One New People Creating a New Humanity

John Claypool, in his Lyman Beecher Lectures, tells the story of a merchant out in the Midwest who had identical twin sons. The boys' lives became inseparably intertwined. From the first they dressed alike, went to the same schools, did all the same things. In fact, they were so close that neither ever married, but they came back and took over the running of the family business when their father died. Their relationship to each other was pointed to as a model of creative collaboration.

One morning a customer came into the store and made a small purchase. The brother who waited on him put the dollar bill on top of the cash register and walked to the front door with the man. Sometime later he remembered what he had done, but when he went to the cash register, he found the dollar gone. He asked his brother if he had seen the bill and put it into the register, and the brother replied that he knew nothing of the bill in question.

"That's funny," said the other, "I distinctly remember placing the bill here on the register, and no one else has been in the store since then."

Had the matter been dropped at that point—a mystery involving a tiny amount of money—nothing would have come of it. However, an hour later, this time with a noticeable hint of suspicion in his voice, the brother asked again, "Are you sure you didn't see that dollar bill and put it into the register?" The other brother was quick to catch the note of accusation, and flared back in defensive anger.

This was the beginning of the first serious breach of trust that had ever come between these two. It grew wider and wider. Every time they tried to discuss the issue, new charges and countercharges got mixed into the brew, until finally things go so bad that they were forced to dissolve their partnership. They ran a partition down the middle of their father's store and turned what had once been a harmonious partnership into an angry competition. In fact, that business became a source of division in the whole community, each twin trying to enlist allies for himself against the other. This open warfare went on for over twenty years.

Then one day a car with out-of-state license plates drove up in front of the store. A well-dressed man got out and went into one of the sides and inquired how long the merchant had been in business in that location. When he found that it was over twenty years, the stranger said, "Then you are the one with whom I must settle an old score."

"Some years ago," he said, "I was out of work, drifting from place to place, and I happened to get off a boxcar in your town. I had absolutely no money and had not eaten for three days. As I was walking down the alley behind your store, I looked in and saw a dollar bill on the top of the cash register. Everyone else was in the front of the store. I had been raised in a Christian home and I had never before in all my life stolen anything, but that morning I was so hungry I gave in to the temptation, slipped through the door, and took that dollar bill. That act has weighed on my conscience ever since, and I finally decided that I would never be at peace until I came back and faced up to that old sin and made amends. Would you let me now replace that money and pay you whatever is appropriate for damages?"

At that point the stranger was surprised to see the old man standing in front of him shaking his head in dismay and beginning to weep. When he had gotten control of himself, he took the stranger by the arm and said, "I want you to go next door and repeat the same story you have just told me." The stranger did it; only this time there were two old men who looked remarkably alike, both weeping uncontrollably.

The Claypool story points to the great truth of the Christian life: Christ does not just bring peace; He is peace. The visitor to the alienated brothers did not just bring peace; his very presence was peace. He stepped into the situation and by his very presence brought peace. Through peace, a restored family, a renewed family, was possible.

So, also, is Christ. He does not give lessons in peace, write a code of peace, enforce a routine of peace, or command a discipline of peace. He is Peace when He shows up. Perhaps the greatest picture of that in the last war-torn century was on Christmas 1914. During World War I, the British soldiers were in one trench facing east and the German soldiers were opposite them in another trench facing west. No-man's-land was between them. They were dug into a stalemate, killing one another and gassing one another. Yet out of one of the trenches came a lone voice singing, "Silent night, Holy night." Soon other voices joined this voice. Germans were singing "Stille Nacht, Heilige Nacht" in German while the British sang the same words in English. Some crawled out of the trenches, greeting their enemies on that icy Christmas; this was a miracle of grace.

Yet they crawled back into their trenches and started to slaughter one another again the next day. Only, for the sake of Christ, would that all humanity could crawl out of our trenches and apartments and gated communities and slums and high rises and tents in the desert and mansions in the suburbs and tenements and hovels and meet in the no-man's-land of our time. In this time, the presence of peace would make a new people, a new creation, a new world. This is what Coca-Cola sold a silly vision of—that if we all could drink colored sugar-water, the world would sing in perfect harmony. What a pity. Louis Armstrong sang of a beautiful world where he dreamed of unity. That world is possible only through Christ.

So, then, this new humanity cannot rest on human ideas. From the left or from the right, political philosophies do not create the new humanity. We are not made new through the theories of those who reject the kingdom of God for notions of humanity rooted in liberal tolerance. Getting along with one another is essential, it is necessary. But these theories tend toward atheistic self-worship where humanity attempts to replace God with ourselves. Liberalism will not bring a new humanity, no matter how hard it tries. Moreover, conservative philosophies fare no better. No amount of vapid patriotism, phony challenges to oppressed people to self-improve, or requests to say "peace, peace" when there is no peace will help us. The new humanity comes with the recognition that human ideas will not accomplish the aims of the kingdom.

We are saved through our submission to Jesus Christ and our willingness to repent. Then, and only then, will God allow us to see ourselves revealed in Him as His new people.

When we reflect on these things, we realize that all of this culminates with Christ's ministry of making peace, breaking walls, and creating a new humanity. "He came and preached peace to you who were far away and peace to those who were near. For through Him we both have access to the Father by one Spirit" (Eph. 2:17–18).

Sermon on Political Division
Text: 1 John 4:18
Title: God, Politics, and the Church—There Is No Fear in Love
Preacher: Rich Villodas

Introduction

Here's the reality, friends. A number of people in our congregation will be voting for Donald Trump next month. And a number of people will be voting for Joe Biden. Some will abstain, and some will maybe write in their favorite superhero. Regardless of all of this, the first thing I need you to hear is this: No matter who you vote for, you are welcome in our church. The only thing I ask as your pastor, is that you would take the teachings of Jesus seriously; that you would see politics through the gospel of the kingdom, and not the gospel through your politics; that you would be curious about why your brothers and sisters here see things differently. And that you would live humble, prayerful lives.

What is it that God wants for this congregation in this tumultuous time? I think it's pretty clear. God desires our freedom, joy, compassion, humility, and discernment. It's in that spirit that I want to talk about the role fear plays in our lives, and what it has done to us—throughout history, and in our time.

The apostle John writes simple, prophetic words to us. In 1 John 4:18, the apostle writes, "There is no fear in love. But perfect love drives out fear."

Fear makes us do some crazy things. Well, let me speak for myself. Fear makes *me* do crazy things. A couple of years ago I was surfing the internet. I had read an article, and before clicking to another open tab on my computer, I saw one of those strange ads that show up from time to time. The ad, which looked like a news article, had a picture of a slimy looking creature and was titled, "Life Threatening Creature Discovered." I curiously clicked the link and learned all about this life-threatening creature, which in hindsight, probably didn't exist.

Later that night my family paid a visit to my in-laws' home in Long Island. I went out to their backyard to take their dog out, when I saw what seemed like that slimy deadly creature from the article. Being the anxious and protective person I am, I thought, "I better kill this thing fast." I start looking

Rich Villodas is the Brooklyn-born lead pastor of New Life Fellowship, a multiracial church with more than seventy-five countries represented, in Elmhurst, Queens. He holds a Master of Divinity degree from Alliance Theological Seminary. He is the author of *The Deeply Formed Life*. Sermon adapted from www.richvillodas.com.

for something to smash this creature. After hastily looking around, I found a large brick. In the process of me trying to kill it, the brick slipped out of my hand and almost crushed my foot (of course, I was wearing sandals at the time).

That's when I looked closer to see that it was a snail. A blasted snail. I could be wrong, but it looked as if the snail shook its head at me in disbelief. I almost lost a toe because of fear—and came close to killing a helpless snail in the process. Fear has a way of accessing a part of our brain that makes it difficult to think clearly. Now, this head-shaking backyard story is pitiful, yes, but it's also a picture of our world. Throughout a given day, we are told who and what we should fear. And when something similar passes in front of us, we take out our bricks.

Fear is the currency of political hostility and every other kind of division. It's the energy behind cable news. And yes, while there is much to be afraid of in our world, there's a way of relating to fear that leads to greater social pain and fragmentation.

In today's message, I want us to contemplate a foundational truth:

We are not called to deny our fears, but to resist being formed by them.

Consider voting for a minute. It's easy to see who and what people are voting for. But what we don't see is what's beneath the surface—the things that are forming us. The fear beneath us. The fear under them. Day in and day out, we are confronted with fear. And like the brick almost falling on my foot, fear causes irrational behavior that puts our lives, and the lives of others, in danger.

But how do we live from a different place? How do we demonstrate, especially in our interactions with others, this gospel truth that love pushes out fear? This is where we come to 1 John 4, in what is one of the most important passages for this political and social moment.

In this portion of Scripture, the apostle John is trying to help a community of Christ-followers live in the way of love. John writes to them as a spiritual father. Over and over, he calls them "my dear children." There's great affection that John has for these people. In this letter he writes to them about many topics:

- Forgiveness
- Our relationship to the world
- Sin and mercy
- The centrality of Jesus
- The Incarnation

Through all this rich theological reflection John comes back consistently to *love*.

In verse seven of chapter 4, he writes, "Let us love one another, for love comes from God." Then he writes, "Whoever does not love does not know God, because God is love." He continues in verse ten, "This is love: not that we loved God, but that he loved us and sent his Son as an atoning sacrifice for our sins." Over and over, John is trying to instill in his spiritual children the importance of love. And then he gets to a point that has many implications.

There is no fear in love. But perfect love drives out fear.

Fear and love can't remain in the same space at the same time. Only one can stay. And this is the challenge before us. There is a gospel truth and a cultural reality. The gospel truth is: *Perfect love casts out fear.* However, the cultural reality is: *Paralyzing fear casts out love.*

Yes, perfect love casts out fear, but what we are seeing in our day is *paralyzing fear casting out love*. We often think of hate being the opposite of love. But it's important to see the contrast John is making here. How can you love well, when fear is present? The answer is, you can't.

This is what we are seeing in our world, and I want you to pay attention to it. We are in an intense season in which we are seeing the politics of fear forming us deeply—the politics of fear dominating our lives. We have been covertly and overtly shaped to see people who are different as people to fear. And here's the dangerous truth: We don't even give critical assessment to it.

Take, for example, the cultural symbols of our day. We are at a point where hostility and fear are constantly manifested through the well-known symbols of our culture.

For example, for some, fear comes when we see someone wearing a MAGA hat.

For others, fear comes when we see someone wearing a #BlackLivesMatter shirt.

For some, fear comes when we see someone waving the American flag.

For others, fear comes when we see someone waving the rainbow LGBTQ+ flag.

Frankly, much of the fear is generated by the surrounding culture—especially social media and cable news. We have succumbed to Cable News Discipleship, unaware of the Powers and Principalities forming us in particular ways.

American author and journalist Eric Sevareid once wrote, "The biggest big business in America is not steel, automobiles or television. It is the manufacture, refinement and distribution of anxiety."[1] Hear this clearly: *our panic is often generated by profit.* The profit of large corporations seeking to make a buck—or a billion. We are being played by the powers when we uncritically allow them to tell us whom we should fear. Those powers come through pastors, leaders, politicians, and the media. In the process, fear drives out love.

Now, don't get me wrong. There are legitimate reasons to be afraid. I've heard people offer legitimate fears around this election—around the fear of fascism, fear of religious liberty being eliminated on college campuses, fear of how climate change is being handled, fear of the future of healthcare.

All of this is important to name, but what I'm getting at here is the destructive power of fear as a political and social strategy.

In the wildly successful Pixar movie *Monsters, Inc.*, the monsters would scare kids at night because the screams powered the city. It was the energy source of the city. When seen as a metaphor for our cultural moment, it rings true to our lives. This film is not just a delightful family movie, but an illustration of a fallen world powered by fear.

The media profits from fear. Politicians use fear as a strategy for votes. Fear is one of the most powerful motivators. And it's one of the most destructive forces. What happens when fear forms us? For one, our relationships with each other are marked by self-protection and suspicion. This leads us to seeing the world through the lens of survival, which produces the instinct to crush our opponents.

But fear is not to form our social imagination as followers of Christ. The world will not heal when fear is the primary motivation behind our engagement with the world. This is what John wants us to see. We are to be set on a different trajectory. A trajectory of love.

Perfect love casts out fear.

When I talk about love, I'm not talking about sentimentality. I'm not talking about being nice. Love is the most powerful force in the world. Love is concerned with the well-being and flourishing of another, which means, justice is an act of love. Policy can be an act of love. Holding people accountable can be an act of love. Speaking the truth can be an act of love.

Forgiveness is an act of love.

We see this most profoundly in Jesus Christ.

In Jesus, love casts out fear. In Jesus, we don't have to fear judgment. Why? Because Jesus was judged in our place. In Jesus we don't have to be afraid of God. Why? Because Jesus demonstrates that God has been for us all along. In Jesus, we don't have to live suspicious of God's love. Why? Because God's

---

1. Eric Sevareid, *This Is Eric Sevareid* (New York: McGraw-Hill, 1964), 17.

love is not contingent on what we do. God's love is perfect. The gospel casts out fear because it announces that there's nothing that can separate us from God's love.

The question, then, is how do we live into this? How do we carry this truth from John to our relationships with others? Frankly, I think it requires two commitments.

First, we must resist Cable News Discipleship.

I learned that the average Christian spends an hour or two a week under the teaching of their local church but as many as thirteen hours a day consuming other forms of media: listening to podcasts, scrolling through Twitter, or watching cable news.

This is a recipe to have us drive out love in the name of fear because we are constantly being fed content made to produce anxiety, hate people on the other side, or buy some product.

I used to joke that when I became a Christian, I was in church all the time. I went to the men's service, the women's service, the prayer meeting, the youth meeting, the home small groups. I was constantly having my imagination shaped by Jesus. Yes, I was a "church rat," but I was mentored by men and women to see the Bible as the primary source where we work out our salvation.

I learned that our social talking points are to be shaped by Holy Scripture. I was instructed to work through difficult community issues through the wisdom of the Proverbs. I was trained to process the difficult feelings of my soul through the Psalms of David. I was formed to work through matters of injustice by paying attention to the Prophets. I was led to think about neighbor-love through the words and actions of Jesus.

To have love drive out fear requires us to put boundaries around the things we watch, giving our attention to what God has done in the narrative of Scripture. Which leads to an important question: how much corrosive news are you consuming? What are you feeding yourself day after day? Are your social and political talking points informed more by Sean, Tucker, Rachel and Lemon, or by Matthew, Mark, Luke, and John?

Second, love drives out fear when we work hard to see the humanity of others.

I know this is hard for many of us to receive in this moment. But every person is made in the image of God. Every person is loved by God. I know it's hard to see their humanity, but beneath so much of us, there are wounds. So much of the dysfunction in our world stems from wounds we all carry.

I'm not talking about ignoring the character and sins of political leaders. There is a level of decency and humility and civility that leaders must have to lead others. Again, I'm not presenting love as a sentimentalizing act. I'm not suggesting we ignore injustice or maintain false equivalencies.

I'm talking about resisting the fear that casts out love.

As followers of Christ, we are not called to simply receive the love that casts out fear. We are called to give expression to that love as well. And make no mistake about it: to love in this way requires the work of the Spirit.

In closing, listen to how John ends this chapter.

We love because he first loved us. Whoever claims to love God yet hates a brother or sister is a liar. For whoever does not love their brother and sister, whom they have seen, cannot love God, whom they have not seen. And he has given us this command: Anyone who loves God must also love their brother and sister. (1 John 4:19–21)

Amen.

<u>**Sermon on Reconciliation**</u>
Text: Acts 10–11
Title: Intentional Journey toward a New Community
Preacher: Sandra María Van Opstal

Introduction

For those of you who don't know me, the most important description of myself that illustrates what I'm about is this: I love people.

My husband and I live on the west side of Chicago in a predominantly Latinx and Black community. I regularly attend Zumba class because it's a great way to get to know my neighbors. My husband and I don't have a washer and dryer at our house because going to the laundromat allows me to regularly hear stories from people in my community. One of my favorite things to do is watch the kids on my street and imagine what their lives are like and who they're going to grow up to be. I love all kinds of people!

However, I must admit that as much as I really *love* people, there are some kinds of people I just don't like. I know as Christians we're not supposed to admit this, but if we're being honest with ourselves, we all know people who are just a little bit hard to love. Maybe they're difficult to deal with, or they make us uncomfortable, or maybe they make us see things in ourselves that we don't want to see. Can anyone relate?

Most of us will at some point in our lives interact with people who are very different from us—different races, ethnicities, cultures, socioeconomic backgrounds. I am a Latina, daughter of immigrants from Colombia and Argentina, who was raised in a predominantly white suburb of Chicago, where I was always one of the only ethnic minorities in my class. I was the kid who was different from everyone else. When I came to know Christ as a teenager, I remember hearing that God has unified all people—that we are reconciled and considered one humanity in God's eyes. Many of you have probably heard this too. So, some of you may ask, then, why do we need to talk about our differences? Why is reconciliation a necessary topic in the church? Let me tell you why. Yes, the Scriptures tell us we are unified. But why, then, is it so hard for us to live like this is true? Why do our cities, schools, and churches tend to be so segregated? Why do so many people actively avoid other kinds

Sandra María Van Opstal, a second-generation Latina, pastors at Grace and Peace Community on the west side of Chicago. She holds a Master of Divinity degree from Trinity Evangelical Divinity School. She is the author of *The Next Worship*.

of people, whether consciously or subconsciously? We don't have to look very far to see the impact of deep divisions in our society. Not only do we see them displayed on the news, on social media, and in our neighborhoods, but we also see them in our churches.

Reconciliation is a topic that tends to be avoided in the church because sometimes we don't know where to start. Most of us, when we hear the word "reconciliation," immediately think of the interpersonal dynamic by which two people come together to reconcile their differences and restore their relationship—whether it's friends, family members, or spouses. But oftentimes we forget that reconciliation is also communal and systemic, meaning it can happen between communities of people and in the context of the societal structures in which we live. We can't seek to live as reconciled people unless we understand the systems that are harming us and our neighbors.

Thankfully, the Scriptures have a lot to say about what true reconciliation looks like. The Scripture I'd like to share is the story of Peter and Cornelius in Acts 10–11. This story impacts me every time I hear it or study it because I see myself in it. We know the story of Peter and Cornelius is significant for three reasons: first, it is the longest narrative in the book of Acts, which describes the growth of the church and the work of the Holy Spirit. The story is covered in portions of chapters 9, 10, and 11. Second, the story of when Peter and Cornelius meet sits right in the middle of the launching of the mission of the church to the gentiles. In Acts chapter 1, the disciples are told, "You will be my witnesses . . . to the ends of the earth"—and right here in this story is where that mission begins. Finally, this story is about two people who should never have met—a Jew and a gentile—so it's a strange story that causes us to stop and listen closely.

The whole story is quite long, so I will just share from Acts 10:23–48, since it summarizes what happened between Peter and Cornelius. I absolutely love this story in Scripture because it teaches us three very important things about reconciliation: (1) reconciliation is initiated by God, (2) reconciliation requires intentionality, and (3) reconciliation creates a new community. Let me spend a few minutes exploring each of these points.

In the first section of the story, we find out that reconciliation is initiated by God. We read that Peter was in Joppa, minding his own business, praying and communing with God, as good Jewish men did. He wasn't an enlightened cross-cultural minister who had read lots of books on reconciliation—no, he was doing his own thing when God initiated with him. On the other end, we have Cornelius, a gentile, who is in his house when the Lord shows up through an angel and calls him to go and send for Peter. God initiates with both of them. The main characters in this story are not Peter and Cornelius, but God himself, who by his sovereignty calls out to them with something important to do.

As I studied this picture of the church in the book of Acts and watched the life of Jesus, I became convinced that God explicitly calls all of us to reconciliation—from all of our different backgrounds and perspectives—to be together as one. The Scriptures call us to this reality that we are one new humanity. We read about it again in Ephesians 2:15–17. We see it again in John 17:20–23. Here's the thing: we can't just believe this cognitively. We must believe it volitionally with our lives and the way we live. God did not throw a sheet in front of me and say, "You are to be a minister of reconciliation!" My call came from the Scriptures—and I believe God calls all of us to reconciliation through his Word.

So now that we know that God calls us all to reconciliation, what's next? We see clearly through the Scriptures that reconciliation requires obedience and intentionality. Peter and Cornelius were attentive to what the Lord called them to, and they obeyed. Peter knew that the voice was from the Lord, but he was still reluctant. He was reluctant not just because he personally didn't like the gentiles—no, it went far deeper than that. The societal structure he lived under was set up in a way that kept the two groups apart. There existed a great deal of laws that told him whom to be with, what to eat, what to do—and hanging out with gentiles was against their law. Peter also lived in a culture with a long tradition of these laws, so he had a community of people around him who would reinforce divisions. His family made sure he'd never have to interact with "those people." They kept him nice and safe. And so, it wasn't Peter's fault—he was merely perpetuating the separatist attitudes that had been passed down to him for generations. But his obedience takes him somewhere else. Most gentiles had been taught to hate the Jewish people, so possibly the biggest surprise of this story is that Cornelius invites Peter to step into the house of a gentile. Imagine how that went. Cornelius probably was not very smooth. He was not cross-culturally trained, hadn't been to a good Christian school, and hadn't done summer global missions. When Peter entered Cornelius's house, Peter probably said something to this effect: "You know I'm not supposed to be here. But the Lord told me to come, so here I am."

Talk about awkwardness for both of them!

Let me tell you a little bit about the messiness in my own heart. I already shared that there are some people who are hard for me to love. I have to come to grips with this every time I cross into a young, hip, wealthy neighborhood and enter Whole Foods. I walk around observing the people doing their shopping, and I find myself scowling and, under my breath, saying, "Man, white people with money from the suburbs don't even get it! What kind of world do they live in?!" My judgmental comments aren't stemming from a personal dislike of the people inside the store—I don't even know them!—but my issue is that the minute I step foot into the store I am reminded of the people and places in our society that practice economics that are disenfranchising my community. And when I make these grumpy and judgmental comments to my husband (who, by the way, grew up in a rich, white suburb), he looks at me and says, "Um, you have issues." And he's right! I shouldn't be judging. I understand that all of us, no matter who we are or where we're from, are trying to get to a place of flourishing. But if I'm being honest, it is very hard to be in relationship with or trust people who support policies that marginalize my community. This is something that I reckon with every day as a person of color and a Christian who is called to reconciliation.

Christians must be intentional in how we live our lives, and we must think about how our actions affect others. When we interact with someone from another culture or socioeconomic background, it's easy to make assumptions about who they are and project all the negative things that we've ever experienced onto them. We have to let go of our misconceptions. Scripture calls us to learn to be in community with people who help us see different perspectives. But true reconciliation requires us to go deeper than simply interpersonal relationships. The communal and systemic layer demands that we consider which people are being hurt or marginalized and seek justice for them. The people with power, typically those in the cultural majority, must be able to identify their advantage and intentionally learn about the human and pastoral concerns of the vulnerable communities. This means being informed on the issues that are on their minds every day.

For example, imagine you meet someone at your workplace who is a refugee from another country, and you begin to build a friendship with this person who has a very different life experience than you. But you don't stop there. You begin to learn that there is a large community of refugees from that country settling in your city, and you become curious about what human concerns they are facing as they settle into a new life. You begin to educate yourself on the issues that affect refugees and begin to ask what role your church could play in welcoming them by learning from websites like wewelcomerefugees.org.

This is true reconciliation because we are taking our relationship deeper and making the effort to understand their concerns. We must not only invite others to our tables, but we must go to theirs to understand what it's like to be displaced. What keeps us from delving deeper? Is it that we're uncomfortable? Or is it that we're afraid that we won't do it well? Are we afraid to ask dumb questions? Or are we just not ready for God to expose what is in our hearts?

Finally, reconciliation should be done in a community, and as a result it creates a *new* community. It's not just about individuals coming together; it's about creating a new community that practices mutuality and concern for one another and the systems that are at play. In Acts chapter 11 we see Peter bring his community in Jerusalem along in his journey of reconciliation with the gentiles. When Peter returned to Jerusalem after witnessing firsthand the conversions of the gentiles, his community responded with, "I can't believe you ate with those people."

Peter's community couldn't accept the call to reconciliation because there were too many systemic roadblocks at play preventing them from loving the other. Peter could have given up on them, given that they clearly didn't understand the significance of what had happened. But Peter had a calling to his community, so he stayed with them, was patient with them, and trusted that God would do something for them. The Jewish people saw that Peter's heart had changed, and they needed to experience that through him in order to embrace a completely new worldview. Sure enough, we see that the gospel that spread in Jerusalem was one that brought everyone from every tribe, nation, and language together, just as God had intended. Imagine if Peter had given up on them!

Think about what is happening in your community today. Let's say you're in a small group with a few parents from an ethnic minority background, and they are concerned about an educational policy that would restrict the school from teaching the history of racism in our country. Perhaps you should lean into that and seek to understand why this issue is so important to them, and maybe even attend a board meeting where this is being addressed. Or maybe some kids in your church are interested in attending a protest addressing the relationship between the police and the Black community, but it makes the church leaders uncomfortable. Perhaps this means you should ask questions about why the kids care about this issue, and even consider going with them as a way of learning about concerns facing your community.

The journey of reconciliation is distinct for each of us. If you're part of a marginalized or ethnic minority group, you may be holding on to anger or distrust that will make this road challenging. If you're part of the majority community, you may be holding on to long-held ideas, assumptions, or stereotypes about others that make it hard to grasp the bigger picture. We are all grappling with our own issues that we have to work out, and it's not easy. We won't have all the answers at once. The effort won't be 50/50. It is a long journey, and we must be willing to trust God.

I have wanted to say to the Lord a hundred times, "I don't want to have anything to do with those Whole Foods-going, skinny jeans-wearing people who just don't get it!" And do you know what the Lord has done? The Lord had me marry a white man from a wealthy upbringing who has every allergy known to humanity—gluten free, dairy free, peanut sensitive—so guess what? I am always at Whole Foods confronting my issues! The Lord sure has a sense of humor, doesn't he? But God has had me stand in this place of tension because it matters to the witness of the church. God knew what I needed to get a grip on the messiness in my heart. I won't say it has been easy, but I am better for it. And now my hope and prayer are that other Christians would seek to know me, understand the concerns of my community, and attempt to live in a way that doesn't marginalize us further. This would be true reconciliation, and what a witness that would be to the nonbelieving world! People are tired of hearing us preach a message of unity that we don't live out in our churches. People are tired of hearing us talk and waiting to see us live in such a way that shows the love of Christ.

Yes, Christians are already unified; the Scriptures say we are one. Yes, we are reconciled; the Scriptures say we are reconciled. Yes, we are one humanity; the Scriptures say we are one humanity. But if this is true, then we need to act like it. Imagine if the most diverse communities in our society were churches, as we see in the book of Acts. How might God want to use you toward this vision? What is he calling you to be intentional about? I pray for us all, that we would grow not just in having different people present in our churches, but in creating space for those voices to come alongside us so that all may know the glory of God and preach a gospel that declares that he is the God of *all people.*

Sermon on Sexism
Text: Genesis 1:27–28
Title: Equal in God's Eyes
Preacher: Paul A. Hoffman

Introduction

Has anyone here heard of or seen the 2017 movie *Battle of the Sexes*? For those who may be unfamiliar, it's a critically acclaimed film starring Emma Stone, who won an Oscar for Best Actress in the musical *La La Land*, and Steve Carrell, who played Michael Scott on *The Office* TV series. *Battle of the Sexes* loosely depicts the real-life Battle of the Sexes II, a famous tennis match between tennis pros Billy Jean King and Bobby Riggs. The event took place on Sept. 20, 1973, at the Houston Astrodome and was heavily promoted by ABC. The winner was set to win $100,000 and the loser, zip. It's estimated that ninety million people worldwide watched this match. Anyone curious who won? Sorry, but you'll have to google that *after* the sermon!

Here's the point: it's pretty obvious this epic tennis match drew a massive television audience because it was a competition between a woman, Billy Jean King, and a man, Bobby Riggs. And the contest resulted in only one winner and one loser.

But what if I told you God's perfect plan for the sexes is not *competition* but rather *collaboration*? In fact, that's what God's Word teaches in the first chapter of the Bible, Genesis 1. Specifically, today we're going to explore what Genesis 1:27–28 has to say regarding God's purpose and plan for how men and women are to interact.

Now, before you turn there, let me give you some context. Many scholars believe Genesis 1 provides a snapshot of how God created everything. Then, in Genesis 2–3, the author zooms in and offers more detail regarding how God created the first human beings. My goal is to examine just two verses, Genesis 1:27–28, and draw some broad concepts from them.

I invite you to turn with me to Genesis 1:27–28. [Read Gen. 1:27–28]. The first lesson we learn here is that:

1. Males and females are equals because they share God's image (1:27)

Verse 27 indicates both males and females are made in God's image. Generally speaking, to be made in God's image has at least two implications. The first is *resemblance.* Males and females carry God's likeness; they convey something of God's identity. Scholar Barnabe Assohoto explains: "We should be able to recognize the Creator in the men and women we see around us."[1] Like God, males and females have the capacity to reason, to create, to live as moral and spiritual beings in the world.

The second implication is *relationship.* Because God creates males and females in his image, both have the capacity to know God, to have a personal and direct relationship with him. That means the God who hung the stars in the sky and calls them each by name, wants *you* to talk to *him,* to share your dreams and fears with him. He loves you, likes you, and even wants to spend time with you. That is mind-blowing to me! Someone say, "Hallelujah!"

We need to recognize that Genesis 1:27 was a revolutionary statement in the ancient world. Historian Gordon Wenham writes this: "Ancient oriental kings were often seen as bearing the image of their god, but Genesis affirms that every human being is made in God's image."[2] That's radical: males and females, young and old, rich and poor, plebians and princes, all are created in God's likeness. Ladies and gentleman, regardless of your background or upbringing, you are equally valuable because you share God's image. Can I get an "Amen!"?

We now arrive at the second point of Genesis 1:27–28, which is this:

2. Males and females are equals because they share God's image and *blessing* (1:28a)

Did you notice the first three words of verse 28: "God blessed them"? In the original language the verb "to bless" means "to bestow favor, approval, or praise." God gives his affirmation and praise to males and females. When God looks at you, he delights in you. He thinks, "Wow! You are so handsome; you are so lovely. What a masterpiece! I am so proud to be your Creator." When God speaks blessing, he's referring to your intrinsic worth. You are worthy, period. He doesn't need you to *do* anything, *earn* anything, *prove* anything, or *be* anything. You are precious to him regardless of your height, the size of your waist or biceps, your GPA, your credit score, or the number of social media followers you possess.

1. Barnabe Assohoto and Samuel Ngewa, "Genesis," in *Africa Bible Commentary: A One-Volume Commentary Written by Seventy African Scholars,* ed. Tokunboh Adeyemo (Grand Rapids: Zondervan, 2010), 11.

2. Gordon Wenham, "Genesis," in *New Bible Commentary: 21st Century Edition,* ed. Gordon J. Wenham, J. A. Motyer, D. A. Carson, and R. T. France (Downers Grove, IL: IVP Academic, 1994), 61.

And you need to know that you are his priceless treasure regardless of whatever pain, hardship, or abuse you've experienced. If someone has mistreated you, demeaned you, or said "you are worthless," or "no one will ever love you," or if someone made you feel gross, cheap, or used, your heavenly Father doesn't cherish or value you any less. No human act can alter his opinion of you. God blesses you.

To drive this home, I invite you to speak this truth aloud in unison on the count of three: "God blesses me!" Ready: 1, 2, 3: "God blesses me!"

That's not all; it gets better. Not only are males and females equally valuable because they share God's image and share God's blessing, but third and finally, they share God's mission. Look at the second part of verse 28: "Be fruitful and increase in number; fill the earth and subdue it. Rule over the fish in the sea and the birds in the sky and over every living creature that moves on the ground."

That brings us to today's Big Idea:

3. Males and females are equals because they share God's image, blessing, and mission (1:28)

Although you are intrinsically valuable to God, he esteems you so much he's given you a vital mission. We could also call it a command, since the verbs used in verse 28 are actually imperatives. This mission is twofold. First, to be fruitful, to increase and fill the earth. Males and females, through the holy covenant of marriage, are to populate the earth. I hope you understand what I'm referring to, because it's going to get weird if I have to explain it any further, and . . . that's not the kind of sermon I am preaching today! And . . . I think many of us have already reached our comfortability quotient at this point!

The second part of the mission is to subdue and rule over the earth. We are to exercise authority over the animals, birds, and plants. Now, to be clear, dominion does not imply domination. Men and women are equally tasked with the responsibility of caring for, cultivating, and nurturing creation rather than destroying or abusing it. God calls males and females to be wise and faithful stewards and not reckless teenagers who trash the place, like a frat or sorority party that's gone off the rails. Here's the key: both men and women participate in God's mission to be fruitful and rule over creation.

Bottom line, the takeaway of Genesis 1:27–28 is *males and females are equals because they share God's image, blessing, and mission.*

You may be thinking, "Okay, that's nice, but now what? How does that idea apply to my daily life?" Well, as mentioned at the beginning of the sermon, men and women are to live as collaborators, and not competitors. Genesis 1:27–28 makes this abundantly clear. We're not to face each other as rivals. Instead, we are to face forward as colleagues and teammates who've been given the same value, same affirmation, and same mission by our Creator. There's no battle and no losers, only winners.

Having said that, let me suggest a few practical steps you can take this week. First, pray and ask the Holy Spirit to show you a member of the opposite sex he would have you bless and affirm. It could be a spouse, a family member, a coworker, or a neighbor. Go to that person and tell him or her that he or she is valuable to God because he or she is made in God's image, that God approves of him or her and that God has a special mission for him or her. There's someone in your life who needs your encouragement. Your words could inspire and cheer that person, especially if he or she feels unnoticed or unappreciated. Proverbs 16:24 says, "Gracious words are a honeycomb, sweet to the soul and healing to the bones." Go and dispense some nourishment and healing.

Next, ask the Spirit of God if he would have you intervene in a conflict and serve as his peacemaker or reconciler. God could be asking you to step into this disagreement and bring the parties together. I am not talking about a shallow, "you kids shake hands and make-up" type of deal. But to help them work through their conflict in a productive and healthy way. If God leads you down that road, please keep something in mind: if one person is demonstrating any sexist or disrespectful attitudes, behaviors, or language, you need to—gently but firmly—confront it. If that person professes to be a Christian, tell him or her their attitude is sinful and dishonoring to God, because the person he or she is mistreating is made in God's image and is precious to him.

My third and final recommendation is this: spend some time reflecting on your relationships with members of the opposite sex. Are you overlooking someone God wants you to invest in, or mentor, or partner with for some Spirit-ordained assignment? It could be a person who's living on the margins and oftentimes ignored: a teenager from a broken home, a single parent who's overworked and stressed out, or a senior citizen with no family. Utilizing appropriate boundaries, how could you engage him or serve her?

Conclusion

Why bother to do any of this? Because Genesis 1:27–28 teaches that *males and females are equals because they share God's image, blessing, and mission.*

As I close, let's take a moment to dream together. What would it look like if we as a church community honored our Creator and lived out Genesis 1 in an authentic way? What would happen if we promoted mutual respect, honor, and collaboration between the sexes? How might God flood our community with his love, joy, peace, and hope? Wouldn't our homes and businesses become places of flourishing and growth? You want this, don't you? Let's pray.

Sermon on Unity

Text: John 17:1–19

Title: What Are You Praying For?

Preacher: Matthew D. Kim

Introduction

Being asked questions about our spiritual life can be rather off-putting or even annoying. Well-meaning questions from well-meaning persons, such as: "How's your spiritual life?" "How are you doing with God?" Or my personal favorite: "How are you sinning today?" If we're honest, we don't appreciate being bothered with these spiritual probes. It feels icky. They've crossed the line. We want to keep spiritual questions private between me and Jesus. We don't want to be asked about our spiritual journey because that's off-limits in our individualistic worlds.

Yet, is that the case for those who are called to be in Christian community? No, Jesus wanted us to live in Christian community and to keep each other accountable. If you don't mind (being that you don't really have a choice, haha), let me ask you this hopefully less invasive question: What are you praying for these days? Maybe for you, like me, prayer has been especially difficult or discouraging in this season and you wonder whether prayer is meaningful or effective.

Jesus teaches on prayer several times in the Gospels. But in John 17, Jesus models prayer for us as he prays to God, the Father. We're taken to an intimate moment that Jesus shares with his heavenly Father. Turn with me to John 17. What does Jesus pray for especially as he draws near to the end of his earthly ministry? I'm so glad you asked: let's examine Jesus's prayer and see what we can learn from it.

1. Pray that God's glory will be revealed through us

Today, we'll be exploring the first two parts of Jesus's prayer, and next week we'll look at verses 20–26. Here, in verses 1–5, we immediately take notice of the posture in which Jesus prays. Verse 1 tells us that Jesus looked toward heaven. He recognizes that God, the Father, is exalted high above the earth. But, at the same time, Jesus demonstrates the intimate relationship that he has with his Father. And he starts his prayer by saying: "Father, the hour has come. Glorify your Son, that your Son may glorify you." Jesus seems to be self-interested, but he's not. Ultimately his desire is for God, the Father, to be glorified. In fact, in every facet of Jesus's life his goal was to glorify God.

Throughout this prayer, known as Jesus's high priestly prayer, Jesus prays that God's glory will be manifested through his life. This season of COVID-19 has been one of the most challenging seasons in any living person's experience. Perhaps the last thing on our minds is whether I'm glorifying God or not. Maybe we're just trying to stay sane and get through another day.

Yet Jesus's focus has been laser sharp with an eternal purpose. He acknowledges in verse 2 that God is the one who grants eternal life. In verse 3, Jesus says that eternal life is "that they know you, the only true God, and Jesus Christ, whom you [the Father] have sent." Again, Jesus focuses on God. It is only through knowing God and his Son Jesus that we have everlasting life. Then, in verse 4, Jesus prays: "I have brought you glory on earth by finishing the work you gave me to do." Jesus says, "God, I have brought you glory on this earth through my life." Can we say this, friends? God, I have glorified you throughout my life.

Jesus got it right. Every part of his life sought to bring God glory. That's the first prayer that we can emulate today. Pray that God's glory would be revealed through us—from the moment we wake to the moment we sleep, God be glorified through me. The reason why Jesus was able to live for God's glory was because he had experienced an intimate relationship with him. Put differently, Jesus had unity with God. He was united with God in mission and purpose. We see this close relationship in verse 5, where Jesus concludes this portion of his prayer: "And now, Father, glorify me in your presence with the glory I had with you before the world began." As the Son of God, Jesus knew God so personally that he shared God's glory. He loved his Father so much that Jesus lived to bring God glory. We can share in this prayer and pray that God's glory would be revealed in our lives.

Now, Jesus's prayer shifts from himself to his disciples. How is God's glory revealed? This leads us to the second part of Jesus's prayer concerning his disciples. Look with me at verse 6.

2. Pray for our unity, protection, and holiness

What does he pray for next? In verses 6–10, Jesus tells his Father that his disciples have accepted his word and that they believe in him as their Messiah, their Savior. As Jesus shifts the direction of his prayer from himself to his disciples, we notice that Jesus prays for three major things concerning his apprentices: their unity, protection, and holiness. The heart of his request starts in verse 11. He asks for the preservation of unity. Jesus says, "So that they may be one as we are one." Among all the millions of things that Jesus could ask for, why does he ask for unity?

A. Jesus prays for our unity

We are living in a divided nation, and sometimes we are a divided church. In his challenging book *The Church of Us vs. Them*, David Fitch underscores the myriad ways by which American evangelicals have become pitted against each other. He says: "Our witness, as a people, to the life, death, and resurrection of Jesus Christ has become tainted with the ugliness of enemy making."[1] Living to promote one issue, one doctrine, one belief, one ideology has led to the demise of the American evangelical church. Rather than uniting around our common faith in the person and work of Jesus, we have partitioned ourselves over biblical, theological, and cultural minutiae. Fitch calls this phenomenon feeding the "enemy-making machine."[2] Every time a Christian prioritizes arguments that aren't central to the gospel, we feed the enemy-making machine another meal.

If you've been using social media or reading the news lately, you know how divided Christians are on pretty much every single issue. Denominational infighting continues. Pastors battle other pastors on Facebook and Twitter. Christians spew out vitriolic hate messages toward one another. It's so bad that authors like Douglas Bursch needed to write a book—his is called *Posting Peace: Why Social Media Divides Us and What We Can Do about It*.[3] We are so fractured that we don't know what to do, and worse yet, maybe we're so numb that we don't even care.

Disunity occurs any time we value being right about nonessential doctrines, ideas, and matters more than we love the people who may disagree with us. Sure, as Bible believing Christians there are some things worth fighting for. One of those doctrines is the Trinity. The Trinity is a beautiful reflection of unity among the three persons of the triune God: Father, Son, and Holy Spirit. They are three distinct persons and yet one God. It's a mystery that no person can completely understand. And yet the triune God is a model for believers that we can be different and yet be one.

Why does it matter for Christians to be unified? Skip down with me to verse 23: "I in them and you in me—so that they may be brought to complete

---

1. David E. Fitch, *The Church of Us vs. Them: Freedom from a Faith That Feeds on Making Enemies* (Grand Rapids: Brazos, 2020), 8–9.
2. Fitch, *Church of Us vs. Them*, 29.
3. Douglas S. Bursch, *Posting Peace: Why Social Media Divides Us and What We Can Do about It* (Downers Grove, IL: IVP, 2021).

unity. Then the world will know that you sent me and have loved them even as you have loved me."

Friends, as believers in Christ, what differentiates us from nonbelievers who don't know Christ? What will tell the world of God's love? It's our unity. It's our oneness and unity in Christ. It is the unity of believers that demonstrates the power of the gospel to an unbelieving world. Francis Chan writes: "It's great that you share the gospel with those you love, but it's our unity that will cause them to actually believe your words."[4] We can only accomplish more for the kingdom of God through unity by supporting, encouraging, and even helping one another to press on. Donald Grey Barnhouse tells this story:

> Several years ago, two students graduated from the Chicago-Kent College of Law. The highest ranking student in the class was a blind man named Overton and, when he received his honor, he insisted that half the credit should go to his friend, Kaspryzak. They had met one another in school when the armless Mr. Kaspryzak had guided the blind Mr. Overton down a flight of stairs. This acquaintance ripened into friendship and a beautiful example of interdependence. The blind man carried the books which the armless man read aloud in their common study, and thus the individual deficiency of each was compensated for by the other.[5]

Satan is working against the kind of unity this story describes. In fact, he wants us to see everyone's deficiency as something to divide over. He wants Christians to stop worshiping together because we disagree over some nonessential theological or biblical issue. He wants us to be divided over science, politics, race, ethnicity, culture, and everything else. Will you take a few moments now and ask God, "With whom do I have disunity? Is there any person in my life that I dislike or even hate at this moment?" Who makes you angry? Is there a broken relationship that needs reconciliation? Pray for this unity that Jesus speaks of. As Jesus prays, seek unity.

B. Jesus prays for our protection

The second thing that Jesus prays for his disciples concerns their spiritual protection. We've been talking so much the last two years about protection from this virus and protection from racial violence. But Jesus also has another type of protection in mind. Verse 12 says: "While I was with them, I protected them and kept them safe by that name you gave me." Then, in verse 15, he

4. Francis Chan, *Until Unity* (Colorado Springs: David C. Cook, 2021), 28.

5. "Blind and Armless," Bible.org, February 2, 2009, https://bible.org/illustration/blind-and -armless.

prays: "My prayer is not that you take them out of the world but that you protect them from the evil one." Jesus was clear that he wanted his disciples not to retreat from the world, but to be protected from all types of danger: from Satan, from evil, from sin, from physical harm. But now that he is leaving, Jesus prays for his disciples' well-being. Jesus asks God to protect them.

Wake up, Christians! Engage, Christians! We're asleep, spiritually speaking. We are living in a time of great spiritual warfare. This is what Jesus prayed for his disciples—that God would protect their souls—and this is what I'm praying for you. I'm praying for our spiritual protection—that God would guard us from the garbage and filth that this world holds so dearly. I'm praying for our integrity. I'm praying for our purity. I'm praying for godly values to be promoted in the home. I'm praying for unity. I'm praying that your spiritual compass would be directed by the word of God and not the values of media and society. Jesus prays for unity, protection, and finally, holiness.

C. Jesus prays for our holiness

Lastly, in his prayer for his disciples, Jesus prays for holiness. He prays in verses 16–18: "They are not of the world, even as I am not of it. Sanctify them by the truth; your word is truth. As you sent me into the world, I have sent them into the world. For them I sanctify myself, that they too may be truly sanctified."

Brothers and sisters, we are called by Christ not to be like the rest of the world. Rather, more and more in this world where morality seldom exists, we must pray for holiness. If we are Christians, we have a large target on our backs. Satan wants us to lose faith in God and fall into despair. Satan wants us to fall into unhealthy habits that will destroy us and our families. Satan wants us to be disunified. How does this happen? Not pursuing God and God's Word.

No wonder George Barna, a Christian statistician, says that we are witnessing steady decline in church attendance, prayer, and morality among professing Christians.[6] More than ever before, we must pray for spiritual protection. God provides clear teachings on right versus wrong in the Bible. We must pray that our morals are defined by what the Bible says and not what the world dictates. The lack of morality is why there is little difference between the way Christians and non-Christians live their lives.

The word that Jesus uses, which is translated here as "sanctify," is the verb *hagiozō*. It's where we get the word "holy." It means "to separate or to be set

---

6. Barna Group, "Signs of Decline & Hope among Key Metrics of Faith," March 4, 2020, https://www.barna.com/research/changing-state-of-the-church.

apart for good use or a good purpose." Jesus prays that God would sanctify his disciples and set them apart for God's holy work. When we think of holiness, we often think of boredom. But developing in holiness is exciting. When people's lives change from a life without Christ to holiness, there is nothing more attractive. C. S. Lewis once wrote to an American friend, "How little people know who think that holiness is dull. When one meets the real thing . . . it is irresistible. If even ten percent of the world's population had it, would not the whole world be converted and happy before a year's end?"[7]

Before Jesus left his disciples, he prayed for their sanctification—that they would be holy and set apart to do God's work. Jesus said in verse 18, "As you sent me into the world, I have sent them into the world." Jesus has sent us out to the world to do his great work. In order to be a part of what God is doing, we must also seek sanctification and seek maturity through holy living.

What will it take for Christians to live holy lives? Are we fully surrendered to Jesus, and will we pursue unity with fellow Christians? At the end of Jesus's prayer, we see that Jesus cares about two things: (1) God's glory and (2) his disciples' unity, protection, and holiness. He models for us a prayer that shows his heart for us as the Savior. What are we praying for these days? This week I want us to remember that the church brings all glory to God through unity, protection, and holiness. The church brings all glory to God through unity, protection, and holiness.

7. C. S. Lewis, *Letters to an American Lady* (Grand Rapids: Eerdmans, 1967).

INDEX